Reading Jeremiah in Africa

Bungishabaku Katho provides an important and welcome addition to our rich corpus of Jeremiah studies. The particular gain of this exposition is that he reads Jeremiah through the context of African political culture. He shows the ways in which the text makes especially compelling sense when read in this context. The gain for Western readers is to see that our conventional readings of the prophet are culturally conditioned, so that a very different cultural context permits us to see much that we had not been able to see. I readily concur with his verdict that much of the text sounds "as though it had been written by a prophet of our own time." As this is true in African context, so it is equally true in Western context. Given the broad and deep crisis in our culture, attention must be paid to this careful and discerning study.

Walter Brueggemann, PhD
William Marcellus McPheeters Professor Emeritus of Old Testament,
Columbia Theological Seminary, Decatur, Georgia, USA

This is something genuinely new under the sun – a fresh reading of the most anguished biblical prophet against the background of contemporary Africa. Katho's textual analysis is equally informed by experiences of wrenching social crises and by the vibrant hope that sustains African Christians. Western Christians need to learn from this book what it is to read the Bible within the context of a faith community that knows its future depends entirely on the mercy and grace of God.

Ellen F. Davis, PhD
Amos Ragan Kearns Distinguished Professor of Bible and Practical Theology,
Duke Divinity School, Durham, North Carolina, USA

In this important book, we hear the voice of Jeremiah speaking through the voice of a courageous African scholar and church leader to his beloved – but troubled – continent and its Christians. It is a careful, perceptive, honest, and ultimately hopeful treatment of Jeremiah in light of Africa, and of Africa in light of Jeremiah. Katho's work is also a model for all Christians of contextual theological interpretation of Scripture.

Michael J. Gorman, PhD
Raymond E. Brown Professor of Biblical Studies and Theology,
St. Mary's Seminary & University, Baltimore, Maryland, USA

Bungishabaku Katho, a Jeremiah scholar by his own right, looks at the African continent through the lenses of the prophecy of Jeremiah. Just as Jeremiah's ministry was to a people God loved, Katho relates Jeremiah's message to the African situation from the point of view of love for the continent and a deep desire that the continent returns to and maintains that which Yahweh loves – justice, righteousness, and loyalty to God, among other virtues – as expressed in many anthems and constitutions of African nations.

A departure from Yahweh's will leads to judgment, but Yahweh is both a God of judgment and a God of forgiveness, restoration and blessings. In this book, Katho's voice is clearly shouting, "my beloved continent, let us return to Yahweh and his ways as we deal with each other and seek to serve God." This book is an excellent exposition of select passages from Jeremiah and a message for Africa each of us should read, reflect on and apply.

Samuel M. Ngewa, PhD
Dean of Graduate School,
Africa International University, Nairobi, Kenya

Reading Jeremiah in Africa

Biblical Essays in Sociopolitical Imagination

Bungishabaku Katho

© 2021 Bungishabaku Katho

Published 2021 by HippoBooks, an imprint of ACTS and Langham Publishing.

Africa Christian Textbooks (ACTS), TCNN, PMB 2020, Bukuru 930008, Plateau State, Nigeria
www.actsnigeria.org

Langham Publishing, PO Box 296, Carlisle, Cumbria CA3 9WZ, UK
www.langham.org

ISBNs:
978-1-83973-213-3 Print
978-1-83973-504-2 ePub
978-1-83973-505-9 Mobi
978-1-83973-506-6 PDF

Bungishabaku Katho has asserted his right under the Copyright, Designs and Patents Act, 1988 to be identified as the Author of this work.

All rights reserved. No part of this publication may be reproduced, stored in a retrieval system or transmitted, in any form or by any means, electronic, mechanical, photocopying, recording or otherwise, without the prior written permission of the publisher or the Copyright Licensing Agency.

Requests to reuse content from Langham Publishing are processed through PLSclear. Please visit www.plsclear.com to complete your request.

Unmarked Scripture translations in this work are the author's own.

All Scripture quotations marked NIV are taken from the Holy Bible, New International Version®, Anglicised, NIV®. Copyright © 1979, 1984, 2011 by Biblica, Inc®. Used by permission. All rights reserved worldwide.

Chapter 2 first appeared as "Idolatry and the Peril of the Nation: Reading Jeremiah 2 in an African Context." In *Anglican Theological Review* 99, no. 4, edited by Stephen E. Fowl, 713–728. Chicago: Anglican Theological Review, 2017. Used with permission.

Chapter 6 first appeared as "Knowledge of YHWH and True Glorification: A Contextual Reading of Jeremiah 9:22–23." In *Old Testament Essays* 17, no. 1, 78–102. Pretoria: Old Testament Society of South Africa (OTSSA), 2004. Used with permission.

Chapter 9 first appeared as "Seek the Peace of the City . . . for in Her Peace There Shall Be Peace for You (Jeremiah 29:4–9)." In *Old Testament Essays* 26, no. 2, 378–1364. Pretoria: Old Testament Society of South Africa (OTSSA), 2013. Used with permission.

Chapter 10 first appeared as "The New Covenant and the Challenge of Building a New and Transformed Community in DR Congo: A Contextual Reading of Jeremiah 31:31–34." In *Old Testament Essays* 18, no. 1, 109–123. Pretoria: Old Testament Society of South Africa (OTSSA). Used with permission.

British Library Cataloguing-in-Publication Data
A catalogue record for this book is available from the British Library

ISBN: 978-1-83973-213-3

Cover & Book Design: projectluz.com

The publishers of this book actively support theological dialogue and an author's right to publish but do not necessarily endorse the views and opinions set forth here or in works referenced within this publication, nor guarantee technical and grammatical correctness. The publishers do not accept any responsibility or liability to persons or property as a consequence of the reading, use or interpretation of its published content.

*To N. Feli Vicky, with love and gratitude
and to
Bryant M. Kaumbo, Nolan B. Anyete, Khylah N. Kaumbo, and Bradely Kaumbo,
my grandchildren*

Contents

Acknowledgements xi

Introduction 1

1   Called to Serve in a World Coming to an End 9
     Jeremiah 1:1–19

2   Idolatry and the Peril of the Nation 31
     Jeremiah 2:4–8

3   Agonizing for a Blind People 47
     Jeremiah 4:19–22

4   Poverty and Knowledge of God 65
     Jeremiah 5:1–6

5   The Anatomy of a Dysfunctional Community 85
     Jeremiah 9:2–9

6   The Secret of True Greatness and Power 105
     Jeremiah 9:23–24

7   The Use and Abuse of Political Power 129
     Jeremiah 22:13–19

8   Weak Leadership and the Dismantling of Judah 153
     Jeremiah 24:4–7

9   Seek the Peace of Babylon: Constructive Presence in Exile 173
     Jeremiah 29:4–9

10   New Covenant and New Community 191
     Jeremiah 31:31–34

Bibliography 211

Acknowledgements

I finished writing this book in February 2017 in Grand Rapids, Michigan. I want to express my profound gratitude to the Issachar Fund, especially its president, Kurt Berends, for his continuous help to my ministry and scholarship. The entire staff of the Issachar Fund were so friendly and supportive during my time in Grand Rapids that I often felt like a member of that wonderful team. Merely to name everyone who helped me seems insufficient, but nonetheless I cannot avoid doing so: Mike Hamilton, Sarah Hohnstein, Sarah Merrilees and Deb Sisson – thank you for counting me as one of you.

I also want to thank the Board of Shalom University for allowing me to take a long six-month leave that allowed for transition in the leadership of Shalom University as I was stepping down after fourteen years as the university's president.

It took me a whole year to work with my editor, Steven Van Dyck. Steven not only helped to make my English better, but he also gave careful attention both to my argument and my articulation of it.

It would have been difficult to complete this project without the help of Ms. Rose Ansobi, my assistant at the Jeremiah Center for Faith and Society. Rose worked hard to reduce the number of people and friends who wanted to see and talk with me while I was writing this book. I heard her arguing often with those who insisted that it was important to see me without any appointment and those who called to talk to me. May the Lord Almighty bless her for all the help she gave me.

Finally, I am glad to dedicate this book to Negura Feli Vicky, my loving wife, in thanks and affection, and to our grandchildren Bryant Kaumbo Mutamba, Nolan Baraka Anyete, Khylah Negura Kaumbo, and Bradely Kaumbo. My choice to become a scholar and writer has had consequences for my family, as my wife knows better than any other person. This time, she allowed me to be away for six months. I am not sure that other relatives understand what it means to be apart for that long, just for the sake of writing a book! But the good news is that while I was away, two of our grandchildren kept her very busy and happy. We thank God for each one of them.

Introduction

The book of Jeremiah contains difficult material that poses many challenges for readers trying to understand its message, bridge the gap between our time and the socio-historical context of the seventh century prophets, and apply this message to the modern context. Unfortunately, instead of helping the reader surmount these barriers, most modern scholars of Jeremiah prefer to emphasize the complex elements of the prophetic book, making it almost impossible for ordinary readers to understand it. One can only wonder about the relevance to most Christians of some works on Jeremiah produced in the last twenty-five years. Recent titles such as *Troubling Jeremiah*,[1] and *Jeremiah (Dis)placed*,[2] show how complicated things have become for those who simply want to listen to God's voice in their context. Some people now regard Jeremiah as one of the most difficult books of the Bible.

However, many scholars have realized that the vitality, growth, renewal, impact and survival of the African church will depend on the right interpretation and application of the whole word of God, including the message of "difficult" books such as Jeremiah. This also means that the African church can no longer continue reading the Bible only from a Western perspective. There is an urgent need to produce an interpretation of Scripture that is profoundly biblical and addresses African issues. This emphasis on African issues implies a shift away from a merely spiritual understanding of the Bible toward a broader approach that also interprets the Scriptures as giving voice to a call for the divine gift of liberation and *shalom*. In other words, biblical interpretation in Africa must embrace public political responsibility and seek justice and well-being for all in a continent that is facing challenges on many levels.

In this endeavour, the greatest challenge for African Bible scholars is certainly methodological, especially as regards the inclusion of local, contextual resources in the interpretation of Scripture. These local resources must consider the oral dimension of the Bible, for it is important to note that most of the texts of the Bible existed in oral forms before they were fixed in writing.

---

1. A.R. Pete Diamond, Kathleen M. O'Connor, and Louis Stulman, eds. *Troubling Jeremiah*. Sheffield: Sheffield Academic Press, 1999.

2. A.R. Pete Diamond, and Louis Stulman. eds. *Jeremiah (Dis)placed: New Directions in Writing/Reading Jeremiah*. New York: T&T Clark, 2011.

Acknowledgement of the oral dimension of what we today call the Bible offers a real advantage to African interpreters, for most African cultures still favour oral communication. So this book uses African proverbs, sayings and poems to illustrate some key points in the interpretation of Jeremiah.

Another dimension of the interpretation of the Bible in Africa is the recognition that most biblical texts were produced by and for struggling communities. They were not private works, produced by a few specialists for a limited audience of scholars and their students, as is the case with much of our writing today. The Bible reflects the experiences and struggles of people in real-life situations. Our struggle in Africa against issues like poverty, war, the displacement of people, and political turmoil likewise demands a new reading of Scripture. It is important for African interpreters to bear this communal dimension of the Bible in mind, though our use of this approach must be based on the solid foundation of rigorous textual analysis.

My goal in writing these essays is to demonstrate that once the complexity of the book of Jeremiah has been acknowledged and worked through, much of the text sounds as if it were written by a prophet in our own time. As a follow up to my 2017 commentary on Jeremiah,[3] I now show how ten selected passages from the book of Jeremiah can speak to our context and help us connect the challenges of contemporary Africa with the challenges faced by the people of Judah, including war, injustice, corruption, idolatry, abuse of power, and the crisis of refugees and exile. In this way, God's warnings to the people of Judah becomes relevant for us in Africa today.

This book is also an exercise of the imagination as I dream of a new Africa that knows God and prospers. It seems to me that this is how Jeremiah himself understood his ministry – a ministry that sought to instil and nurture a new understanding that was different from the consciousness of the dominant culture of his time.

In chapter 1 (Jer 1:1–19) I reflect on what it meant to be a prophet of Yahweh in a decaying country. It becomes clear that there is no way to be a true prophet of Yahweh and avoid suffering in a context where both spiritual and political leaders refuse to listen to God. The chapter sets the stage for the book by introducing Jeremiah, the nature of his calling, and the kind of ministry to which he is being called. Yahweh clearly shows his prophet that his ministry is going to be difficult. Throughout the nineteen verses in the chapter, God constantly warns Jeremiah that he must be ready for the challenges to come, and that he must resist being terrified by those in power. Jeremiah

---

3. Robert B. Katho, *Jeremie & Lamentations* (Carlisle: LivresHippo, 2017).

would be engaging with the leadership of Judah – kings, princes, priests and the people – who would literally fight against him. Yet it is important to note that the chapter ends with Yahweh's renewed promise to protect his servant. The chapter's conclusion raises several questions for us to reflect on: How do we define a prophetic ministry today? Who is a prophet today in Africa? How should the African church live out its prophetic role in the image of Jeremiah? How can African churches and theologians deal with false prophets and idolatry?

In chapter 2 (Jer 2:4–6, 8), we look at Yahweh lament that Israel has turned away from him to serve idols. The prophet offers a diagnosis of what has gone wrong with the people of Judah: They have walked away from Yahweh, the centre of life and the centre of true power and vision for the well-being of the community.

Yahweh engages his people through a question, "What fault did your ancestors find in me?" (2:5 NIV). This is a surprising question coming from the sovereign God. It signals that Judah's condition is at a critical point and that the real problem was idolatry. The people had grown tired of God. Yahweh was no longer needed. He was no longer the centre of their life and interest. They wanted autonomy from Yahweh, and no one was asking, "Where is Yahweh?" (2:6). They were taking God for granted and following futile idols, and in the process they had become futile themselves. Like two sides of a coin, these two evils, the sin of omission (forgetting God) and the sin of commission (walking after idols) were the basis of Yahweh's accusations. Four groups of leaders are accused of being responsible for this crisis: priests, teachers, prophets, and politicians.

When God is rejected, something or someone else is put in his place; either a person (in the form of a personality cult or dictatorship, for example) or a system or doctrine. The consequence of abandoning Yahweh to serve other gods was a loss of direction for the nation and a separation of the people from the source of their worth. Jeremiah's diagnosis of Judah's problem provides a key to understanding the current situation in Africa.

Reflecting on Jeremiah 2 is helpful in attempting to understand what ails Africa and why the continent is in such a mess. A short look at its recent history reveals that Africans face ongoing social and political backwardness and spiritual struggles.

Chapter 3 (Jer 4:19–22) analyses Jeremiah's lament for his dying nation. The people of Judah, especially the leaders, are accused of being foolish, stupid, lacking understanding, not knowing Yahweh, and being wise only in doing evil. More particularly, the prophet accuses them of numbness and inattention to the real problems of their society and holds them accountable for the disaster that this evil is bringing to the nation. The prophet wishes that his compatriots and their leaders would open their eyes to see the coming destruction, but they do not care. Everyone lives in denial, everyone is preoccupied with their own interests, the nation's well-being is not a priority for the people or their leaders. This creates great emotional and spiritual pain for the prophet, who experiences the evil in the land on a daily basis.

Social injustice does bring disaster, especially when leaders refuse to listen to God or to the voice of wisdom and, as one sees too often in Africa, are consumed by the desire to loot and cling to power and position. There is little doubt that Africa's plight is at least partly attributable to its leaders' lack of wisdom and understanding. As a consequence, many Africans have been scattered all over the world, and often those who have left their home countries are viewed as fortunate by their peers. Those who remain, especially the intellectuals, are often forced to join the forces of corruption in order to prosper or survive. Those who refuse to play along expose themselves to danger and are regarded as enemies of the society and its corrupt leaders.

Chapter 4 (Jer 5:1–6) takes the reader into the streets of Jerusalem, which were much like the crowded streets and marketplaces of Africa. God commands Jeremiah to search the streets and marketplaces of Jerusalem to find one righteous person who acts with justice and strives for honesty so that God may spare the city. Upon finding no one who is righteous, the prophet concludes that he searched in the wrong places, that is, in the streets and marketplaces, and among the wrong people, the poor. Jeremiah decides to go to search among the rich, to find out whether there is a single person there who acts justly. Despite his strong hope, he soon learns that they too are unrighteous.

This chapter seeks to answer the question: Why does Jeremiah think that to search in streets and marketplaces and among the poor was to search in the wrong places and among the wrong people? It seems that for Jeremiah, the extreme poverty of the poor made it easy for them to behave like people who did not know Yahweh. They told lies (sometimes in order to get something for themselves and their families), made promises they did not keep, and stole when necessary. They lacked a proper knowledge of Yahweh. This kind of poverty, I argue, is not to be regarded as virtuous; it is an enemy of faith, rendering God's people vulnerable to temptations. Jeremiah associates the knowledge of Yahweh with a way of life that shows faithfulness to God, but for the poor, faithfulness to Yahweh was secondary to the need to survive.

The main argument of this chapter is that poverty is an obstacle to faith in God in Africa because it destroys human dignity. Severe poverty has a terrible impact on spiritual, psychological, and physical health; it creates a sense of meaninglessness. While many Africans love the Lord Jesus Christ and his church, severe and persistent poverty and the inability of the church to deal with the real issues facing the poor in Africa prevent many African Christians from fully enjoying their relationship with God.

Chapter 5 (Jer 9:2–9) describes how Judah as a society has been destroyed internally by its own corruption as a result of not obeying the law. The refusal to live by the law shows that Judah has broken the covenant, and consequently has ceased to be God's covenant community. There is moral decay in the society and people are concerned with themselves, not with the needs of others. Their refusal to observe moral and ethical norms has led to a breakdown of social order.

Once the covenant was broken, any claim to knowing God that Judah made was false, because to know Yahweh means to follow his commandments as expressed in high ethical earnestness in our actions. Because of breaking the covenant, Judah is broken, a debased society characterized by malicious and deceitful speech that destroys community and oppression of the weak to smooth the way for the powerful and increase their wealth and control over the weak.

These evils point to a lack of concern for building the just community that God desires. Jeremiah describes a situation where the people of Judah were taking advantage of their fellow citizen to advance their own interests, without regard for the word of God. It is the sum of these social evils that Jeremiah calls "the lack of knowledge of Yahweh."

The situation is no better in Africa. The church has not done enough to help Christians understand their calling in society. More specifically, the church has failed to emphasize the formation of virtues in believers. Consequently, Christians in Africa have too often not prioritized the cultivation of the Christian virtues, and as a result they make little difference in the society and are largely not concerned with building a community of hope.

Chapter 6 (Jer 9:23–24) discusses the relationship between the knowledge of Yahweh and true glorification for both individuals and the community. More precisely, the chapter discusses three things in which people or nations trust and in which they glory: intellectual knowledge, power, and wealth. The prophet Jeremiah offers an alternative to this view and argues that human beings and nations should glory only in knowing Yahweh. It is this knowledge, says Jeremiah, that should guide our use of intellectual knowledge, power, and wealth if we want to build a just community, one that is obedient to Yahweh. Otherwise, the misuse of our intellectual knowledge, power, and wealth leads to suffering, breakdown of community, and eventually the death of individuals and nations.

In the context of Africa, this passage forces us to confront the question of the failure of leadership characterized by the selfish and idolatrous use of intellectual knowledge, power and wealth against the godly understanding and use of power, wisdom and wealth for building of our nations.

Chapter 7 (Jer 22:13–19) reflects on the abuse of power by those in leadership in Judah. The chapter attempts to analyse the relationship between the use and misuse of power/authority and the breakup of national life. According to Jeremiah, Israel's social and political ordering was authorized by Yahweh's sovereignty through his law, and consequently it did not reflect the will of any political rulers, systems or parties. Thus, and this is important in any society, the power of the state as a creation of Yahweh is culturally bound to the norms of the word of God and not to any human philosophy or ideology, such as democracy.

In the context of Africa, this chapter examines the concept of democracy, which is often promoted as the best form of governance in Africa and the solution to the continent's political problems. I argue that Western democracy is not necessarily the solution to Africa's governance problems, but rather the imposition of yet another Western concept and experience. Democracy should not be applied in Africa without reflection. This is because democracy sometimes produces overzealous populist leaders who do not always deliver on their promises. We all know that campaign slogans such as "hope and change we can believe in," "stronger together," or "making Africa great again," are often just empty slogans of governments that come to power through democratic processes. In the name of democracy, many African countries have wasted a great amount of money organizing fake elections whose results are known before voting take place. We in Africa might need to redefine and reconceive democracy so that it is a system capable of putting in place godly leaders who promote stability in our countries.

Chapter 8 (Jer 24:4–7) continues with the subject of leadership, and, more specifically, the consequences of weak leadership. Jeremiah describes King Zedekiah as a weak and fearful leader who was unable to stand up to his princes and unable to listen to Yahweh and make decisions that would have saved Judah. During his reign, the nobles were divided between those who supported his rule and those who did not. Zedekiah was a weak and a confused king with no real power. We see others deciding for him and forcing him to act against his will and against Yahweh. This division at the top leadership level and King Zedekiah's poor decision-making were partly responsible for Judah's demise. In our modern context, we see terrible disruptions fall on our countries when a president's closest advisers control the president to advance their interests.

Using case studies in Africa, this chapter demonstrates that confusion in leadership breaks down a nation and that, particularly during a time of national crisis, there is a need for a good, wise, and strong leader who can carefully scrutinize the situation and listen to different voices and who knows how to filter relevant information to save the nation from chaos.

Chapter 9 (Jer 29:4–9) deals with the concept of "peace/*shalom*." Most of the references to *shalom* in the book of Jeremiah are negative. They are related either to the false concept of peace that was being promoted by the political and religious leaders in Judah, or to the oracles of false prophets opposed to Jeremiah's ministry. The argument in this chapter is that the assurances of peace offered by Jeremiah's opponents (false prophets, political and religious leaders) were mostly grounded in a false sense of security motivated by the traditions of Israel's inviolability as God's covenant people and the promised survival of the Davidic dynasty. However, the people of Judah went into exile, and Jeremiah uses the word *shalom* in 29:7 to urge the exiles of Judah in Babylon to seek the peace of the city where they now lived. The hard question this chapter tries to address is: How can exiles seek the peace of their enemy? Jeremiah responds to the question in two ways: First, the exiles must first accept that they are not in Babylon because of the military power of Nebuchadrezzar[4] but because they broke God's covenant; and second, they need to know that Yahweh has not forgotten his people despite their current situation in exile.

This passage is evaluated in the context of the millions of refugees and internally displaced people in Africa today. It is common to find that refugees are creating problems for the cities to which they have fled. This is mostly done out of their sense of hopelessness. In fact, there is much in today's world that creates despair over the future of our continent: poverty, wars, ethnic conflict, climate change, Ebola and COVID and other endemic diseases, HIV/AIDS and corruption to name a few. However, the Bible is clear that there is a bright future for the people who have hope in God and in the Lord Jesus Christ. God has not given up on the world or Africa. He is invested in the future destiny of

---

4. In the Old Testament, the name Nebuchadnezzar appears in two different forms: "Nebuchadnezzar" and "Nebuchadrezzar." Because the official Babylonian documents use Nebuchadrezzar to designate the king of Babylon, many scholars now believe that the name's original and official form is Nebuchadrezzar, which means "Nabu protect my first born." This is the spelling used throughout this book.

humanity. Jeremiah reminds us that in the current deep crises in the continent, we as the people of God still need to act with courage, determination, and hope as a sign of God's affirmation that the current crises will not have the final word. Terrifying times like those in which we live call for people of courage and faith like Jeremiah, who will stand and show in action their God-given hope for the bright future that God has announced for humanity.

Chapter 10 (Jer 31:31–34) analyses Yahweh's promise to make a new covenant with Israel/Judah after the exile. Judgement has already been rendered against the people of Israel because they broke the covenant with Yahweh. Some of them were in exile and others were about to follow them. It was at that time that Yahweh announced that he would forgive his people and make a new covenant with them. In this new covenant, Yahweh himself will empower his people to know him properly. The right knowledge of Yahweh in the new covenant will change the life of the renewed community. The forgiven and renewed community will have a common and shared access to the knowledge of God and will become a forgiving community. Similarly, as this chapter argues, Christians in Africa, despite the poverty, war and ethnic divisions in which they live, should remember that they are a forgiven community and always strive to live like a community that knows Yahweh, that is, a community characterized by justice, forgiveness, and the desire to live and grow together in love and peace.

1

Called to Serve in a World Coming to an End

Jeremiah 1:1–19

¹ The words of Jeremiah, son of Hilkiah, one of the priests who were at Anathoth in the land of Benjamin, ² to whom the word of Yahweh came in the time of Josiah, son of Amon, king of Judah, in the thirteenth year of his reign. ³ And it continued in the time of Jehoiakim, son of Josiah, king of Judah, until the end of the eleventh year of Zedekiah, son of Josiah, king of Judah; that is, until the deportation of the people of Jerusalem in the fifth month.

⁴ And the word of Yahweh came to me:
  ⁵ "Before I formed you in the belly, I knew you;
  and before you came forth from the womb,
  I set you aside [I declared you holy] (to be) a prophet to the nations."
⁶ But I said, "Ah Lord Yahweh, look, I do not know how to speak, because I am only a young man [boy]."
  ⁷ But Yahweh said to me, "Do not say 'I am only a boy,' because wherever I send you, you will go, and whatever I command you, you will speak. ⁸ You must not be afraid of them, because I am with you to deliver you. The word of Yahweh."
  ⁹ And Yahweh stretched out his hand and touched my mouth. And Yahweh said to me,

> "Look, I have put my words in your mouth. ¹⁰ See! This day, I have given you authority [I have appointed you] over the nations and over the kingdoms, to pluck out and to pull down, to destroy and to demolish, to build and to plant."

¹¹ And the word of Yahweh came to me: "What do you see, Jeremiah?"

And I said, "I see a branch of an almond tree."

¹² And Yahweh said to me, "You have seen it correctly, for I am watching my word, to carry it out."

¹³ And the word of Yahweh came to me a second time: "What do you see?"

And I said, "I see a pot being boiled, with its top turned away from the north."

¹⁴ And Yahweh said to me, "Disaster will blow down from the north upon all the inhabitants of the land. ¹⁵ For look! I am calling all the clans and kingdoms of the north – declares Yahweh!

> They will come and each will set up his throne
>   at the entrance of the gates of Jerusalem;
> and against all its walls round about,
>   and against all the cities of Judah.
> ¹⁶ And I will speak my judgements against them
>   for all their evil in forsaking me,
> in sacrificing to foreign gods,
>   and in worshipping the work of their own hands.

¹⁷ But as for you, brace yourself like a man! Stand up and speak to them everything that I command you. Do not be terrified because of them, or else I may terrify you before them. ¹⁸ And this day I have made you a fortified city, an iron pillar, a wall of bronze against the whole land; against the kings of Judah and its princes, against priests and the people of the land. ¹⁹ They will fight against you, but will not overcome you, for I am with you to deliver you" – It is the word of Yahweh!

Historical and Literary Context (vv. 1–3)

The book of Jeremiah recounts the last days of Judah, which culminated in the destruction of Jerusalem and its temple and the deportation of its people to Babylon in 587 BC. Beyond simply narrating events, the book is a meditation on the downfall of Judah as a nation, why this calamity befell God's people, and the struggle of the prophet to save his beloved but stubborn people from national collapse. M. Moorehead gives a vivid description of the atmosphere in Judah:

> It was Jeremiah's lot to prophesy at a time when all things in Judah were rushing down to the final and mournful catastrophe; when political excitement was at its height; when the worst passions swayed the various parties, and the most fatal counsels prevailed. It was his to stand in the way over which his nation was rushing headlong to destruction; to make an heroic effort to arrest it, and to turn it back; and to fail, and be compelled to step to one side and see his own people, whom he loved with the tenderness of a woman, plunge over the precipice into the wide, weltering ruin.[1]

Some may dismiss this description as outdated, but nothing can more aptly capture the heart of Jeremiah's ministry and struggle. We are forced to ask: What was the cause of this catastrophic situation in Judah? Jeremiah's answer is clear: It was the failure of Judah's spiritual and political leadership.

The first three verses thus provide the general context of the entire book by identifying the person of the prophet who carries this word, and the political context of his ministry. As Walter Brueggemann rightly argues, "the word of the Lord is not a romantic or floating spiritual notion. It can be precisely linked to a chronological process."[2] In this specific process, the prophet mentions three kings of Judah who reigned during the nation's last years as a political entity: Josiah (626–609 BC), Jehoiakim (609–598 BC), and Zedekiah (598–587 BC). We know of two other kings during this period, Jehoahaz (609 BC) and Jehoiachin (598 BC), who reigned for only three months each and thus did not play a significant role in the final ruin of the nation.

Jeremiah's was an unwelcome voice in Judah's corridors of power, and he constantly clashed with the governing authorities. The outsider from Anathoth was a troublesome presence, a constant reminder that even royal power is ephemeral and that Yahweh himself watches over each of our steps and stands ready to judge. Every act of a king has consequences for the nation's political, social, spiritual, and economic life. This was particularly true for Judah, called by Yahweh to serve as an example of godly leadership for other nations.

---

1. Quoted by G. Campbell Morgan, *Studies in the Prophecy of Jeremiah* (London: Fleming A. Revell, 1931), 10.

2. Walter Brueggemann, *A Commentary on Jeremiah: Exile & Homecoming* (Grand Rapids, MI: Eerdmans, 1998), 22.

The kings of Judah always knew that leadership is more than human strategizing and manoeuvring for power. Leadership is about following the law, listening to God's voice and establishing justice. Leaders who try to manipulate and rule by a calculated understanding of power end in failure. This is a universal principle, applicable to far more than just the kings of Judah.

Jeremiah's short introduction ends with the sentence "until the deportation of the people of Jerusalem in the fifth month" (v. 3). The book of Jeremiah does also recount events following the deportation, but its historical and theological focus is on the death of the kingdom as a consequence of the perversion of God's model for leadership.

Read in this light, this passage and indeed the entire book of Jeremiah resonates with us in Africa. Our suffering and failure are not fortuitous. We can understand them given our leadership and how we live as citizens of our nations. But there is another dimension: each nation needs its own Jeremiah, someone called by God to remain faithful despite all the hardships arising from living under bad leadership, someone who can shine in the darkness as a reminder to the establishment that there is an ultimate judge of the universe. This Jeremiah can be a person, a group of people, or an institution.

The Prophet's Call (vv. 4–5)

Jeremiah's call is introduced by the standard formula: "And the word of Yahweh came to me" (see also vv. 11, 13; 2:1; 16:1). The whole sentence could be literally translated as "And the word of Yahweh came to me, saying." However, most English translations do not translate the word "*lë'mōr*" (saying). If we to integrate that word into the sentence in a natural way, we could come up with the translation: "and this is how the word of Yahweh came to me." The prophet is giving his own account of the revelation he received from Yahweh. The use of a first-person pronouns ("me" and "I") in this section of the book may indicate that these words were written down by a scribe (Baruch?) at Jeremiah's dictation (see Jeremiah 36).[3]

Taking encouragement from Jeremiah's example, let me give my own first-hand testimony to my own calling by God to serve in Bunia in the north-eastern DR Congo. Having read it, you may read Jeremiah's account of his call with new eyes.

---

3. See also Jack R. Lundbom, *Jeremiah 1–20: A New Translation with Introduction and Commentary* (New York: Doubleday, 1999), 230.

My own call

Before looking in more detail, many people have asked why I decided to stay there, despite its many troubles. In fact, in 2003 when one of my students heard that I was in Nairobi and planning to return to eastern DR Congo, he drove for several hours to visit in an effort to dissuade me. I was taken aback by his final observation when he realized his efforts had failed: "My classmates and I used to say that you were the best of all our teachers. However, it now seems to me that something has gone wrong with your mind. How can you decide to go to Bunia, when everybody is running away?" I never told him why I was going back. But this is my story, the story of my call.

In 2002, I was in South Africa working on my PhD at the University of Natal (now KwaZulu-Natal) while my wife and our four children remained in Bunia. The financial support for my research allowed me to travel three times a year for a short visit to the family. Communication with the family was very difficult given that there was no telephone service in eastern DR Congo, and email service had barely arrived in our part of the country. On 12 September 2002, I received an email message from someone in Kampala, the capital city of Uganda, our neighbouring country. The message said, "Where is Katho? If someone can contact him, let him know that his family is in great danger in Bunia." But I had no way to contact my wife to learn any further details. Later that week, I received another message with a first list of about sixty-seven people in my village who had been killed, including close friends and relatives. This was the massacre that took place at Nyankunde, in which about one thousand four hundred people were killed in September 2002. Finally, two weeks later, around midnight, I got a call from my wife. She had managed to escape with the children and was calling from Nairobi.

These events generated an intense wave of discouragement in me. I struggled with the question of whether it made any sense for me to go back home. I decided to look for a job in South Africa or elsewhere, anywhere I could live peacefully with my family. Eventually I was offered a position. However, the night before I was to sign the contract, I was troubled by a strange vision: someone woke me up and pointed at a very dark place with people walking in darkness. He then asked me a question: "What do you see there?" "I see a very dark place," was my answer. He then said to me: "that is your home country." He then gave me a torch and told me to illuminate the dark place with the torch. Then once more: "How do you see it now?" I answered that the place was very bright. He said: "I am sending you back with this light, into your country, for the school and Nyankunde. I do not allow you to stay here or go anywhere else." So I obeyed and went back.

When I reached Bunia in September 2003, Bunia Theological Seminary had been evacuated since March and the campus was crowded with some one thousand three hundred displaced people. I began my ministry as a pastor to these displaced people on the campus. This was the beginning of a very difficult journey. I spent the first four weeks without any money, relying for food on displaced people, themselves receiving food from the UN (ever since then, I have a great dislike of yellow corn meal, having eaten nothing else every day for four weeks).

Seven months later, my younger brother was killed in a car accident. At my urging, he had headed to Nyankunde to help build latrines for people returning to their village. Unfortunately, the car that was taking him to Nyankunde was involved in a terrible accident. Though I never doubted my call, I struggled with the idea of a God who could so clearly talk to me and then allow so much suffering in my life. After the car accident, my brother was in the hospital for nine hours before passing away. During that time, I cried: "Oh! Lord, you cannot let this boy die. He has nothing to do with you. Your call was to me, not to him. I am the one who sent him. If you want, please kill me, not my brother. He is innocent!" I was overcome by guilt and cried for months. Three weeks later, while trying to visit Nyankunde myself, I was arrested by two heavily-armed child soldiers (around 11 and 14 years old) who almost killed me. As they ordered me to remove my jacket and lie down so that they could shoot me, I said in my heart: "God, I am going to die now, and I am ready to meet you. You will tell me why you messed up my life and that of my family. I did not know that you were calling me back only to see my brother and be killed. Is this how you reward people who remain faithful?"

These events in my life help me to read Jeremiah from a totally new perspective. When he becomes discouraged and begins to lament and protest, I remember my own life. I know that my experience has helped me not to be fearful in a context of constant threats. Having understood that my life is completely in God's hand, I am free to move even in very dangerous parts of my region that are under rebel control.

As I say, my story has shaped my reading of the ministry of Jeremiah. But I must admit that I am still puzzled when I hear many people happily claim to have been called by God. Do they know what such a call means? Even today, I struggle to understand God's call, just as Jeremiah did.

Jeremiah's call

Jeremiah's call comes in the form of a dialogue between Yahweh and his prophet. The dialogue is initiated by the one who calls, clearly identified by the pronoun "I" in the sentence: "Before I formed you in the belly, I knew you; and before you came forth from the womb, I set you aside [I declared you holy], to be a prophet to the nations." Scholars have interpreted this passage in different ways. Jack R. Lundbom compared the call of Jeremiah with the calling of kings in the Ancient Near East. In Egypt and Assyria for example, kings were believed to be called by gods. They were not ordinary human beings.[4]

This type of call characterizes most of the prophets in Israel. We see God calling his servants in a similar manner in the accounts of the ministry of Isaiah (Isa 6), Ezekiel (Ezek 1–3), and Samuel (1 Sam 3:1–14). What stands out here is Jeremiah's understanding of predetermination. Jeremiah has been called by God not before he was born but even before he was conceived.[5] Jeremiah appears to suggest that Yahweh, who knows us intimately, has chosen some people for some specific ministries and prepares them in secret until the day he reveals it to them and begins working with them (Pss 22:10–11; 139:13–16; Gal 1:15–16). The one called can protest (as Jeremiah does), but this is a sovereign decision that cannot be changed because it is Yahweh's will. Even kings and other powerful leaders who try to oppose the prophet's message will be defeated. They may arrest, torture or even kill the messenger, but they will never be able to stop the words of Yahweh. Jeremiah may experience fear, or resist the call because the mission is hard, dangerous or revolting, but nothing will change God's will because he predestined his messenger before he was even conceived. The prophet is a mere instrument in the hand of Yahweh.

Understood this way, this passage becomes very important and underlines at least two things. First, it helps us understand the nature of the God who calls. Yahweh is not an idol, a statue, or an invented deity. Nor is he dead, as some people claim. He is the living God who enters into personal conversation with his servants to clearly communicate to them his will and what he expects from them. Many atheists seek to expel God from the world that he has created. Richard Dawkins, among the most militant of the "New Atheists," has gained a global reputation for his polemics against the existence of God, and thus, against any ultimate purpose behind the existence of human beings in this

---

4. Lundbom, *Jeremiah 1–20*, 231.

5. Lundbom (*Jeremiah 1–20*, 231) suggests that "no other prophet has such an advance appointment. Moses – who in Deuteronomy is the prophet *par excellence* – and Samuel were destined for special ministry from birth (Exod 2; 1 Sam 1). The 'servant' of Second Isaiah is also said to have been 'formed in the womb' (Isa 44:2, 24; 49:5), and 'called in the womb' (Isa 49:1). In the NT, John the Baptist is filled with the Holy Spirit 'from the womb' (Luke 1:15), and Jesus' infilling with the Holy Spirit is announced before birth (Matt 1:20; Luke 1:35). The clearest echo of the present call comes in Paul's statement in Galatians 1:15, where he says '(God) set me apart before I was born.'" This is an interesting comparison, but we will not discuss it at this point.

world. For him, human beings are mere survival machines or robotic vehicles, whose evolution has blindly programmed them for self-preservation, through the instrumentality of "selfish molecules known as genes." But Jeremiah's experience shows us that God does exist and does enter into dialogue with human beings. It may be futile to try to demonstrate the existence of God. The best way to prove that he exists is to try him, to ask him to reveal himself to us.

Second, the call narrative highlights the fact that whoever claims to be on a mission for God must first hear his voice and be assured that God is the one sending them. Prophetic literature reveals intense prophetic activities undertaken by both true and false prophets. Not all those who call themselves prophets have been called by God. In the Old Testament, the true prophets were those like Jeremiah, inspired by the Spirit of God to deliver a specific message for a specific purpose, during a specific period. Their message was often unpopular, and sometimes not vindicated even during their lifetime. By contrast, the false prophets preached what their hearers wanted to hear, and often lived comfortably.

In the New Testament, it is written that the church is built upon the foundation of the apostles and prophets, with Christ himself as the chief cornerstone (Eph 2:20). The early church did not choose prophets, nor did prophets choose themselves. They were chosen by the Holy Spirit, who set aside select believers to receive and deliver God's revelation. At the same time, and because of the danger of false prophets, the church was warned to "test the spirits to see whether they are from God" (1 John 4:1 NIV).

Africa has seen a multiplicity of prophets, especially in the African Instituted Churches and Pentecostal churches. Some of these new African prophets resent being tested by the word of God as recommended in 1 John 4:1. Many are willing to resort to manipulative practices in ministry, to the extent of brainwashing their spiritually weak and desperate followers. I was once surprised to read on the wall of one of these churches in Kinshasa, an announcement – in large capital letters – of the scheduled time for "prophetic consultation," when members and neighbours could come with their problems, to receive solutions from "the prophet" on the spot. This is a non-biblical understanding of prophetic ministry, an invention of our time. Very often, these self-declared prophets take advantage of the dire conditions and ignorance of their followers. They impose on them a demand for strict moral perfection, warning them that failure to abide by their prescriptions may open the door to (new) demon possession. The prophet will dictate to people what to eat and not to eat. Some have gone so far as to ask their followers to divorce their spouses in order to "be delivered." One consequence of such abusive activity is the growing number of street children who have been thrown out of their homes after being accused of sorcery. The question of (false) prophecy is one of the gravest challenges facing Christianity in Africa today. Failure to profoundly reflect on it and to find an adequate response threatens the future of Christianity on the continent.

Jeremiah's Excuses (v. 6)

Jeremiah reacts to Yahweh's call with very polite excuses: "Ah! Lord Yahweh, look, I do not know how to speak, because I am only a boy." There are two interjections in the sentence: *'ăhâ* (Ah!) and *hinnēh* (look! or behold!). Many commentators have rightly noticed that this double exclamation in the same sentence expresses shock and alarm. But more than alarm, it expresses a kind of desperation in the young man. Jeremiah realizes that he has been caught up by Yahweh, and he appears to understand at once that this is the beginning of a very strange life. He knows that Yahweh will never change his mind to let him go. We can reflect on just how strange this new life is for Jeremiah from four perspectives.

First, as the son of a priest, he knows the nature of a call to a prophetic ministry – how different and in many ways unattractive it was compared to the socially comfortable living of a priest – and he is aware that beginning with that call, something has deeply changed in his life. To be called is to have limits imposed on one's life, to be restricted. The person called is no longer the same, nor are they free to do whatever they want, when and as they want. This is the meaning of the verb *hiqdaštîkâ* (I declared you holy, I consecrated you). The concept of consecration contains the idea of being set apart, of having been elected and cleansed for divine service. The person called has become a different person.

Second, the context of the region at the time of this calling was very complex. This was a time of conflicts and wars among the nations. Jeremiah's entire life was shaped by these constant regional conflicts. The destruction of Israel, the northern kingdom (721 BC), was still very fresh in the memory of the people of Judah. The intense trauma caused in the kingdom of Judah by Sennacherib's campaign of 701 BC was far from forgotten (2 Kgs 18–19). Egypt and Babylon were constantly fighting for regional supremacy, with a baleful impact on smaller nations like Judah. The entire context was one of terrible sociopolitical turbulence, and in such a situation, the appropriate response of a national leadership would be to mobilize its military, intelligence, and sociopolitical force to respond to the challenge, to resist the enemy and to assure the survival of the nation. When nationalist and jingoistic appeals are so prevalent and powerful, it is not easy to declare the defeatist message that Jeremiah was expected to deliver to his nation. A message to the king that his army will never be able to resist the enemy was nothing short of high treason, and it could have been severely punished as the entire book of Jeremiah demonstrates. It is true that at this point, Jeremiah did not know the content of the message, but he knew from his experience that being a prophet always meant navigating against the current of majority opinion. God will never call a prophet just to repeat what is being said by everyone else. He will never call them to entertain or try to please people, as happens today in too many African churches. This is why Jeremiah tried to present an excuse, to evade his calling. The responsibility laid on Jeremiah, the true prophet of Yahweh, was overwhelmingly massive, given his age, and his social and political context.

Third, being a prophet to the nations (v. 5) required great intellectual capacity, knowledge and political skills and maturity. To contextualize this passage, it would be like calling a young boy from DR Congo to speak to the President of South Africa or Egypt during a time of political tension or war. This was the case with Jeremiah, caught up in the geopolitical machinations of superpowers like Babylon and Egypt. Even addressing smaller nations like Philistia, Sidon, Damascus, Edom, and Moab required enormous courage and determination since they were mostly enemies of Judah. No wonder Jeremiah felt some initial inadequacy for this task. However, when one reads the book in its entirety, it becomes clear that Yahweh never intended to send him physically to those nations, as the call seems to imply; rather, God meant that his message to Judah would have international implications (Jer 27:1–11; 34:1–5).

Fourth, there was the challenge presented by Jeremiah's young age. In traditional Africa, during a time of war, a message opposing the powers might be tolerated from a mature adult. Leaders might be prepared to listen to someone with experience and wisdom. But in a crisis meeting convened by the village elders during a time of war, conflict or any other crisis, young men are present only as observers. They are not allowed to speak. They listen to the elders, gleaning wisdom for the time when they themselves will become leaders. For a young man like Jeremiah to shout out a defeatist message, out of line with what the elders and the political and spiritual leaders had already decided, would by completely unacceptable.

Looking at the reasons for Jeremiah's objection to becoming a prophet, we can understand why his reaction is so different from what we witness in many churches in Africa. Today, African "prophets" are eager to use every public opportunity to lay claim to a special revelation from God. They think that being a prophet is an honour and a reason for boasting, rather than trembling. They should listen to Henry Mottu who said: "Whoever does not tremble before his call is a blind man."[6] And to Bruno Chenu, who reminds us that "a good prophet is a dead prophet."[7] It may indeed be true that whoever does not tremble before the immensity of God's calling is not a true prophet. Jeremiah did not find anything to boast about; he knew that God's call contains something sublime that makes us shiver.

My prayer is that the African church and "powerful" African prophets will heed this message and listen to Paul, who reminds us that we should only boast about our weakness and suffering (2 Cor 11:16–30). We should also listen to Jesus himself, who, "being in very nature God, did not consider equality with God something to be used to his own advantage; [but] . . . humbled himself by becoming obedient to death – even death on a cross!" (Phil 2: 6–8 NIV).

Yahweh's Reaction (vv. 7–8)

Yahweh's gentle reaction to Jeremiah suggests that he acknowledges the merits of the young man's argument. He knows that being a prophet is a very difficult calling. Indeed, throughout his ministry, Jeremiah will seek to free himself from the burden of responsibility for declaring this divine word, for which he has become an object of mockery (Jer 20:8). Instead of entering into a discussion with Jeremiah, Yahweh gently overrules his argument and moves forward with the plan: "Do not say 'I am only a boy,' because wherever I send you, you will go, and whatever I command you, you will speak." In other words, this call and the dialogue are intended more as a declaration of Jeremiah's new life and ministry than as an invitation that he can accept or decline. Yahweh has made a choice; he chose his servant before the servant was conceived, and it is not open to the servant to reject or to change his plan.

In his answer to the prophet, Yahweh tells him, "whatever I command you, you will speak." The verb to command ($ṣwh$) is a perfect answer to Jeremiah's claim that he does not know how to speak. Jeremiah does not need to know what to say. He is to speak what Yahweh will command him to speak. God's glory is manifested more powerfully when we humans recognize our inadequacy. This reminds us again of Paul's struggle in 2 Corinthians 12:9 when

---

6. Henry Mottu, *Les Confessions de Jérémie: Une Protestation Contre la Souffrance* (Genève: Labor et Fides, 1985), 33. Own translation.

7. Bruno Chenu, *Prophétisme et Église* (Abbaye de Saint Maurice: Edition numérique, 1981), 30. Own translation.

God told him: "My grace is sufficient for you, for my power is made perfect in weakness" (NIV). Thus, the prophet does not need to be an older person with a lot of experience because what he is to do is not based on what he knows; it is based on what Yahweh wants him to do, and he will go where Yahweh wants him to go. He is not allowed to amend or alter anything that Yahweh will ask of him, even when his life is threatened.

We see this clearly during the siege of Jerusalem by the Babylonian army. At that time, Jeremiah was constantly threatened and was very often in extreme peril. It would have been easy to modify God's word in order to save his life. So, for example, when Zedekiah sent people to get Jeremiah from prison, and asked him, "Is there any word from Yahweh?" Jeremiah knew that there was indeed a word. However, he also knew that to declare that word might cost him his life. But he had no choice: "Yes," Jeremiah replied, "you shall be handed over to the king of Babylon" (37:16–17). What boldness!

More evidence of the dangerous nature of Jeremiah's ministry comes from the final encounter between the king and the prophet a few days before the fall of Jerusalem. The king again asks him whether he has a word from Yahweh for him. And the prophet responds: "If I give you an answer, will you not kill me? Even if I did give you counsel, you would not listen to me" (38:14–18). It seems to me that this is the true nature of prophetic ministry, a ministry that constantly brings great danger and even death into the life of the servant of Yahweh when a country has fallen apart, or when a nation is in the hands of dictators. Jesus, the final and greatest prophet, likewise spoke truth to power, and the political and religious power structures colluded in his death.

There are numerous examples throughout African church history of Christian leaders who have served God in extremely difficult political contexts and have paid with their lives. One of them is Janani Jakaliya Luwum, the Anglican archbishop and primate of Uganda, who was assassinated by the Ugandan president Idi Amin in 1977. In a paper on the legacy of the archbishop, George Piwang-Jalobo quotes the Right Reverend Henry Okullu:

> Janani Luwum had a role to play in the affairs of his nation. He refused to tremble before Idi Amin. He faced him . . . Archbishop Luwum was not seeking martyrdom; and church leaders should not seek martyrdom. But they must not run away from it. As the situation worsened during Luwum's last days, his wife, Mary, pleaded with him continually to run out of Uganda. The Archbishop refused putting it clearly that he had no guilty conscience on Amin's accusations. Sometimes it is said that it is the

privilege of the great to watch catastrophe from a terrace. Luwum refused to run away and watch catastrophe from the terrace. He put down his life for the sheep. It is said that he kept telling his brother bishops: "We must see the hand of God in this." He saw God's hand in everything that was happening in those days before his murder.[8]

On 16 February, the day Luwum was murdered, Amin summoned all the top religious leaders of Uganda to the presidential palace. After a short meeting, he asked all other leaders to leave and told Luwum to stay behind. As his colleagues were leaving, Luwum whispered to Bishop Festo Kivengere: "They are going to kill me . . . I am not afraid." Tragically, his premonition was correct. The following day, a patently false report was issued saying that the archbishop had died in a motor vehicle accident. According to some reports, the archbishop was actually shot dead by Amin himself after having refused to sign a false "confession" of treason.

"They are going to kill me . . . I am not afraid." These were the last words of the Archbishop Luwum to his colleagues. And it is with almost the same words ("You must not be afraid of them") that Yahweh encourages his prophet in verse 8. We hear Jeremiah himself asking King Zedekiah: "Will you not kill me, if I tell you the truth?" This is really the essence of the prophetic calling. And it should not be different for Africa today. Like the Ugandan archbishop, Jeremiah will be sent to deliver tough words to kings, princes, soldiers, priests, false prophets, scribes, ambassadors of foreign nations, and the people of the kingdom. For Jeremiah to assume such a heavy responsibility entailed grave risk, since the political and religious establishments and the general public wanted to close their ears to Yahweh's words of warning and judgement. Jeremiah will indeed be afraid and he will suffer. Yahweh did not promise to protect him from suffering, but to rescue him from the real threats that he will face during his ministry. As John Thompson states,

> It may be sound theology to say, "One man with God is a majority"; but when that one man faces the crowd, in the hour of actual confrontation he needs more than theoretical theology. Nothing less than the deepest conviction that God will be with him will

---

8. George Piwang-Jalobo, "The Legacy of St Janani Luwum: 1922–1977" (unpublished paper, 2006).

suffice. The reassuring word that Jeremiah received, "Don't be afraid of them! For I am with you to rescue you," was a necessity.[9]

Several times during his ministry, when Jeremiah was under pressure, persistent persecution, or mockery on every side, he seems to have doubted Yahweh's assurance (12:1–4; 20:7–18). But this is a natural response, demonstrating real suffering on the part of an authentic messenger from Yahweh. Delivering a true message in times of trouble does bring suffering and pain. It is impossible to stand up against such pressure unless you clearly hear God's voice assuring you that God's presence is with you.

Yahweh's Commission (vv. 9–10)

In verse 9, the prophet shares a specific experience of a divine vision: "Yahweh stretched out his hand and touched my mouth." The first eight verses were a conversation between Yahweh and the prophet. Verse 9 introduces a new element in the prophetic call: direct contact between the human prophet and the divine. This experience reminds us of Isaiah's inaugural vision (Isa 6:6–7). However, the difference between the two visions is that in Isaiah, the touching of the prophet's mouth with a burning coal helped to cleanse his whole body, whereas for Jeremiah, the weight is on the divine "words," the ministry of the spoken word being given to him as confirmed by the following sentence: "Look, I have put my words in your mouth." This experience of Yahweh touching the prophet's mouth and putting his word in his mouth clearly reminds us of the promise in Deuteronomy 18:18: "I will raise up for them a prophet like you from among their fellow Israelites, and I will put my words in his mouth" (NIV). The prophet from Anathoth certainly must have known this passage, and it would have afforded him strong encouragement during the long periods of suffering in his ministry. Jeremiah will be a speaking prophet, a bearer of the "word that will decide the future of the city, the temple, the dynasty and, indeed, the nation."[10]

After the first encounter (vv. 4–5), a short reaction from the prophet (v. 5) and Yahweh's commission (vv. 7–8), verse 10 provides more clarity on Jeremiah's call and the authority that goes with it: "See! This day, I have given you authority [I have appointed you] over the nations and over the kingdoms." It is important to note that this authority cannot be detached from the call or

---

9. John A. Thompson, *The Book of Jeremiah* (Grand Rapids, MI: Eerdmans, 1980), 149.
10. Brueggemann, *Commentary on Jeremiah*, 25.

the divine origin of the message. It is not an authority that comes from wealth, worldly power, or political manipulation. As the ministry of Jeremiah will consistently demonstrate, the prophet from Anathoth was a fragile person, but his authoritative words profoundly shook the establishment in Jerusalem. This is another confirmation that God's power and glory manifest themselves in weak, fragile human bodies.

The same verse spells out specific actions that will determine the painful ministry of Jeremiah. These actions are listed in six verbs: "pluck up," "break down," "destroy," "demolish/overthrow," "build," and "plant." The first four actions are negative, to declare that Jeremiah's ministry will be characterized by Yahweh's severe judgement. They probably indicate that the prophet will be at war against the falsehoods of the people of Judah and beyond. This will be a war against the illusions of the people, caught up in a logic that will end up destroying them. For Judah in particular, it will be a war against whatever ends up diverting them from the covenant with Yahweh. As I will describe in the following chapters, it is this falsehood that finally brought judgement in terms of destruction and exile.

However, the last two verbs reveal that there is hope beyond judgement. The prophecy of Jeremiah does not end with destruction and exile. The prophet will finally announce a time of restoration for the nation after the judgement (see chapters 8–10 in this book). God is able to work newness, creating new possibilities in situations that seem hopeless and closed.

Some commentators find it curious that there is no account of Jeremiah's reaction to this appointment and commission such as we see in Isaiah (6:8). They think that, in part, the reason is to be found in the purpose of the call narrative, which is not intended to be a full account but only to establish the authority and authenticity of the ministry that is to follow.[11] This might be true, but why should Jeremiah respond? Whoever has had such an encounter with Yahweh knows that despite all forms of resistance and excuses, God does finally prevail. This was the case with Moses and Jonah. And this is true in the real-life experience of every Christian who has been called to a significant ministry. One could think of C. S. Lewis' hugely impactful ministry, yet his calling was a long-drawn-out process that only became clear in retrospect. In this particular passage, the person of the prophet is no longer a subject or an interlocutor but rather an object of God's choice and sovereign decision.

---

11. Peter C. Craigie, Page H. Kelley, and Joel F. Drinkard Jr, *Jeremiah 1–25*. Word Biblical Commentary (Dallas, TX: Word, 1991), 11.

In his commentary on the book of Jeremiah, Brueggemann persistently argues that the survival or destruction of Jerusalem is not related to the city's own capacity for life and survival but is determined solely by the sovereign will of Yahweh, and that the prophet's word is subordinated to the irresistible purpose of Yahweh.[12] This is a very difficult issue to deal with, for nobody really knows God's intention (Deut 29:29; Dan 2:22; 12:9; Prov 25:2). However, I find Brueggemann's argument problematic because it undermines the very essence of prophetic call and ministry. I do not see why Yahweh would call Jeremiah if he had already decided the fate of Jerusalem. In his sovereignty, Yahweh surely knew what would happen, but he did want his servant to keep warning the people and their leaders. What if they had listened to Jeremiah and repented as King Hezekiah did in 2 Chronicles 32 and as the people of Nineveh did when Jonah preached (Jonah 3)? When God invites his people to "settle the matter" (Isa 1:18 NIV), it is a true invitation. Is it not the same with us? Doesn't God always speak to us and call us to repentance?

Two Visions (vv. 11–16)

Because the mission is difficult (vv. 4–10) one more assurance is needed to confirm to the prophet that God's word will be faithfully carried out, even to the smallest detail. Brueggemann's argument that we do not need to linger over the question of the phenomenon of vision[13] misses the point. It seems to me that the prophet will need several such visions from now on to encourage him, to confirm his call, and to keep him going. When the going gets tough, one needs more assurance. Those who have worked in very difficult situations understand the importance of renewed visions from God at each step.

The new vision consists of two very similar signs. In both cases, Yahweh asks a question of Jeremiah. The prophet responds, and Yahweh gives the interpretation of the vision. The dialogue initiated in verse 5 continues here, but with a different attitude on Jeremiah's part. He no longer protests; he quietly receives instructions and the narrative moves forward smoothly.

In the first vision, Jeremiah is shown a branch of an almond tree. The almond tree is the first tree to bud during spring. All who have visited the region will confirm that Anathoth, Jeremiah's home village, is still a centre for almond cultivation. So, Thompson is right to report that "the modern visitor to the area in the very early spring is promised the memorable and

---

12. See, for example, Brueggemann, *Commentary on Jeremiah*, 27.
13. Brueggemann, *Commentary on Jeremiah*, 27.

unforgettable sight of almond trees[14] in bloom and in great profusion around the village of 'Anata.'"[15] However, the prophet does not say that this vision came during springtime, although that is possible. Jeremiah was told to look, and Yahweh asked him to tell what he saw. Jeremiah saw a branch of an almond tree (*šāqēd*).[16] And Yahweh confirmed that he saw rightly because Yahweh is watching or is early (like the almond tree in spring) on the watch (*šōqēd*)[17] to accomplish his word (judgement).

It can be hard for modern readers to grasp the meaning of this vision, for it involves a play on two Hebrew words that sound very similar: (*šāqēd*) (a branch of an almond tree) and *šōqēd* (the verb "to watch"). The almond tree is the first tree to bud after winter. It is therefore the tree that anticipates spring by preparing itself to put forth new life in its branches. So in the vision the almond tree symbolizes Yahweh's action. Yahweh is watching to accomplish his word at the right time.

To be more concrete, this is how one can imagine the conversation:

Yahweh: What do you see, Jeremiah?
Jeremiah: I see an almond tree (I see a *šāqēd*)
Yahweh: You are right, because I will watch (I will *šōqēd*) to accomplish my word.

The emphasis is not on the fact that the almond tree is the first to bud after winter. That was known to anyone who lived in Anathoth or Judea. The important point being communicated is that Yahweh is watching and waiting to fulfil his purposes in the midst of a rebellious people. This was the point hidden to Jeremiah's contemporaries, and this was the message he was commissioned to proclaim. The man from Anathoth was to remind the people and their leaders that Yahweh's eye sees every aspect of their life, private or public. This is an important point, since the people of Judah – especially their spiritual and political leaders – imagined that they were the masters of history. They thought that the future rested solely on their decisions without listening to Yahweh's voice through his prophet, and that whatever they did would not have any consequences for the life of the nation that would exceed their control. This message was also relevant for other nations, including the superpowers of Egypt and Babylon. It was Jeremiah's mission to remind them that Yahweh reigns;

---

14. *Prunus dulcis*.
15. Thompson, *Book of Jeremiah*, 153.
16. Pronounced *shaqed*.
17. Pronounced *shoqed*.

he is watching and he has the last word in the life of every nation, whether a superpower or not! This point is relevant in any era, including our own, and all leaders must be reminded to humble themselves before the watching eye of the Lord of the universe. But how aware are we of this need? Have not our world political systems put in place strong leaders, whose strength tempts them to arrogantly assume they are in total control of their life and nations? There are African leaders who have not yet learned from the personal or national failures of leaders such as Mobutu, Idi Amin, Bokassa, and too many others.

The second vision (vv. 13–16) is of a large pot set on a fire and boiling furiously. The literal translation of the Hebrew would be "a blown pot," emphasizing the intense heat as a fire is fanned under the pot. The boiling liquid in the pot is overflowing in a southerly direction. The explanation of this second vision was straightforward: disaster would soon flow from the north to destroy Judah. The image of a boiling pot to describe raging wars was well known in the Ancient Near East.[18] Both the prophet and those who heard him describing this vision would understand that he was announcing imminent war and devastation.

It is possible, depending on the timing of this utterance, that this vision in fact addressed a specific political crisis occurring towards the beginning of Jeremiah's ministry. Many of the politicians in Jerusalem may have been thinking that the real threat to their country would come from Egypt (this became a reality in 609 BC when King Josiah was killed by Pharaoh Necho and Josiah's son Jehoahaz was deported to Egypt three months later). But Jeremiah corrects this wrong thinking, warning them that the real danger is coming from the north, not Egypt. This had been true throughout the experiences of both Israel and Judah, which had suffered periodically throughout their histories at the hands of Amorites, the Assyrians, and other armies descending from the north.

Verses 15 and 16 provide more detail concerning the vision of the coming disaster. A coalition of enemies would come against Jerusalem and all the other cities in Judah to destroy them. The conquering enemies would set up their thrones at the entrance to Jerusalem to deliberate over its fate. The setting up of thrones at the gates of Jerusalem and other cities symbolizes the defeat of Judah followed by its total control by the enemy. This message of defeat was the last thing the politicians of Jerusalem were willing to hear. Such a prophecy would have provoked great resentment in Jerusalem at any time during Jeremiah's

---

18. Lundbom, *Jeremiah 1–20*, 241.

ministry. Even after the fall of Jerusalem in 586 BC, many politicians could not accept Babylonian rule. They regarded it as only a temporary setback.[19]

Why the Judgement on Judah? (v. 16)

Verse 16 is the first passage in the book of Jeremiah that clearly summarizes the evils committed by Judah that have brought judgement on the nation: Yahweh's people have forsaken their God by turning to foreign gods, offering sacrifices to them, and worshipping the work of their own hands. Because of this evil, Yahweh announces that he will judge the nation. The Hebrew word *mišpāṭîm* (pl. "judgements") are sentences meted out in court (Jer 4:12).[20] This concept becomes central to the book of Jeremiah. It connects this statement with verse 10, where Yahweh announces his judgement in terms of plucking out and pulling down, destroying and demolishing, before building and planting again.

The problem of Judah according to this passage is theological and moral: the breaking of the covenant. Yahweh has demonstrated his faithfulness and power in the past by liberating his people from Egypt and leading them safely through the horrendous desert to the promised land. The promised land itself was Yahweh's gift to his people. In the course of doing these things, Yahweh entered into a covenant with them. On Yahweh's side, this covenant required his continuous protection and blessing of his people. For Israel (and now Judah), it required recognition of Yahweh as their unique Lord to whom they were to remain faithful. Faithfulness to the stipulations of the covenant would bring blessing, while its rejection would mean a curse on the nation. The entire book of Jeremiah is concerned with Judah's abandonment of the covenant stipulations and its consequences.

But how do we understand and explain this abandonment of Yahweh by the people of Israel/Judah after they have experienced all the goodness of God? What is it that pushes people to abandon God and serve idols? Brueggemann calls it the sin of theological, political, and historical autonomy, the nullification of Yahweh's governance of public life.[21]

This is neither only an ancient problem, nor a problem only for Judah. We face the same challenge today, perhaps more acutely than during the time of Israel/Judah. David Bentley Hart calls it "modernity's highest ideal, its special understanding of personal autonomy." He argues that modern man wants

---

19. Thompson, *Book of Jeremiah*, 155.
20. Lundbom, *Jeremiah 1–20*, 243.
21. Brueggemann, *Commentary on Jeremiah*, 29.

absolute freedom. He hates to have a criterion by which his autonomous choices will be judged. He identifies any judgement that stands higher than the unquestioned good of free choice itself as in some sense an infringement upon his freedom.[22] Thus, the tendency of modern, civilized society is the search for absolute autonomy that completely excludes God or tries to eliminate him from the memory of human beings. This gives rise to the claim that God never created human beings; instead, the origin of the universe and the existence of life including human life are attributed to a random and undirected chemical process – chance plus time. Because atheistic evolution is driven by random mutations, it would be possible for our world to have been inhabited by living beings totally different from us: six-eyed beings, with five arms and six feet, three heads, and propelling themselves on their back. This is the world of Richard Dawkins, Samuel B. Harris, Daniel Dennett, and others of the New Atheists who are working very hard toward the exclusion of God from our world.

However, while Hart's understanding fits well with the Western individualistic mentality, in Africa, the crisis of faith and the abandonment of God is of a different nature. It does not consist of the total and open denial of God. Only rarely does one hear an African openly confessing that he does not believe in God's existence, even if there are many Africans not associated with any church. Our real problem is that many people do not want God to control their life, their politics, their economy, and even their church. The Rwandan genocide provides an extreme example: a church that becomes a site for the massacre of its own members on an ethnic basis cannot claim to know God.

It may be that we have created our own gods, made in our image. Thus, the abandonment of God in Africa very often happens when an allegiance to worldly desires (ethnic identity, glory, wealth, or power) is elevated to an unreasonable degree and conditions our thinking and actions. It is the lack of confidence in God that pushes people to idolatrous practices. Idolatry here does not mean atheism; rather, it means not trusting the God whom we confess. It actually means abandoning God. The abandonment of God and idolatry do not describe two separate realities; they are the same. This was also Judah's problem, and the book of Jeremiah is full of condemnation of lip-service by idolatrous people.

Understood this way, the practice of idolatry creates dysfunctions in the community at both the local and national levels. If it is not confronted,

---

22. David Bentley Hart, *Atheist Delusions: The Christian Revolution and Its Fashionable Enemies* (New Haven, CT: Yale University Press, 2009), 21.

idolatry can gnaw at a society until it is completely destroyed as people distance themselves from God in their aggressive pursuit of self-centred and egoistic goals. Very often, this is done by excluding others, and by prejudicing the weaker members of the community. This is the opposite of the vision of a community that covenants with God. The vision of Yahweh, the God of covenant, is of a society shaped by justice. A covenant community is a community that fears God and that works for justice.

How did Jeremiah address the issue of idolatry? This book will seek to answer this question. But how can we deal with it in the church today? Paul addresses this painful question by calling for the conversion of our imagination, to conform it to the mind of Christ (1 Cor 2:16; Rom 12:1–2). For Paul, this conversion is possible only through the power of the cross. Seeing the world through the cross of Jesus energizes us, enables us to see the world differently and to live in conformity with the vision of the kingdom of God and to live out our new identity as Christians (1 Cor 5:16–17).

Conclusion (vv. 17–19)

As an introductory chapter, Jeremiah 1 does not deal with details. These will follow, in the succeeding fifty-one chapters. It simply sets the stage for the book by introducing the prophet, the nature of his calling and the kind of ministry to which he is being called. Yahweh shows clearly to his prophet that his ministry is going to be very difficult. Throughout the nineteen verses of the chapter, God constantly warns his prophet that he must be ready for the challenges to come: "But as for you, brace yourself like a man! Stand up and speak to them everything that I command you. Do not be terrified because of them, or else I may terrify you before them" (v. 17). God makes it clear that Jeremiah is going to engage specifically with the leadership of Judah: kings, princes, priests, and also with the people (v. 18), who will literally fight against him (v. 19a). In such a context, it is important to note that the chapter ends with Yahweh's renewed promise to protect his servant (v. 19b).

The chapter's conclusion raises several questions we need to reflect on. In the light of this chapter, how do we define a prophetic ministry today? Who is a prophet today in Africa? How should the African church live out its prophetic role in the image of Jeremiah? How can African churches and theologians deal with the question of false prophets and idolatry raised in this book?

2

Idolatry and the Peril of the Nation

Jeremiah 2:4–8

⁴ Hear the word of Yahweh, house of Jacob, and all the families of the house of Israel.

⁵ Thus says Yahweh:
"What evil did your fathers find in me,
 that they walked away from me,
and went after vanity,
 and became vain in the process?
⁶ And they did not say, 'Where is Yahweh?
 Who brought us up from the land of Egypt,
who guided us in the wilderness,
 in a land of dryness and utter darkness,
in a land through which no one passes,
 and (where) no one settles?'
⁷ I brought you into a fertile land,
 to eat its fruit and its good produce;
but when you went in, you defiled my land
 and changed my heritage into an abomination.
⁸ The priests did not say,
 'Where is Yahweh?'
Those who handle the Torah did not know me.
 The shepherds rebelled against me,
and the prophets prophesied by Baal;
 they walked after things that do not profit."

Historical and Literary Context

Chapters 2–6 of Jeremiah 2 belongs to what is known as the "Foe from the North" unit. The theme that runs through these five chapters is Judah's unfaithfulness and Yahweh's punishment of his people through an enemy coming from the north. Chapter 2 opens the section with the description of Yahweh's accusation against Judah because of its idolatry. This prophecy chapter must have been uttered at the beginning of Jeremiah's ministry, before Josiah's reformation in 622 BC. Thus Judah's idolatry may reflect, in part, its vassal status to a foreign power (Assyria) which required acknowledgement of the Assyrian gods.[1]

In his commentary on Jeremiah, John Thompson makes the point that chapter 2 consists of an arrangement of several originally independent segments dealing with the same theme that are brought together to serve a theological purpose.[2] For example, verses 4–13 can be distinguished as a separate unit from other units in the chapter by the pronouns used. Here, the feminine singular pronoun is used for the person addressed, whereas in the rest of the chapter the pronoun used for the addressee is masculine and plural.

Thompson also points out that in the context of the whole chapter, verses 4–13 form a bridge between the statement of Israel's early devotion to Yahweh (vv. 1–3) and the description of its present state of bondage to Assyria (vv. 14–19). This gives a clear sequence of events in the chapter: Israel's early devotion (vv. 1–3), Israel's apostasy (vv. 4–13), and the tragic results of this apostasy (vv. 14–19).[3] In this chapter, I wish to focus on the section on apostasy in verses 4–6 and 8.

The study of Jeremiah 2 is very important for us in Africa because it shows how Israel started well with Yahweh only to end in apostasy. It is easy for a country to slowly but surely abandon its primary vision of justice, unity, love, and progress. The national anthems of most African countries, which were composed at the time of independence from colonial rule, contain such a primary vision: the need for building a better nation on the basis of unity, justice, and love, and sometimes include a prayer to God to bless the nation. Some of the first (post-independence) constitutions of these countries also contain such a primary vision. But when a country abandons its vision and

---

1. Peter Craigie, P. H. Kelley, and J. F. Drinkard, *Jeremiah 1–25*, Word Biblical Commentary (Dallas, TX: Word Books, 1991), 28.

2. John A. Thompson, *Book of Jeremiah*, New International Commentary on the Old Testament (Grand Rapids, MI: Eerdmans, 1980), 160.

3. Thompson, *Jeremiah*, 167.

embraces vanity, it finally destroys the whole nation with its people. As I look into this text to discover what went wrong between Yahweh and his beloved people of Judah, I will also be looking at the story of Africa and trying to understand what is going wrong in the continent.

Israel's History Matters (v. 4)

When we go to a hospital for the first time, the doctor always starts with questions about our medical history. They carefully take detailed notes of what we tell them in order to construct a correct picture of the state of our health. They understand that our health is heavily influenced by the past: the places where we have lived, our families, the activities we have been involved in, past behaviours, and past experiences, all have important information that can help to explain our present health conditions. It is the same with society at large. The history of a society helps us to understand its present condition. If we get to know a society's past, we will be able to understand the reasons for most of its problems. This was true for Israel in Jeremiah's time and it is true for us in Africa today.

In Jeremiah 2:4, the prophet takes his contemporaries back to their past, to the history of Israel, to help them understand the root of the problems they were facing. Jeremiah's telling of Israel's history starts with an invitation to hear. History must be explained accurately and heard correctly. If we delight in hearing pseudohistory, it will give us a false understanding of ourselves and our values.

This passage opens in verse 4 with an appeal to the house of Jacob and the families of the house of Israel to "hear the word of Yahweh." In chapter 2 this "word" is mainly a review of Israel's history.

Some commentators struggle to understand why this verse refers to the "house of Israel," which no longer existed in Jeremiah's time since the expression "house of Israel" was the designation of the tribal league at the time of the Judges (1 Sam 7:2, 3) and of the kingship of Saul and David (2 Sam 1:12; 6:5). Holladay, for example, thinks that the verse originally introduced a message to the northern tribes and is simply a poetic synonym for "house of Jacob," as in Amos 3:13, functioning as a reminder that the people of Israel were God's chosen people.[4] Thompson, argues that this oracle might have been spoken at a covenant festival during which the people of the southern

---

4. William Holladay, *Jeremiah 1: A Commentary on the Book of the Prophet Jeremiah Chapters 1–25*, Hermeneia (Philadelphia, PA: Fortress, 1986), 85.

kingdom of Judah would have been addressed as representing "all the tribes of the house of Israel."[5]

My understanding of the passage is different from their views. It seems to me that Jeremiah is here using his prophetic imagination to remind his audience about the whole history of Israel (not only Judah), a history of failing to obey God and instead following after delusion. In this sense, we do not need to see it as addressed either to the northern kingdom (*contra* Holladay) or to a particular Judean festival (*contra* Thompson). It might be that the prophet simply wanted to show his audience the root of their problem. I see the passage as showing a continuity of history. Though the northern kingdom no longer existed, the prophet saw the need to show his contemporaries that their situation was linked to that of their fathers (v. 5), or that their present state of apostasy really began with their fathers, at the very beginning of their history with Yahweh.

In the same way, the question with which Yahweh opens his case against Judah in verse 5 relates to the beginnings of the history of Israel as a nation, and not only to the history of Judah. According to Jeremiah, history is a good teacher that tells us why we find ourselves in a particular situation. This is true for every single society. Cicero acknowledges this in his often-quoted saying: *historia magistra vitae* (history is the teacher of life).

This understanding is important for us because how we choose to live both socially and spiritually in our own time will affect future generations. We are shaped by the society into which we are born and it is often extremely difficult for us to break free from its mould. Unfortunately, as human beings, we mostly concentrate on the present, on things of immediate interest to us. We rarely think about the consequences of our actions for the generations to come. If one thinks, for example, of the many blessings God bestowed on Israel, it is distressing to see the many ways in which Israel showed its ingratitude to God. In the same way, it is distressing to see how life for most people in Africa is marked by suffering and death, even though the continent is teeming with God-given riches. Sadly, the perception of Africa in the world today, mostly as a result of media reporting that focuses on the bad things happening on the continent, is of people dying from hunger, endless wars, malnourished children, broken communities, and so on. The image of Africa in the West is of a doomed continent destroyed by war, crime, corruption, HIV/AIDS, refugees, and people fleeing their countries.

---

5. Thompson, *Jeremiah*, 167.

How do we explain this disaster? How did Africa get here? Why do we Africans seem paralysed and unable to change our situation? Can Jeremiah help us understand the causes of our problems and how to overcome them? My argument is that, just as Jeremiah began by urging the people of Israel to look at their past relationship with God, so we, the people of Africa, must start by examining our history so that we can understand the origin of our problems.

Basil Davidson, for example, links the current crises in Africa's social and political institutions with the denial of its past. Colonization made African history a *tabula rasa*, destroying many of the structures that had sustained life on the continent for centuries, and creating systems and processes that were unknown to Africans. The imperial structures stripped African communities of their history and traditions, destroyed the harmony that existed between societies, and left African people disorganized and destabilized. Africans were taught that in order to be civilized, they needed to adopt a Western/European way of life. Unfortunately, those who did never became true Europeans but ceased to be authentic Africans.

Regarding spiritual matters, it is important to be reminded that in traditional Africa, religion explained and regulated the entire life of individuals and societies. Values could not be divorced from religion; the spiritual and physical dimensions of our world could be distinguished but not separated. In traditional Africa, farming, daily activities, celebrations and religion went hand in hand. Religion regulated meetings, burial ceremonies, weddings, conflict resolution, and so on. Ethics could not be conceived of apart from religion. Nothing could be given a natural explanation without appealing to the supernatural.

This type of spirituality does have its weaknesses. For example, it can kill the spirit of initiative and innovation because it underestimates people's own contributions to shaping their future and regards all outcomes as controlled by God. However, colonialism largely destroyed the spirituality of Africans by bringing in some of the worst elements of Western philosophies such as humanism, which taught that everything, including human beings, has a natural explanation that is not linked to the supernatural. The undiscerning adoption by some Africans of these philosophies and the resulting moral relativism has been devastating both for individuals and society and has led to spiritual confusion. One consequence is that many people think they can do without God. They can steal, kill, and tell lies because religion and God mean little. They need God and religion only when in pain and need.

God has not only been privatized; he has been isolated, manipulated, weakened, and silenced. Can this explain why some who profess to be Christian are corrupt politicians, unfaithful government officials, and morally dubious businessmen and women? Does the same spiritual confusion underlie the superficiality of faith on the continent, despite the phenomenal growth of the church in Africa? There is an urgent need to rethink what it means to be an African Christian.

Yahweh Abandoned by His People (v. 5)

Verse 5 starts with an important rhetorical question: "What evil did your fathers find in me, that they walked away from me?" The word here translated "evil" or "fault" is *'evel*. As a verb, it means to act wrongly or unjustly. It is evil in an ethical, moral sense. Its antonym is *tsadik* (good behaviour, righteousness, covenantal kindness, or justice). The question implies that some moral failure in Yahweh might have forced the Israelites to depart from him. In the immediate context of verses 1–3, which describe the relationship between Yahweh and Israel as similar to that between a husband and wife, and in the context of the whole Old Testament, this passage reminds one of Deuteronomy 24:1, which speaks of a man divorcing his wife when he finds some indecency in her. In Israel, a wife was not allowed to divorce her husband, but in this text, Israel as Yahweh's wife decided to divorce him, which was against nature. This is a pathetic story of the broken relationship between Yahweh and his beloved people.

Theologically, the type of wicked actions encompassed by the word *'evel* have absolutely no part in the character of God (Deut 32:4; Job 34:10). The rhetorical question thus expresses Yahweh's shock at Israel's rejection. It makes him look evil and unable to care for the needs of his people and impugns his character.

Though there is no attempt to immediately respond to this allegation, it is clear that there was no fault in Yahweh. The ancestors of Israel are the ones to be blamed because they were the ones who walked away from Yahweh their God and led the whole nation in rebellion against him. To "walk away" (from God) comes from the verb *rachaq*, which means "to be or become distant, remote, be removed or remove oneself, withdraw, make distant, walk away, go far away." Many commentators understand the expression "walked away from me [Yahweh]" to mean going after Yahweh's rivals or after other gods (idols) in order to serve them.[6] This is contrasted with walking after Yahweh in verse 2 of this chapter, where it is said that Israel followed Yahweh in the desert during the time of love.

The heart of Judah's problem is thus expressed in one single verb: *rachaq*. This walking away from Yahweh has significant social implications. It is also to walk away from the center of life, of true power, of true vision for the wellbeing of the community. It leads to a loss of direction for the future and a distancing from the source of human worth. This distancing from God also means a sense of autonomy from Yahweh, a revolt from his commandments, an unwillingness to obey his law, a deviation from godly principles, and a loss of initial vision in relationship with his transcendence. It is this loss of worth that creates disintegration in human reasoning and leads to the spiritual death of the leadership (represented by the fathers in v. 5) and the entire nation.

Once a leader abandons the source of true power, leadership becomes dysfunctional and brings only death, corruption, poverty, and suffering. This is because the owner of true power, life, and social justice and order has been done away with. This is the problem reflected in the entire book of Jeremiah. We know from our experience in Africa that such leaders lack self-confidence; they are like empty vessels since they have no other greater power and example to imitate. Instead they trust in pseudo experts like false prophets, soothsayers, praise singers, witch doctors, magicians, diviners, and even some religious leaders who, like them, have lost direction.

When God is done away with, something or someone else is put in his place: either a person or personality cult, dictatorship, a system, or a doctrine (like communism, socialism, capitalism, Mobutism, or Nkrumaism). In one way or another, this was what happened to the people of Judah when they distanced themselves from Yahweh. This result also sheds light on the situation in most African countries today where it seems that people are walking in darkness: the darkness of war, hatred, ignorance, poverty, corruption, and tribalism. In both Israel and Africa, this darkness symbolizes the loss of direction.

Throughout its history, Israel flirted with idolatry (Jer 3:23; 11:12; 44:17–25). This specific passage does not tell us how exactly the people of Judah went after idols; these details will come later. Jeremiah 2 thus functions as a hypotext, that is, a text that serves as a summary of the message of the entire book. However, we know that idolatry can take several forms: it can be open

---

6. Thompson, *Jeremiah*, 167. He notes that in secular treaties of the day, a rebel vassal who went after some other ruler was understood to have renounced allegiance to his overlord. This is probably what the accusation meant in this passage.

for all to see, for example, in the sense of seeking help from other supernatural forces through magic, witchcraft, or divination (1 Sam 28:1–25), or hidden in the sense of replacing God in our life with the desire for material goods, power, and other things. For Uchenna B. Okeja, the dominant forms of idolatry in Africa are witchcraft and magic. He paints a horrifying picture of modern idolatrous practices by African people, Christians and non-Christians alike:

> The manifestation of the phenomena of magic and witchcraft in contemporary Africa is so endemic that one can, without risking any ambivalence, say that it is pathological. In the schools, market place, church, government and other offices, streams, rivers, homes, forests, the floor of the stock exchange market, newspapers, bridges, government houses, state and federal houses of assembly, senate house, football stadium and even at the presidency, etc., the feeling, reports or affirmation of the manifestation of these phenomena is commonplace. There is, in short, so much belief, fear and purposeful recourse to the phenomena of witchcraft and magic in Africa, or at least in the part I am conversant with.[7]

This description is probably exaggerated and the situation may vary from one place to another. However, it shows the dark side of African faith and helps to explain why the continent is lagging behind in terms of development, human rights, and social justice. Erich Leistner confirms this when he says, "The fact that witchcraft and sorcery is not about to be 'modernized' is underlined by the reality of African elite – professors, other academics, theologians, ministers, state presidents, professionals, living by it."[8] These leaders are like the "fathers" of the book of Jeremiah. Peter Geshiere acknowledges the strong connection between African politics and witchcraft by arguing that "it is especially this version of sorcery/witchcraft as an accumulative force that prevails in more modern forms of politics."[9]

Jeremiah 2:5 states that the fathers walked after *hevel*, a word that literally means "vapour" (Isa 57:13; Prov 13:11; 21:6; Ps 144:4) and metaphorically means "vanity, nothingness, nonsense, incomprehensibility, deceit, senselessness,

---

7. Uchenna B. Okeja, "Magic in an African Context," in Scott E. Hendrix and Timothy J. Shannon, ed., *Magic and the Supernatural* (Oxford, UK: Inter-disciplinary Press, 2012), 104, at http://eprints.hud.ac.uk/id/eprint/14117/1/MagicandtheSupernaturalmagic1ever101232012.pdf.

8. Erich Leistner, "Witchcraft and African Development," *African Security Review*, March 2014, www.researchgate.net/publication/263332101.

9. Peter Geschiere, *Modernity of Witchcraft*, trans. Peter Geschiere and Janet Roitman (Charlottesville, VA: University Press of Virginia, 1997).

worthlessness, or unprofitableness." Whatever the exact meaning of this verse, it is clear that it assumes a close association between vanity and idols. For Yahweh, idols are vanity because they have turned Judah away from its primary vision, from its initial relationship with God, and from its mission.[10] As a result of following idols, Judah lost its value and identity and became useless for Yahweh. People pursuing vanity or who have become vanity get nowhere. No wonder most African dictators end their life miserably in exile or in prisons – think of Idi Amin of Uganda, Mobutu Sese Seko of Zaire (DR Congo), Hosni Mubarak of Egypt, Blaise Compaoré of Burkina Faso, and Jean-Bedel-Bokassa of the Central African Republic.

The worthlessness of which Jeremiah speaks is not to be understood in abstract terms. It is visible in real-life situations in our countries, communities, and lives and manifests itself in evils such as social injustice, corruption, poverty, suffering, ethnic division, fear, and uncertainty. In Jeremiah, there is a strong relationship between the knowledge of God and social justice on the one hand, and idolatry, war, and exile on the other as far as national and community life is concerned (5:1–9, 27–28; 7:5–7; 9:23–24; 21:12–14; 22:1–5, 13, 16–17; 23:5–6). Consequently, idolatrous practices in Judah threatened the missiological function of the nation by obscuring the worship of Yahweh, the true and living God, and by skewing the just social shape of the nation, and also endangered the very life of Judah as a nation.

From this analysis, it might be right to say that the true problem between Yahweh and the people of God (as described in v. 5) was that the Israelites moved away from their relationship with God and started pursuing useless things and idols. As a result, they themselves became *hevel*, that is, useless or worthless. Hosea 9:10 warns us that people become what they worship.

Trivialization of God (vv. 6–7)

Verse 6 elaborates that the failure of the Israelites resulted from their loss of spiritual memory, an abandonment of their history with Yahweh, that is, the abandonment of their primary vision. More specifically, the prophet accuses them of not asking the question, "Where is Yahweh?" The importance of this question is evident from the fact that it is repeated in verse 8.

---

10. There is a nice metaphor here. In Exodus (13:21–22; 40:36) and Numbers (9:17), the Israelites followed the cloud to guide them during their travel to the Promised Land. This was the presence of Yahweh as their guide, but now Jeremiah accuses Israelites of following a vapour (vanity) instead of that pillar which they followed in the desert.

The question "Where is Yahweh?" is followed by two participles: *hama'aleh* (*hiphil* participle, the masculine singular of *'alah*, which means "to bring up") and *hamôliyk* (*hiphil*, the participle masculine singular of *halak*, which means "to lead, to bring in"). With clear reference to Egypt and Canaan, the question invokes a constant possibility of Yahweh's performing similar acts of rescue to those he performed in the Promised Land, where Yahweh "brought in" the people of Israel after "bringing them up" from Egypt. In this sense, the question can be understood as representing what was supposed to be a constant call or cry of the Israelites to Yahweh for help during a time of need and crisis, just as their ancestors cried out to him in the wilderness when they were coming from Egypt, and in the promised land when they were threatened by enemies.

The failure to ask "Where is Yahweh" can also be taken as evidence that Judah had grown accustomed to God; they were so at ease with God that they had taken him for granted and ignored him. Yahweh was no longer the centre of Judah's life and they did not call on him in time of danger. Instead, the people chose to go after idols, which are ironically implied to be more helpful than Yahweh. Thus, the issue at stake in Judah, according to this text, was the question of Yahweh's effectiveness in directing the life of the entire community, and the awareness of the people that Yahweh was present in daily activities, whether the people were following him or not. It is important to see how not asking the question "Where is Yahweh?" is here linked with the issue of going far from Yahweh, that is, after idols.

Yahweh wanted to retain a close relationship with the people so that they would keep calling on him during their time of need. To call upon, or to cry to, Yahweh was a central construction and practice in Israel's faith. In Exodus 2:23–25 and 1 Samuel 7:8, Yahweh had answered his people's cry. To cry out to, or call on, somebody for help is a sign of friendship with them, recognition of their superiority, and confidence in them. In Israel's case, this confidence in God was rooted in concrete historical facts that had proved the effectiveness of the one upon whom they were to call for help. For this reason, the question "Where is Yahweh?" is linked with important historical and theological events that characterize the deity from whom Israelites distanced themselves.

First, in this verse, Yahweh reminds the people how he brought them up from Egypt. The book of Exodus relates how an enslaved people were turned into a flourishing multitude that prospered under the most difficult political, environmental, religious, military, economic, and social conditions in Egypt under Pharaoh.

Second, the deliverance of Israel from Egypt is associated with Yahweh's guidance through hardships in the wilderness. In other words, without Yahweh, the people of Israel could not have been freed from their slavery or survived in the wilderness. Even if someone else could have delivered them, it would have been impossible for the Israelites to reach the promised land.

The wilderness through which Yahweh's gentle and sure guidance led the Israelites was a threatening place, a place that was hostile to the life of human beings. Yahweh demonstrated his power and his effectiveness by taking the people safely through it. What is being underlined in verse 6 is not simply the fact of crossing the wilderness and entering the promised land but the danger the people faced and the impossibility of the entire journey without the strong hand of the Lord to guide and protect them. This should have created confidence in the people that Yahweh was totally dependable. God's faithfulness throughout these events should have remained perpetually in the memory of the Israelites. Faith is not a simple theory to be recited, it is not just words or concepts; it is the awareness a people have of God's goodness demonstrated in their past and present situations.

One then understands why, in this verse, Israel's experience of God's past faithfulness serves as the basis for the present generation's condemnation. It is the people's ingratitude despite Yahweh's care and his miraculous interventions on their behalf that constitutes the basis for his judgement. This is clearly a crisis of failing to remember God's goodness and taking his care for granted. The real nature of this crisis does not so much consist in the denial of God, but in the *trivialization* of Yahweh. The people of Judah might not have forgotten that Yahweh exists, but at some point, God had stopped being useful for them. They might have thought that Yahweh was not effective and was not delivering on their needs in the way they wanted him to respond to them. Verse 8 will help us to understand how the leaders failed to help the people cope with the new situation because they did not care about them.

Failed Leadership (v. 8)

Verse 8 elaborates on the nation's defilement by describing why things went wrong. Here the prophet names four groups of people who are accused of being the cause of evil in Israel. All four groups were leaders in the nation.

The first group is the priests. Jeremiah accuses them of not asking, "Where is Yahweh?" The priests had the responsibility of representing the people of Israel before God. They also gave general instructions and specific guidance for the nation. They were supposed to instruct Israel in the way of Yahweh so that the nation would remain holy, that is, distinct from all other nations, and become a testimony of Yahweh's distinctiveness from the gods of other nations.

Exodus 19:6 states that Israel as a nation was "a kingdom of priests and a holy nation" (NIV). In other words, the holy nation or the priestly people had the responsibility of mediating the knowledge and the blessing of Yahweh to other nations (compare with Exod 15:11–17; 19:5–6; Lev 20:22–26), and the priests had the enormous obligation of turning Israel into a kingdom of priests. In this way, the failure of the priests was actually a failure of the entire nation to know Yahweh and to make him known to the nations.

Yet priests frequently failed in their responsibility. For example, Aaron is reported to have participated in the making of the golden calf (Exod 32); Micah's priest decided to disobey for prestige and prosperity (Judg 18:19–21); Eli and his family were judged because of inconsistent character and the wickedness of his sons (1 Sam 1–2). In Ezra 10:18, the priests were blamed for marrying foreign women. Finally, in Malachi, priests were blamed for abusing their role of offering sacrifices (1:7–8), and failing to instruct the people in the proper ritual behaviour (2:7–8).

The accusation against the priests in Jeremiah 2:8 is not based on what they did not do but on what they did not say. The priests neglected or forgot to tell the story, that is, to remind the community of the faithfulness and uniqueness of Yahweh, and of their responsibilities as a kingdom of priests. Not only is it important to tell a story, but more importantly, to tell *the right story*. This recalls Malachi 2:7, which states, "For the lips of a priest ought to preserve knowledge, because he is the messenger of the LORD Almighty and people seek instruction from his mouth" (NIV).

In Africa, we know the danger of telling the wrong stories. Wrong stories can lead to death. There are wrong stories told in Africa of tribalism, hatred, child witches, and so on. Stories that tell us that we are Hutus against the Tutsis (Burundi and Rwanda), Lendu against Hema (DR Congo), Dinka against Nuer (South Sudan), black against white (South Africa), Kikuyu against Luo (Kenya), Dyula against Baoulé (Ivory Coast). The result of believing these stories is ethnic confrontations, ethnic hatred, and sometimes bloodshed. Tribal and ethnic identities do exist, but they are not in themselves conflictual, just as individuals are not intrinsically in conflict simply because of their ethnic differences. Ethnicity becomes a problem because of wrong stories and manipulation by politicians.

The second group of leaders to be accused of failing in their responsibility are the guardians of the law – the intellectual leadership of Judah. These were the teachers, the scholars. These were probably the Levites, particularly the group entrusted with the business of interpreting the law and religious education. They had been dispersed to live in what were known as the Levitical towns (Num 35:1–8), so that they could watch over the community and give right instructions about God's way of living. The prophet accuses them of not knowing Yahweh. These were the people whose assignment was to study God's word and rightly interpret it to the people. Levites knew God's word well, but they did not know Yahweh in a personal and intimate way. They were well versed in their scholarship, but that scholarship did not bring them closer to the living God. It is possible to know a lot about God without obeying him. This leads to telling a lifeless story about God and damaging the community's life and hope. Christian erudition is supposed to lead to the source of truth (God) and enlighten our minds and hearts to know and obey God. Christian scholarship should not remain a private activity for self-promotion but should be used in ministry for God's glory.

The third group to fail in their responsibility was the shepherds, or political leaders. These were national leaders responsible for the government and the welfare of the people. The prophet accuses them of being engaged in rebellion against Yahweh. The sentence "the shepherds rebelled against me" is to be understood in both its covenantal and political nuances. The duty of the shepherds was to take care of the people, and it mattered a lot how they fulfilled this obligation. What is at stake in this passage is the issue of allegiance. The rebellion of political leaders against Yahweh in this passage might mean they refused to acknowledge Yahweh's sovereignty and ruled the nation without any consideration for him and his law. This is an indication that the political leaders had lost confidence in Yahweh and had been trying to lead the nation relying on their own skills in political and social affairs.

The question "Where is Yahweh?" shows that for Jeremiah, what mattered most was not secular skills or techniques, but petition – trustful asking from and crying to God during the time of national need, and prayer for wisdom.[11] This is the secret of true leadership. Sadly, the royal system in Judah had led the country far from this trust in the Lord and had convinced the citizens that trusting in other gods would prove more helpful for the well-being of the nation than calling upon Yahweh. Unfortunately, this is still a common practice in national leadership, especially in Africa. In at least one of his public speeches, former President Mobutu declared that for the security of Zaire (now DR Congo), he was ready to enter into a pact with Satan. Mobutu was courageous enough to openly declare what is a common practice for most of our leaders. Unfortunately, we have also heard of many church leaders who get involved in occult practices in pursuit of fame and success.

---

11. We are aware that in an era of pandemics such as COVID-19, secular wisdom and good governance are also important and are not dismissed by God. They must not replace God, but they are also gifts from God.

The last group to be identified as the cause of Israel's moral and spiritual failure is the prophets. Prophets were first and foremost preachers of the revelation and the word of God (Isa 1:1; 2:1; Jer 18:18; 27:18; Ezek 7:26). This word came to them (Jer 1:2, 4; 2:1, and other passages), was with them (Hab 2:1), was spoken to them by Yahweh (Jer 46:13), and enabled them to speak in the name of the Lord (Deut 18:20). Almost all true prophets in Israel addressed their messages primarily to the kings, the shepherds of the community.

In general, the content of these messages was either a call to return to the covenant obligation or a warning of judgement and punishment because of the leaders' failure to follow Yahweh's word. However, there were also false prophets who were particularly active in the decades prior to the destruction of Jerusalem in 587 BC, and whose source of inspiration was a surrogate revelation. False prophets might bear the greatest responsibility for a country's disaster.

According to Ezekiel (13:19), people in Judah listened to false prophets more than they did the true ones, and they followed falsehood since what the false prophets said was what the people and their leaders wanted to hear (see Ezek 13:10, 16; Jer 5:30–31; 6:14; 8:11; 23:17; Mic 2:7; 3:5–8, 11). The general content of the message of these false prophets was that Yahweh would never forsake Jerusalem, his holy city, and that consequently, God's people were forever secure despite all the evil they were doing. In terms of this passage, people thought they were secure despite their "walking away" from Yahweh (Jer 6:13–15; Mic 3:5–12). In the same way, it seems that many people did not like the prophesies of true prophets like Jeremiah, because they persistently told people that destruction was sure if the nation did not repent (Isa 28:9, 10; Jer 6:10; 26:9; 29:24–28; Hos 9:8; Amos 7:12, 16; Mic 2:6–11; 3:5).

The last line in verse 8 is climactic. It summarizes the nature of the evil committed by the four groups who have just been indicted. The passage states that these leaders (political, intellectual, religious, and prophetic) "walked after things that do not profit." I have already noted that the verb "to walk after" means to serve, and to walk after any other person or thing apart from Yahweh means to go after idols. These four groups of leaders might have created a system, a "network" that favoured them, but they had destroyed the nation. This links with our own situation in Africa where our political and religious leaders often work together to protect one another. They collaborate not to benefit the citizens but to maintain their own interest. One cannot imagine that some dictators would succeed in maintaining themselves in power for so long without the support (implicit or explicit) of other influential self-seeking groups in the nation. These four groups constituted the elite of Judah, and they bore the responsibility for the destruction of the nation.

Conclusion

The central message of the book of Jeremiah is a call to repentance, the announcement of judgement because of the failure to repent, a promise of exile, and the announcement of a future restoration. But before God issues this message, he tries to reason with the people to help them think about what has gone wrong in their relationship with him. Yahweh takes them back to their history and recalls their past relationship. He starts by asking a central question: "What evil did your fathers find in me?" This is a surprising question coming from the sovereign God. It also signals that things are at a critical point for the nation. The question reveals the real problem with Judah: idolatry. The people were tired of God. At some point, they had decided that Yahweh was no longer needed; God was no longer the centre of their life and interest. People wanted autonomy from Yahweh. Nobody sought God. They took him for granted and decided to follow futile idols and became futile themselves. Like two sides of a coin, these two evils – the sin of omission (forgetting God) and the sin of commission (walking after idols) – are the basis of Yahweh's accusations. The nation's priests, teachers, prophets, and politicians are accused of being responsible for this crisis. These leaders had become corrupt and had failed to care for the people, to listen to their needs and challenges, and to help them remain close to God. They could not help the people because they themselves were in active rebellion against God.

While reading this portion of Jeremiah 2, I was also trying to understand what is wrong with Africa, why the continent is in such a mess. A short look at our recent history helped me to understand the causes of the current social and political backwardness, and the spiritual struggle on the continent. The passage reminds us of the importance of telling true stories of God's goodness and faithfulness, stories of love, peace and unity, and of painting a vision for a bright future if we rely on and obey God.

The main lesson of this chapter is that people end up like what they worship, either for destruction or for renewal and restoration. From the beginning, God did not create humans as independent beings. He made them to be a reflection of himself. Therefore, we are "imaging beings." In other words, people will always reflect something: either God or whatever thing (idol) they have replaced him with. If the people of Africa are dedicated to following God, they will become like him; if they reject God and are committed to following idols, they will become like the idols and will face the judgement from God, which will lead to destruction.

3

Agonizing for a Blind People

Jeremiah 4:19–22

¹⁹ My anguish, my anguish!
   I agonize!
O, the walls of my heart!
   My heart is groaning within me,
   I cannot keep silent.
You have heard the sound of the trumpet,
   O, my soul, the sound of war!
²⁰ Disaster upon disaster is announced
   The whole land is devastated
Suddenly my tents are devastated
   In a moment my curtains!
²¹ How long must I see the standard,
   And hear the trumpet blast?
²² How foolish my people are!
   They know me not.
Stupid children are they
   And void of understanding.
They are wise in doing evil,
   But of doing good they know nothing.

Historical and Literary Context

Many students of Jeremiah have recognized that it is difficult or even impossible to determine with precision the date of this passage within the prophet's career because the text does not give any indication of historical events. Some think that the prophet's words of anguish were not necessarily provoked by the actual invasion and the onset of disaster, as a literal reading of this text suggests, but that they stem from the prophet's imagination, from his mental recreation of the reality of which he speaks.[1] Brueggemann supports this idea and makes the following comment on the passage: "This piece (vv. 19–22) is presented not as a public proclamation but as a scenario of the prophet at home."[2]

However, I would argue that the literary context of this poem provides readers with some clues that can help them determine the probable period of the events narrated in this passage. Jeremiah 4:19–22 belongs to the larger "Foe from the North" unit of 4:5–6:30. In terms of the relationship between Yahweh and his people, the section uses a courtroom format to depict Yahweh as the king who remained faithful to his obligation whereas Judah defaulted on its obligation. In terms of war or calamity, these passages depict Judah's enemies in the following ways: they are coming from a distant land (4:16; 5:15; 6:22), precisely from the north (4:6; 6:1, 22); the enemy is a tenacious and ancient nation, speaking a language unknown to Judah (5:15); its warriors are invincible (5:15) and cruel (6:23); they ride swift, strong horses (4:13, 29) and use war chariots (4:13); they attack swiftly and suddenly (4:20; 6:25); they are armed with bows and spears (4:29; 6:23); and they are well-trained soldiers (6:23) who are able to attack any fortified city (6:4, 5). The dominant message in this whole unit is judgement in the form of invasion, war and defeat due to Judah's forgetfulness and the many offences it has committed in the eyes of Yahweh.

When one reads Jeremiah 4:19–22 in this context, one cannot but be aware of the prophet's anguish for his nation. It seems to me that such a deep emotion cannot arise from a simple mental recreation of the distant past or the remote future. Rather, a present situation or an imminent future situation that God is revealing to his servant must have provoked it. Thus, at the beginning of verse 20, the prophet refers to disasters that are about to descend on the nation. On the assumption that this reading is right, I would argue that it becomes necessary to connect this poetic passage with a specific military event occurring shortly before the time of its composition. The first Babylonian invasion in 597 BC, which led to the first deportation, may fit well into the context of this passage.

---

1. Craigie, Kelley and Drinkard, *Jeremiah 1–25*, 79.
2. Brueggemann, *Jeremiah 1–25*, 54.

According to 2 Kings and 2 Chronicles, Jehoiakin (Jehoiakim's eighteen-year-old son) was placed on the throne in late 598 BC (2 Kgs 24:8–16; 2 Chr 36:9–10), but his reign lasted for only three months. In March 597 BC, Jeohoiakin, the queen mother, the princes, and ten thousand leading citizens, smiths, and craftsmen were taken, along with servants and booty, into captivity in Babylon. All these events took place only eleven years before the final fall of Jerusalem in July 586 BC. If we put together the two military events that marked the end of Judah as a nation, we can understand why verse 20 speaks of disaster after disaster until the whole land is devastated.

Structure

The passage has two parts: (1) a unit in the confessional style depicting Jeremiah's agony on account of Judah's approaching judgement (vv. 19–21); and (2) an oracle stating the reason for the judgement (v. 22).

Jeremiah's Agony for Judah (vv. 19–21)

The entire speech of the prophet in 4:19–21 reflects a high level of emotion on account of the coming judgement on Judah. He starts with a vivid statement of his pain and moves on to speak of Judah's carelessness or numbness in the face of a real danger in verses 19b–20.

Jeremiah's agony (v. 19a)

Commentators differ on the meaning of the first two lines in verse 19. Some believe that verse 19 is meant to emphasize the distressing nature of the message that Jeremiah is delivering rather than to describe his personal emotions.[3] But it seems more likely that "the opening words, a double exclamation ... (my innards! my innards!), attest the depth of the emotions that grip the prophet."[4] This pain may be both physical and psychological.[5] Thus there are those who think of Jeremiah in this passage as someone who is sick to the stomach, an unstable cardiac patient, whose heart flutters and palpitates, creating what

---

3. A. R. Diamond, *The Confessions of Jeremiah in Context. Scenes of Prophetic Drama* (Sheffield: Sheffield University Press, 1987), 119.

4. Timothy Polk, *The Prophetic Persona: Jeremiah and the Language of the Self*. JSOT Supplement 32 (Sheffield: Sheffield University Press, 1984), 53.

5. Holladay, *Jeremiah 1–25*, 160 and Craigie, Kelley and Drinkard, *Jeremiah 1–25*, 79.

seems to be a voice that he cannot control.⁶ But it is more likely that the language here is metaphorical, rather than an indication of severe pains in his bowels – although, as McKane observes,

> the significance of the appearance of מֵעַי [mēʿay/ my innards] is that the pit of the stomach is believed to be the seat of the most intense emotions, and there may be an empirical foundation for this, namely, that this is where there are physical repercussions when one is subject to severe emotional stress.⁷

There are several examples in the Old Testament where the word translated "innards" (*mēʿay*) is used to refer to an emotional state. It can refer to grief (Job 30:27; Isa 16:11; Jer 48:36; Lam 1:20–21), delight (Ps 40:8), or compassion (Isa 63:15; Jer 31:20). Thus, those who view Jeremiah's lament as coming from one who is sick to his stomach are right. Jeremiah is not (physically) sick but he is groaning and extremely anxious, unsettled and frightened because of what God has shown him with respect to what is awaiting his nation.

Jeremiah's emotional state is well summarized in the sentence "I cannot keep silent" (Jer 20:9). This sentence reflects both the prophet's sense of the loss of inner peace and stability, and an intense awareness that he has come under an influence that in some sense has him within its control and demands expression. In short, the prophet finds himself in a very dire situation: as Yahweh's servant, he is bound to warn his people of the coming judgement; at the same time, he labours under a painful awareness of the advanced state of decay in his nation. He knows that the brutal end of his beloved country has come, but that the people and their leaders are refusing to acknowledge it. They are living in denial, in a state of self-deception and wishful thinking, ignoring the fact that the nation has reached the very end of its existence. This was a paralysed nation, destroyed from within by a rampant idolatry, corruption and all manner of social and spiritual evil. The people were incapable of reading the signs of the time because they had lost direction. Once a nation reaches such a pathetic state, destruction is inevitable, whether delivered at the hand of an external enemy (as in Judah's case), or by internal upheaval (as is so often the case in many unstable African countries). Whether Jeremiah is actually hearing the sound of war (v. 19b) or just imagining it as a poet and prophet, he must end up expressing it because it is very painful for him. He cannot keep silent.

---

6. Craigie, Kelley and Drinkard, *Jeremiah 1–25*, 79.
7. William McKane, *Jeremiah 1–25*, 102.

Most African nations today resemble Judah during the time of Jeremiah: deeply corrupt, and so bombarded by external pressures and the accumulated impact of years of bad governance that they have no good economic or political options left, and are thus trapped in their situation, paralysed and apparently helpless to chart a way forward to a better future. This explains the continent's endemic instability. Some have compared corruption in Africa with solid dirt on the cloth of a madman which irritates and attacks his skin. Joe Smith, a British businessman with long experience of Nigerian corruption, is more emphatic:

> Nigerians are deeply ambivalent about it [corruption] – resigning themselves to it, justifying it, or complaining about it. They are painfully aware of the damage corruption does to their country and see themselves as their own worst enemies, *but they have been unable to stop it.*[8] (emphasis added).

This comment touches on the heart of the problem in most African countries, not only in Nigeria: everybody is aware of the corruption, but nobody is willing or able to stop it. As a result, ordinary Africans are swimming in an ocean of corruption, the powerful barely able to stay afloat by playing along, the helpless slowly pulled under by an inexorable system.

Thus, for example, in his address to the State House Anti-Corruption, Governance and Accountability Summit on 18 October 2016, the Kenyan president, Uhuru Kenyatta, confessed that corruption was one issue that had deeply frustrated him and that he was "under pressure" to do something about it. He claimed that his government had done more than all previous administrations since Kenya's independence in 1963 to fight graft: "Show me any one administration since independence that has taken action on corruption like I have done. I have removed everybody. I have done my part, at great expense also, politically, by asking these guys to step aside." He then, with profound regret, asked the audience: "Ladies and gentlemen, what do you want me to do?" Pointing at the auditor-general, Kenyatta stated: "We have the Auditor-General who says Eurobond [money] had been stolen. . . . What do you want me to do? I did not appoint you, I can't even sack you. Corruption is just being used as a political circus."[9]

---

8. Daniel Jordan Smith, *A Culture of Corruption: Everyday Deception and Popular Discontent in Nigeria* (Princeton: Princeton University Press, 2016), cover text.

9. Aggrey Mutambo, "President Kenyatta Rebukes Agencies for Failure to Tame Corruption," *Daily Nation*, 18 August 2020, https://www.nation.co.ke/news/President-Kenyatta-rebukes-agencies-over-anticorruption-fight/1056-3420824-n0srv7/index.html.

Here the Kenyan president seems to confess that he has been defeated by the corruption in his nation, and that there was nothing more he could do to stop it. Such declarations are characteristic of many African leaders, and they explain, to some extent, why the continent is in such bad shape. How would a prophet like Jeremiah react to the African numbness in the face of these social evils? What would have he told the many African leaders who declare themselves unable to stop corruption?

Instead of confronting his compatriots, Jeremiah chooses to lament the fate of his nation. As Brueggemann puts it, "he (Jeremiah) takes his listeners inside his very own person as an attempt to pierce their numbed indifference. He dares to suggest that his wild anxiety is more real than their cynical self-confidence."[10] Sometimes, such prophetic suggestions can only be expressed with adequate force through poetry. This is why the book of Jeremiah is full of poems; poets possess unusual sensitivity and can use their imagination to express things more clearly through the use of symbols, as Jeremiah is doing in this text. In the same way, many Africans who are feeling the pain of a dying continent express their frustration through poems. The corpus of poems by African authors reflecting on corruption, injustice, and war in Africa is steadily growing. Bartholomew Arkoh B. Sarbah is one of these poets:

> Awake mother Africa, awake
> For you lie asleep for long
> Your future is in the balance
> And your dignity fades away with the passing of the days
> Your children are blindfolded
> And we trail destruction in ignorance
> Each day, Mother Africa;
> A layer of your beautiful clothing is molted away

---

10. Walter Brueggemann, *A Commentary on Jeremiah: Exile and Homecoming* (Grand Rapids, MI: Eerdmans, 1998), 58. In another book (*Theology of Old Testament: Testimony, Dispute, Advocacy* [Minneapolis, MN: Fortress, 1997], 625), Brueggemann points out that despite the fact that the prophets are characteristically immersed in public crises, they are not primarily political agents in any direct sense and they rarely urge specific policy. He also adds that prophets are first of all utterers, and that they speak most often with all of the elusiveness and imaginative power of poetry. They use images and metaphors that aim to disrupt, destabilize, and invite to an alternative perception of reality. His conclusion is that the poetic idiom and the elusive quality of imagination together constitute a strategy among the prophets for taking the listening community outside of administered ideology, which is most often identified with royal policy and royal imagination. While this argument needs to be discussed in the light of the ministry of each prophet (for example, I doubt if this will be true for Amos), I agree that it fits well the passage of our investigation, in that the prophet has chosen not to confront anybody but to lament the situation of his nation and show his contemporaries the reason for his lamentation.

> Your heritage escapes the present generation
> And the heroism of the land seems to have perished
> Mother
> Are we truly your children;
> And yet we show no resemblance?
> Are we of your lineage;
> And yet we are world apart?
> Awake from your slumber Mother Africa, awake
> Lest your children perish.[11]

Jeremiah's way of speaking to the community through poetic grieving and lamenting, like that in Sarbah's poem, might not work well in most societies today, which turn away from those who keep lamenting, grieving, and complaining. When a man complains and cries, some will either mock him as a "woman," since men (like Jeremiah) are expected not to cry, or they will dismiss him as a fool. Moreover, some of us do not take heed of the words of the Jeremiahs in our midst. We are in a hurry; we do not care because we have our agenda. It is easier to join in the corruption and other evil practices than to endlessly complain, to no effect. But it probably was not so in Jeremiah's traditional society, where people were sensitive to the emotions of others, especially when the one lamenting was a mature man. Jeremiah's lament expressed his prophetic message in an emotional and powerful way. Unfortunately, though people heard him, they chose not to understand his terrifying message. So, the prophet was treated like a "doomsday spokesman or a pitiful man who had a grudge and sat around crying."[12] As in Jeremiah 29:26, the prophet was actually referred to as a "maniac" who sets himself up as a prophet.

A call for groaning prophets in Africa

I see Jeremiah, the suffering prophet, as also representing another class of good and responsible citizens who are deeply affected by the decaying of their nations due to corruption and other related social ills. Corruption entails suffering for all citizens, but most especially, for the powerless. Kä Mana,[13] a Congolese

---

11. Bartholomew Arkoh Boamah Sarbah, "Awake Mother Africa," 28 December 2016, http://www.poemhunter.com/poem/awake-mother-africa/.
12. Walter Brueggemann, *The Prophetic Imagination* (Philadelphia: Fortress, 1978), 52.
13. Kä Mana, *Christ d'Afrique, Enjeux éthiques de la foi chrétienne en Jésus Christ* (Paris: Karthala, 1994), 153–58.

theologian, gives several examples of how a decaying nation can destroy its own citizens. One of those he mentions is Professor Francois Nkombe Oleko of the Catholic University of Kinshasa.

Professor Oleko was an eminent teacher who was greatly appreciated by his students and the Congolese learned community. The young professor had a kind of quiet, reasonable and beaming faith in the Lord Jesus Christ. His struggle to affirm the relevance of the gospel in the reconstruction of Africa was both genuine and impressive. But after only two years of a brilliant teaching career, Oleko was plunged into a strange spirituality in which he claimed to see visions, receive direct revelations from God, and be able to compose songs and psalms under the direct inspiration of angels.

Many explanations were offered for what had happened to him. Some saw it as a parody of spirituality, motivated by financial considerations, more reprehensible because it was in the midst of a society torn apart by crises. Others claimed that he had become irrational due to the barriers placed in the way of marrying his sister-in-law, whom he loved. For others, it was evidence of mental illness. However, in Kä Mana's opinion, the explanation of Oleko's conduct lay in his country's severe socio-economic and political crisis, a situation for which he was unable to find a solution despite his patriotism, great effort and sacrifice.

Similar issues confront many African scholars who, after studying in the West, decide to come back to serve their nation, determined to help their people. They soon realize that it was a mistake to come back, and that they will be unable to change the situation. Many of them, consequently, become victims of the corruption in their decaying nations.

There are thousands of people like Oleko throughout Africa. Many scholars and other eminent people simply decide to leave Africa or not to return after their studies. Like Jeremiah, they continue to groan for their countries, but they do it from outside. Those unable to remain outside the country, or who decide against all advice to the contrary to remain in Africa, generally end up in various bad situations. Some join hands with the dictators and find themselves serving corrupt regimes and becoming corrupted themselves in the process. George Nzongola-Ntalaja captures the process of this corruption well:

> By depriving scholars of the capacity to lead a financially secure middle-class lifestyle and the ability to conduct serious research, governments have succeeded in making many of them willing collaborators. Instead of following Socrates in remaining skeptical of the defenders of law and order against the claims of social

justice, many of our colleagues have been too eager to follow Plato's footsteps in dirtying their hands in the service of tyrants like Mobutu, Ibrahim Babangida, Sani Abacha and others.[14]

Those who refuse to collaborate with the regime and decide to defend their ideal of a just society suffer at the hands of dictators. This was the fate of Englebert Mveng, the Cameroonian Catholic priest who was found strangled in his home on 22 April 1995.[15] Jean-Marc Éla, another Catholic priest and one of Africa's most renowned theologians, was forced to flee Cameroon in August 1995, and spent the rest of his life in Canada, after having been alerted to a serious risk of assassination.[16]

African scholars and intellectuals who are not assassinated often live in misery, abandoned by the regimes, which resent them. Speaking at a public meeting with all the presidents of his nation's universities and colleges in 2012, Professor Mashako Mamba, then Minister of Higher Education of DR Congo, expressed his fear that at least one professor dies each month at the University of Kinshasa. Unfortunately, he did not want to discuss the causes of these deaths. But there is no doubt that the country's socio-economic crisis contributes to this loss of life.

Thus, in contemporary African society, the intellectual finds themself stuck in the middle, between those in power and the poor who suffer at their hands. But like the prophet Jeremiah, intellectuals should not have a neutral position on the evils in their countries. Those who try to live a neutral life in a suffering continent betray both their education and calling. Jeremiah tells us that abdication of responsibility or neutrality is not a solution. Socially, Jeremiah is a citizen living in clear revolt against an unjust and corrupt government. This is why I call him a groaning prophet. The so-called confessions or lamentations of Jeremiah express his revolt against injustice and blindness.

Those of us who have chosen to live in Africa understand at a personal level this kind of prophetic message and lamentation. We are often driven to cry for our nations, whether in groaning like Jeremiah, in a word of prayer, or in responding to the overwhelming needs of people by doing something

---

14. Georges Nzongola-Ntalaja, "The Role of Intellectuals in the Struggle for Democracy, Peace and Reconstruction in Africa," *African Journal of Political Science*, 2, no. 2 (1997): 12.

15. On the political reason for the assassination of Englebert Mveng, see Achille Mbembe, "Jean-Marc Éla: le veilleur s'en est allé" in *Messager* (January 2009). See also Nathanael Yaovi Soédé, *Cri de l'Homme Africain et Christianisme. Jean-Marc Ela, Une Passion pour l'Opprimé* (Abidjan: Seprim Ivoire, 2009), 81–83.

16. See Nathanael Yaovi Soédé, *Cri de l'Homme Africain et Christianisme. Jean-Marc Ela, Une Passion pour l'Opprimé* (Abidjan: Seprim Ivoire, 2009), 81–83.

to help. Sometimes, our prayers express the hopelessness around us. Like the prophet of Anathoth, we sometimes even revolt against God who seems not to respond to our cries. We can agree with Jeremiah that it is extremely difficult to continue living in a decaying country, where one knows that the future will be worse than the present. In such situations, the common temptation is to seek refuge in other countries. But Jeremiah instead chose to suffer for and with his people as long as this was possible. Moreover, Jeremiah did not suffer simply for the sake of becoming a hero. He had a mission: to announce God's will to his indifferent contemporaries until the dying minutes of his country's life. Likewise, prophets in Africa should not forget their mission, they should not attempt to escape when circumstances deteriorate, should not succumb to denial or cynicism, and should not quickly blend into the political regime to avoid commitment or for an easy life.

The cause of the prophet's groaning (vv. 19b–21)

A Samoan proverb states that "a careless fish will be eaten by the shark." Judah's carelessness or numbness in the face of a real danger becomes clear in verses 19b–20. The "sound of the trumpet . . . the sound of war" (v. 19b) is audible. The trumpet may be that of an advancing enemy or a trumpet sounded to rouse the defenders of the nation, but in either case, it rouses an intense commotion of warriors, "the sound of war."

Verse 20 builds on verse 19 and describes the cruel and devastating effect of the war to come. Jeremiah chooses his words carefully; what is going to happen soon will be disaster after disaster. We know this from experience in Africa. Warfare is attended by starvation, disease, killings, deportations and waves of refugees, destruction, and an enormous range of suffering – physical, psychological, moral, and spiritual.

How the prophet wishes his people could comprehend the terrible danger looming ahead! But they cannot, and so the prophet takes their places, suffering for them in a kind of prophetic substitution. In this way, the prophet found himself isolated and consumed by his anger, fear, and despair. Anger in response to the refusal of his people to come to grips with their situation and the disaster to come; fear because, more than any other person in Judah, he could see the mighty enemy approaching. Finally, the prophet is desperate and frustrated because the people of Judah and their leaders are not willing to listen to his voice, or rather to God's voice. On the contrary, they are deceiving themselves, thinking that they will be able to make peace and survive by their own efforts, without regard to what God is trying to tell them. The text does not hint at any hope for repentance. All hope is gone, and the coming tragedy, which is actually Yahweh's judgement, is unavoidable; indeed, the prophet can already see it coming. Because of this, he is in a state of emotional shock. In this respect, the prophet's suffering is a suffering with God, the prophet's anger is Yahweh's anger, and the prophet's disappointment is also God's disappointment with a people who are unwilling to listen.

It is clear that Jeremiah loves his country; we hear him speak about "my tents," and "my curtains." But the text does not support a view of Jeremiah as an advocate, representing the people in their lament before God and consequently becoming a virtual opponent of God on behalf of the people, as is claimed by some commentators.[17] Nothing in this passage shows that Jeremiah is against God. He knows that Yahweh is within his rights to punish the wicked people. He consequently knows what is going to happen to his beloved nation, and he laments for the country, for his people, and for himself. This explains his grief and cry in verses 19 to 21. The prophet is wondering how much longer he can stand the emotional strain of the experience, witnessing the standard of the enemy raised high and hearing the sound of the trumpet blasts.[18] Jeremiah knows that Judah is a careless fish about to be eaten by a shark!

Jeremiah's prophetic grief and cry in this passage speak powerfully to our situation in Africa. Too often, pastors and other church leaders dissociate the general politics of our nations from their ministry and think that their call is to serve God in the church and not to fight for political issues. They do well in caring for the soul, but this care keeps them too busy, too sure that in doing this they are doing all that God requires of them as shepherds so that they have no margin left to grieve over the direction in which the whole nation is heading. Fortunately, the situation is now changing. Many church leaders in Africa have come to understand the urgent need to engage with political issues in their ministries. For example, Linda Ochola-Adolwa, the executive pastor of Mavuno Church in Nairobi, has rhetorically asked:

> Should we just leave politics to the politicians? Should a few individuals dictate how our lives in the city are lived? We cannot

---

17. For such a position, see H. G. Reventlow, *Liturgie und Prophetisches Ich bei Jeremiah* (Gutersloh: Mohn, 1963), 200.
18. Thompson, *Jeremiah*, 228.

afford to be passive observers while all hell breaks loose around us. Nairobi is not neutral; you must influence or be influenced.[19]

This strong statement should be the vision of the church of Africa in the twenty-first century. There is no way to dissociate our Christian ministry from pressing political and other social issues in our nations. It is not possible to remain passive, especially for Christian leaders, while the continent is burning. We must constructively and persistently engage in dialogue with those in power. In other words, the church in Africa must be bold and forthright, innovative and constructive. At the same time, we must educate individual believers to refuse to be constantly deceived by politicians, most of whom work only for their own interests, as was the case in Judah during the time of Jeremiah. Depending on the reality of each country, both individual believers and the corporate body of Christ in Africa have a part to play in the political realm if we want a transformation of the continent. Jeremiah is showing that we must deeply grieve for national matters and speak out. This will be is easier to do in some countries than in others.

It is interesting to see in Jeremiah a spiritual leader who spent *private* hours in combative prayer with the Lord and was thus equipped for a *public* ministry – grieving for his nation, openly addressing public issues, challenging public opinion, and confronting political leaders. They type of reflexive obedience to political authority that is common in some of our churches simply had no place in his ministry. Jeremiah's view of the ministry derived from his deep grief over both the religious and the sociopolitical life of his nation. He put his faith into practice in public and real-life situations. To use the language of the New Testament (which is borrowed from Isaiah), he was the "light" of his nation, though most of his contemporaries refused to recognize it.

This is one area that needs to be emphasized in the entire continent if Christianity is to remain relevant in Africa. In other words, as far as political engagement is concerned, the church has two roles to play: (1) educate Christians about their civil rights, teach them to resist corruption, and encourage them to actively participate in the building of the nation; and (2) fulfil its prophetic calling by challenging political abuse at all levels. Christianity in Africa will perish alongside African society if it neglects these two responsibilities.

---

19. Steven Lichty, "Religious Motivation for Political Engagement in Kenya," African Studies, Research Report 2012, 31 (University of Florida), 28 December 2016, http://africa.ufl.edu/files/CAS-Research-Report-2012-13-Small.pdf.

Reason for the Judgement (4:22)

In verse 22, there is a sudden change of speaker, mood and language, It is no longer the prophet who is speaking, but Yahweh. Whereas the prophet was complaining, Yahweh is speaking like a schoolmaster. The vocabulary used ("foolish," "stupid," "without understanding") is now informed by Israel's Wisdom literature. The word "foolish" (*'ĕwîl*) appears nineteen times in Proverbs and twice in Job; "stupid" (*sākāl*) appears in Jeremiah 5:21, and six times in Ecclesiastes; "be discerning" (*nĕbônîm*)[20] or the verb "to discern" appears nine times in Proverbs and once in Ecclesiastes. For the alert reader, this first glimpse of verse 22 anticipates what was the problem in Judah, and what Yahweh found lacking in his people. Judah needed wisdom to walk in the way of the Lord, and to know how to relate to God's leadership.

It is significant God refers to those he accuses of being foolish as "my people," and as his "children" (see also Hos 11:1-6). The use of the possessive "my" is significant because it recalls God's choice of the Israelites and underlines his continual love for them as a people, despite the current situation. The Israelites belong to Yahweh who describes himself as their father. This love, expressed by the possessive "me" or "my" can be seen throughout the book of Jeremiah (1:16; 2:13; 6:14; 7:12; 12:1, 6; 18:15; 23:2, 22, 27, 32; 30:3; 33:24; 50:6). This way of talking on the part of God underlines the divine challenge – God dearly loves his people, whom he considers his children, but the very children he cherishes do not respond with the obedience due from loved children, consequently he must punish them.

These beloved children of Judah are said to have become stupid, foolish, and void of understanding. The use of each of these words is important and merits further examination.

First, the people of Judah are accused of being *'ĕwîl* (i.e. stupid). In the Old Testament, the adjective *ĕwîl*/stupid often stands in antithesis to *ḥokmâ*/wisdom, wise (Prov 10:8, 14; 11:29; 12:15; 14:3; 17:28; 29:9). The *ĕwîl*/stupid person is one who is not receptive to advice (Prov 11:29; 12:15), and it is useless to instruct them. They are also those who speak the wrong thing or speak at the wrong time and, as a result, get into trouble (Prov 14:3; 17:28). They are quarrelsome and immoral. In his commentary, McKane emphasizes that *ĕwîl*/stupid is opposed to *ḥokmâ*/wisdom and that true *ḥokmâ*/wisdom expresses itself in practical competence that the stupid person lacks. Thus, such wisdom is beyond the grasp of the fool because "he is not amenable to educational discipline and does not attain the maturity of character and nicety

---

20. *nĕbônîm* here is a *niphal* participle with the meaning of "discerning ones.".

of judgement which lend weight to public utterance."[21] Such a person, even if highly educated, should never be made a leader or become a decision maker in the community. If they somehow do become a leader, their leadership will prove a disaster, and those under them will suffer greatly. Could this be the situation in most African countries? The Ghanaian Bishop Dag Heward-Mills, the founder of the Lighthouse Chapel International, thinks that this is the case:

> Though most of these [African] leaders are highly educated having received knowledge from these prestigious universities abroad, they lack the ability and wisdom to apply the knowledge for the benefit of their people . . . It is this lack of wisdom, that has culminated in developing countries to resort to borrowing and depending on the Western countries for aid and assistance, when the continent is well-endowed with natural resources, which could be harnessed [for] its total development.[22]

Second, the same people are *sākāl*. When used as an adjective or a noun, the word *sākāl* equates with folly, madness, or recklessness. It is normally used in a moral or spiritual sense and indicates an incapacity for doing good and the tendency to always create problems in a community.

Third, they are said to be "void of understanding" (*lo nĕbônîm*). The verb *bîn* (to have understanding) is habitually used to communicate the idea of paying close attention to God's acts. It is also connected with terms meaning "to hear" and "to see," and in such instances it denotes wisdom (Prov 10:23), patience (Prov 14:29), keeping of the law (Prov 28:7), shunning evil (Job 28:28), and perceiving what is right, just, and fair (Prov 2:9).[23] Someone who lacks understanding does not care about listening to advice from others. Again, such a person cannot be a good leader.

In the last part of this verse, Jeremiah uses the verb *yada'* ("to know") twice (both times in the negative form), once with Yahweh as its object ("they know me not") and once with "doing good" as the object ("but of doing good, they know nothing"). Rather than one of these actions depending on the other, they go together, with each requiring the other. Thus, in this passage, to know Yahweh does not mean to know his name or who he is, but to know what he

---

21. McKane, *Jeremiah 1–25*, 189.

22. Dag Heward-Mills, "African Leaders Lack Wisdom," *Ghana Web*, 29 December 2016, https://www.ghanaweb.com/GhanaHomePage/NewsArchive/African-leaders-lack-wisdom-Bishop-Heward-Mills-463110.

23. Terence E. Fretheim, "בין" in *TDOTT*, 1:653.

wants. What he wants is to do good. Thus, to know Yahweh is to know how to do good.

The expression "doing good" is here used in a general sense, without an indication of what it means specifically. Though the meaning of the expression may be unclear to modern readers, it was clear to the original audience who knew what Yahweh was requiring of them and what the prophet was speaking about. Reading this text from our African perspective, it becomes clear that Judah's problem as a society was its lack of wisdom in understanding the prophetic teaching in general and applying it to the socio-economic, political, and religious context of the nation. This wisdom was particularly lacking in Judah's leaders.

Moreover, the use of two contrasting terms "to do evil" and "to do good" in verse 22 can help us understand what it means not to know Yahweh. In Leviticus 5:4, the contrasting terms "do good" and "do evil" are used with reference to the consequence of making a vow. But elsewhere in the Prophets, such as in Isaiah 1:16–17, we see a clear reference to social justice in the pairing "to do evil" and "to do good":

> Wash and make yourself clean.
>   Take your evil deeds out of my sight;
>   stop *doing wrong*.
> Learn *to do right*; seek justice.
>   Defend the oppressed
> Take up the cause of the fatherless;
>   plead the case of the widow. (NIV)

We have the same exhortation in Amos 5:14–15 where "evil" and "good" are paired as substantives:

> Seek *good*, not *evil*,
>   that you may live.
> Then the LORD God Almighty will be with you,
>   just as you say he is.
> Hate *evil*, love *good*;
>   maintain justice in the courts.
> Perhaps the LORD God Almighty will have mercy
>   on the remnant of Joseph. (NIV)

From these two passages, in which the pairing "to do evil" and "to do good" is clearly used in the context of social justice, it is probable that in 4:22, Jeremiah had in mind the issue of social justice in Judah. If so, I would argue that it is the perversion of this social justice that the prophet is considering as the sign of the lack of the knowledge of Yahweh. Said differently, our intertextual reading shows that in Jeremiah 4:2 "to do good and to hate evil" is to do justice in society in terms of encouraging the oppressed, defending the cause of the fatherless, pleading the cause of the widow, and maintaining fairness in the courts. To practise this kind of justice shows knowledge of Yahweh. Therefore, it is the lack of the knowledge of God expressed in the injustice in the society that is bringing judgement on Judah, judgement for which Jeremiah is lamenting in verses 19–21.

Conclusion

In Jeremiah 4:19–22, the people of Judah, and especially the leaders, are accused of being foolish, stupid, lacking understanding, not knowing Yahweh, and being wise only in doing evil. More particularly, the prophet accuses them of numbness and inattention to the real problems of the society; evil that is bringing disaster to the nation. The prophet wishes that his compatriots and their leaders would open their eyes and see that destruction is coming. He tries to help them realize the imminent danger to the nation, but nobody cares. Everyone is preoccupied with their own interest; the national well-being is not a priority for the leaders. The people's complacency causes great emotional and spiritual pain for the prophet, who experiences this evil on a daily basis in the land.

Social injustice does bring disaster, especially when leaders refuse to listen to God or to the voice of wisdom and, as one sees too often in Africa, they become consumed by the desire to steal from their own people and to cling to power – even beyond legal term limits in many cases. There is little doubt that Africa's plight is at least partly attributable to its leaders' lack of wisdom and understanding, as Bishop Dag Heward-Mills and others have argued. As a consequence, many African experts are scattered all over the world, choosing to live outside the continent to escape injustice and evil. Those who have managed to leave their countries are often viewed as fortunate. Many of those who remain, especially the intellectuals, are forced to join the forces of corruption to prosper or survive. Those who refuse to toe the line risk exposing themselves to danger and being perceived as enemies of the society's corrupted leaders. What we hear all too often from the citizens of countries such as Somalia, South Sudan, and DR Congo is that if they had had a choice, they would have been born in a different country. Yet, when foreigners visit some of our countries, they become fond of our beautiful lands. Yes, Yahweh has blessed Africans with a beautiful continent, but Africans and their leaders have too often squandered it. The bad state of many African countries bring pain and, like the prophet Jeremiah, we must refuse to keep silent in the face of injustice.

Does the African church have a solution to the problems in Africa? Jeremiah represents the voice of God and he is a symbol of the church in Africa, the only credible institution that can stand in the gap in prayer to bring about change in the continent. As I am writing these words, far from my home country of DR Congo, I join my compatriots in celebrating the achievements of the Congolese Catholic bishops who skilfully, pastorally, and decisively managed to negotiate an agreement between the opposition and the incumbent President Joseph Kabila regarding an end to his term in office in line with the constitution. There are other Africans, citizens of countries with entrenched leaders, who wish their bishops could achieve the same thing. Unfortunately, their bishops have kept quiet or feared for their lives.

Henri de Lubac, a French theologian who has reflected deeply on the predicament of the traditional church in an anti-traditional age, reminds us that the church in the world is the church amid conflict.[24] The image of the church amid conflict perfectly reflects the ministry of the prophet Jeremiah. If this is forgotten, the church loses it valuable place in the society.

---

24. Henri de Lubac, *The Splendor of the Church* (New York: Sheed & Ward, 1956), 187.

4

Poverty and Knowledge of God

Jeremiah 5:1–6

Run to and fro through the streets of Jerusalem,
    look around and take note!
Search its marketplaces/squares/streets and see
    if you can find one person
who acts justly,
    and seeks truth –
so that I may forgive Jerusalem.
² Though they say "as the Lord lives,"
    they are surely swearing falsely.
³ Your eyes, O Yahweh, do they not look for honesty?
You struck them down,
    but they were not weakened,
you took them to the limits,
    (but) they refused to accept correction.
They made their faces harder than rock;
    they refused to repent.
⁴ Then I thought: these are only the poor,
    they act foolishly;
for they do not know the way of Yahweh,
    the manners of their God.
⁵ Let me go to the noblemen,
    and speak to them,
for they know the way of Yahweh,
    the manners of their God.
But they (too) have broken the yoke,
    they have burst the bonds.

Historical and Literary Context

This text too belongs to the "Foe from the North" unit (4:5–6:30), especially the section concerning judgement on Judah because of its wickedness. According to biblical scholar Laurent Wisser, the section is accepted by the majority of scholars as authentically Jeremianic.[1]

It is not easy to date the material of chapter 5. With much hesitation, Thompson dates the chapter to the early years of Jehoiakim's reign or the end of Josiah's.[2] But he concludes that there are no strong grounds for proposing a specific date for the text. However, Holladay is less hesitant and argues convincingly that the period between 605–601 BC, most probably the autumn of 601 BC, fits the context of this text.[3] He supports his argument with two specific textual elements: (1) the passage hints at Yahweh's law ("the way of Yahweh," "the requirements of God"), material that was appropriate to a season in which the Deuteronomic law was recited (one of those seasons being 601 BC); (2) the phraseology of verse 5 is applicable to the time when Baruch read the contents of Jeremiah's first scroll to the officials and then to the king (36:10–26). Another argument that favours dating the passage near the end of Josiah's reign is its emphasis on social and personal morality rather than idolatry. This might suggest the post-Josianic reformation period, "after the cult centres had been destroyed and the grosser elements of Baal-worship had been eliminated."[4] Bright thinks that *musar* (to correct or chastise) in verse 3b might be an allusion to the death of King Josiah during his campaign against Pharaoh Necho in 609 BC. This discussion suggests that the consensus of scholars points to the very end of Josiah's reign or the beginning of Jehoiakim's as the probable date of this passage. My interpretation of this passage is based on my belief that the oracle was uttered during Jehoiakim's reign (not at the end of Josiah's reign).

In the Streets of Africa's Cities (vv. 1–5)

In Jeremiah 5:1–5 God commands the prophet to search through the streets and marketplaces of Jerusalem to find out whether there is one righteous person who acts with justice and strives for honesty so that he may forgive

---

1. Laurent Wisser, Jérémie, *Critique de la Vie Sociale: La Connaissance de Dieu et la Justice Sociale dans le Livre de Jérémie* (Geneva: Labor et Fides, 1984), 31–32.
2. Thompson, *Jeremiah*, 234. See also Craigie, Kelley and Drinkard, *Jeremiah 1–25*.
3. Holladay, *Jeremiah 1–25*, 176.
4. Thompson, *Jeremiah*, 235.

the city (v. 1). The prophet searches and finds nobody who is righteous. Then he comes to a first conclusion: the search was done in the wrong place – that is, in the streets and marketplaces – and among the wrong people: the poor (v. 4). He decides to go to a different location, where the rich live, to find out whether there is a person there who acts with justice. He goes to the rich (v. 5) with a strong hope that he will find a different situation there. Unfortunately, the rich too, he finds, are unrighteous.

My study of this text is guided by four main questions:

- Why did God send Jeremiah to search for a righteous person in the streets or marketplaces in Jerusalem? Is this choice arbitrary?
- Why did Jeremiah conclude that the search was done in the wrong place, and among the wrong people, the poor?
- Why did Jeremiah assume that the rich must know the way of the Lord, compared to the poor?
- What can we learn from this text in our context?

Jeremiah 5:1 reads, "Run to and fro through the streets of Jerusalem, look around and take note! Search its marketplaces/squares and see if you can find one person who acts justly, and seeks truth, so that I may forgive Jerusalem." Someone from Europe or the United States who visits African cities such as Nairobi, Kinshasa, Lagos, or Kampala for the first time will be surprised by the number of people in the streets. Some of these streets are easily converted into marketplaces, with hundreds of thousands of people, which can make human movement very difficult. It is to such places that Yahweh sent his prophet. As Lundbom puts it, "the mission is to canvass public areas of the city – the streets and souks where merchants and craftsmen have their shops and where people were buying and selling."[5]

Yahweh could have sent the prophet to the temple or private homes, but he chose the streets and marketplaces because in the temple people can hide their behaviour and pretend to be spiritual or religious. In marketplaces their masks slip and reveal their true character and behaviour. Righteousness is not written on people's faces; it is seen in their daily lives and interactions in life situations. So, the best place to observe who people really are is public settings such as marketplaces and city streets.

Concerning the kind of person Yahweh was looking for, the text is explicit that it was a person who acts with justice (*mišpaṭ*) and who strives for honesty (*'ĕmûnâ*). Justice (*mišpaṭ*) means what is just, right and proper, or simply

---

5. Lundbom, *Jeremiah 1–20*, 376.

righteousness. Honesty (*'ĕmûnâ*) is a guiding principle, the God-given norm to ensure a well-ordered society. Accordingly, proper conduct in all spheres of life is to be done in honesty or in conformity with it. The word *'ĕmûnâ* also means faithfulness to the covenant and to the Lord of the covenant. But in the social sphere, it means the character that enables someone to keep their word, to be counted on, and to be faithful in all circumstances. It also means integrity, trustworthiness, and dependability. In the Old Testament, *'ĕmûnâ* is often used as the opposite of *šeqer*, which refers to falsehood, deception, or lying. William Holladay notices that elsewhere in the Bible *'ĕmûnâ* is the object of the verb "to do" (Prov 12:22), but that in this passage, Jeremiah speaks not of "doing *'ĕmûnâ*" or "acting honestly" but of "seeking *'ĕmûnâ*/honesty." The verb "to seek" has a profound meaning; it engages our energy, our will and our consciousness. It is a question not simply of adherence to rules ("do justly") but of wanting, craving, and seeking integrity as well.[6] In other words, honesty is what we should long for in private as well as public life.

Justice (*mišpaṭ*) and honesty (*'ĕmûnâ*) should have differentiated the communal life of the people of Yahweh from that of the people of the other nations. To contextualize it for us today, justice and honesty are the two basic elements that should characterize us as Christians if we are to build a society based on brotherhood and responsibility, where each individual Christian and Christian group is driven by the desire to live by the standard of the gospel for the building of a new society.

Many scholars have noticed a similarity between this text and Abraham's intercession on behalf of Sodom in Genesis 18:23–33. Abraham bargained with God over the number of righteous persons that would be enough to spare Sodom from destruction. Starting from fifty people, he managed to bargain Yahweh down to agreeing to waive the judgement if there were only ten righteous persons there. But in Jerusalem, Yahweh looks for only one righteous person. Does this mean that Jerusalem is ten times as wicked as Sodom? This is what Ezekiel 16:48 seems to suggest. But it is also possible that Jeremiah is here using hyperbolic language to indicate that the great majority of the people in Jerusalem were wicked.

The result of the search for righteous persons in Jerusalem was disappointing for Jeremiah. He found that people in the city were very religious, for they were swearing all the time by Yahweh (v. 2). To swear by God is to use his name as the guarantor of an obligation that someone has assumed. In the event of

---

6. William L. Holladay, *Jeremiah 1: A Critical and Historical Commentary on the Bible* (Philadelphia: Fortress, 1986), 176.

a violation of any duty or agreement, Yahweh would be expected to visit the covenant-breaker with severe judgement. But in Jerusalem, the oaths sworn in Yahweh's name were dishonest; they were *šěqer*: falsehood, deception, lying, pretence, and fraud (v. 2). People used the proper formula for oaths ("as Yahweh lives"), but their intentions were dishonest. Swearing had become a habit, a culture, a mere word. Its meaning and value had been forgotten.

The Decalogue forbids false swearing, for we read in Exodus 20:7 and Deuteronomy 5:11: "You shall not misuse the name of the LORD your God" (NIV). The Syriac version has in fact translated these verses in the Decalogue as "You should not swear falsely by the name of the LORD your God." In the Old Testament, the condemnation against people who swear falsely is also found in Leviticus 5:4; 19:12; Zechariah 5:4; Malachi 3:5.

The prophet then draws his first conclusion: He was searching in the wrong place, the streets and the marketplaces, and among the wrong people, the *dallîm*, the poor (v. 4). How should we understand this verse? Is Jeremiah condemning the poor, or is he justifying their ignorance? Who are these poor, the *dallîm*?

In the Hebrew Bible, the *dallîm* are sometimes identified as the opposite of the rich (Ruth 3:10), or simply as the powerless and insignificant, as opposed to those who have power and influence (Lev. 19:15). Thompson argues that in this context it refers to poverty of knowledge and understanding rather than economic poverty. He adds that verse 5 supports this view because it contrasts the poor with the great, the men of high station:

> The reference may well be to the citizens of Jerusalem, who were insensitive to God's chastening and affairs, which required them to enter into agreements with an appropriate oath. There was no intention on their part to submit their lives and their business dealings to God's scrutiny. They hardly believed that God would care. God was not in their thoughts or in their hearts although they took his name constantly on their lips.[7]

A close look at the text will demonstrate that Thompson's perception of poverty in this passage is a misunderstanding of what it is talking about. In this passage, the poverty is both a lack of knowledge and economic poverty, and each has an impact on the other. In other words, the poor in the streets of Jerusalem were economically poor. They spent their days, and part of the night, in the streets, looking for ways to survive. Their understanding of God,

---

7. Thompson, *Jeremiah*, 238.

who seemed not to respond to their daily needs (while the rich seemed to have everything they needed), might have been profoundly distorted. Their survival and that of their families was more important than keeping the covenant, going to the temple, or telling the truth. Their economic poverty created a poverty of knowledge of, and faith in, God.

The same is true of the poor who today crowd the streets of African megacities. Michela Wrong gives a vivid description of what she observed in Kinshasa, capital of DR Congo,

> In the space of forty-five minutes, as I worked my way through a steaming plate of rice and beans, I was offered the following items without straying from my seat: cigarettes, chewing gum, hard-boiled eggs, cola nuts, spice sachets and carrots (all from a medicinal box aimed at those plagued by bad breath or sore throats), French perfume (two tatty boxes, clearly fake), plastic briefcases and plastic sandals (range of), shoe polish (a small boy knocking his brush against a stool to attract attention), men's trousers, transistor radios (choice of two models), a display of tinny-looking watches and sunglasses, ginger powders, a couple of sports shirts, cheap nylon ties, disposable razors, men's briefs (packet of three), men's shirts, paper tissues, roasted peanuts (in the sachets), grilled prawns (on wooden skewers), socks (variety of colors).[8]

Wrong concludes her observation by noting that, "The traders patiently allowed their goods to be examined and commented on by sceptical but not unfriendly diners, then moved tirelessly on. It was like watching predators on the savannah as they prowled the long grasses and scoured the horizon, searching relentlessly for a kill."[9]

Wrong's description of her experience in only one of the streets of Kinshasa could apply in many African cities. Often they are like walking supermarkets, where the poor stand in the streets and call out loudly to advertise their goods and services to passers-by in the hope of making a sale. This is one of the ways in which the continent's poor people struggle to make ends meet in our cities. It is to such noisy public places that Yahweh sent Jeremiah.

---

8. Michela Wrong, *In the Footsteps of Mr. Kurtz: Living on the Brink of Disaster in Mobutu's Congo* (New York: Harper Collins, 2001), 149.

9. Wrong, *In the Footsteps*, 149.

Barbara's story

The state of the poor in the streets of Jerusalem reminds me of the story of Barbara, a young lady who works in an Internet café in Uganda. She opens the office at eight in the morning and closes it at ten at night. She works seven days a week, without twenty minutes for rest, not even on Sundays. I was in the café late one day and noticed that her employer kept calling every half hour to see whether Barbara had left work before ten. When I asked why she accepted such conditions, why she was not able to ask her employer for a day off, especially on Sunday so that she might go to worship God with other believers (Barbara is a Christian), her answer was simple and straightforward:

> The boss will not accept the request, and if I dare to disagree with him, I will be fired and another person will take this job on that same day. What should I do in this country of misery? I spent four years looking for a job. I even made a bad mistake and became pregnant because I needed money. Now that God offered a job for me, why should I leave it for someone else?

This is a *dal* (a poor person) of our day. Barbara has no choice but to work in that Internet café, almost as a slave, despite the unbearable working conditions. Should she disobey her boss, go to church on Sunday, and lose her job? Will this not force her to go back to selling her body and becoming pregnant again, probably eventually dying of HIV/AIDS? Should she forget about the church and continue with her job? What will be the effect of her decision on her faith if she continues with her job in this way? Does she really have time to pray and meditate on God's word? These are some of the many difficult choices facing the poor in our countries. Poverty does have a negative impact on our faith.

A hermeneutic of compassion

With the reality of the difficult choices that the poor face to secure their livelihoods in mind, Thompson's claim that the poor in Jerusalem were merely merchants making a noise in the streets might not be totally true. They might well have been a mixed crowd of people with different concerns, some of them in dire circumstances. In such a scenario, it might not have been unlikely for the poor to behave like people who did not know Yahweh: telling lies when necessary to get what they needed for themselves and their families, making oaths that they did not keep, or stealing to survive. How many such *dallîm* languish in our prisons because they were forced to steal for the survival of their families?

It seems to me, and this is an important point to make, that Jeremiah looked at the poor who crowded the streets of Jerusalem with compassion. He noticed that something very important was missing in them: They were very busy, trying to meet their basic needs in life, but they lacked knowledge of Yahweh. In such a context, poverty is not a virtue; it is an enemy of faith.

I would argue that Jeremiah was trying to justify the ignorance of the poor. In other words, the poor were faulty but excusable because of the condition in which they found themselves. This is why my translation of verse 4 reads like this: "these are only the poor, They act foolishly; for they do not know the way of Yahweh, the manners of their God." In this passage, knowledge of Yahweh is associated with certain conditions of life. And for the poor, their concern for survival was stronger than their concern for faithfulness to Yahweh.

Jesus had a special concern for the poor people of his time. One day, after teaching many of them for three days, he noticed that the crowd had nothing to eat. He feared that they might faint on their way home, probably because most of them had not eaten for some or all of those days. There is no doubt that those who came to listen to him were very poor people, who were expecting a change in their dire condition. He looked at them with a lot of compassion: "Jesus called his disciples to him and said, '*I have compassion* for these people; because they have been with me three days and have nothing to eat. I do not want to send them away hungry, or they may collapse on the way'" (Matt 15:32 NIV, emphasis added). These were really poor people who came to listen to Jesus. What would have happened to them if Jesus had sent them away hungry? They would certainly have forgotten all his good teachings, and Jesus was aware of this. In the context of his ministry, Jesus knew that eating, healing and hearing the good news go together. If, as Christians we separate the spiritual and physical needs of people, as we often do, our ministry to them will be ineffective.

The majority in African churches are poor people, who come to our services expecting to find a way to be fed and healed. Describing Christianity in Africa, the Gambian-born American professor, Lamin Sanneh says,

> We should take heart because suffering people have found faith and hope. The people who have lined up, determined to enter the church, have eaten of the bread of adversity and tasted the waters of afflictions, and still they press to come into the church. The church exists to welcome precisely such as these, their personal or material circumstances notwithstanding.[10]

---

10. Lamin Sanneh, *Whose Religion Is Christianity? The Gospel beyond the West* (Grand Rapids, MI: Eerdmans, 2003), 33.

What can African churches do to help poor people like Barbara or those crowding our streets? This is one of the pressing questions to the church in Africa. And the future of Christianity in Africa depends on the answer we give to this pressing question.

The conversion of the prophet

There is one more question we need to ask: What happened to Jeremiah during his search? God sent him with a specific mission: to search in the streets of Jerusalem and report whether he had found one person who acts with justice and seeks truth so that Jerusalem might be forgiven. This was a serious mission, and he dared not take it lightly. But the prophet ends up "arguing" for the poor, justifying their ignorance. It seems that something happened in the life of the prophet during his close observation of the life of the poor. My argument is that the prophet was transformed during his search; he was converted after his meeting with the poor in the streets of Jerusalem. In other words, we cannot meet the poor, live with them, and see what is going on in their lives without being changed. It is difficult to spend two days in African slums without being transformed by the experience. Susan Slavin, for example, narrates her unforgettable experience of walking through Kibera slum in Nairobi in 2010:

> We were walking very briskly through Kibera, a slum in Nairobi, Kenya, on a Friday in March of 2010. There were no roads, only dirty, dusty, rocky paths twisting and turning in one direction or another through a jigsaw maze of twig and mud shanties. The air was heavy with stench of humanity mingled with the odor of outdoor charcoal cooking fires. I was not looking where I was going. Instead I was looking down, dodging brown streams of urine and excrement oozing from plastic bags. I was also trying to avoid the myriad small piles of burning garbage. I remember thinking, thank God I'd worn sneakers and not sandals, since the thought of human waste between my bare toes simply grossed me out. I expected a certain amount of physical discomfort with mission work, but I drew the line at walking through human waste with open sandals.[11]

---

11. L. Susan Slavin and Carolis Salvador, *What's So Blessed about Being Poor? Seeking the Gospel in the Slums of Kenya* (Maryknoll, NY: Orbis, 2013), 1–3.

Continuing to reflect more analytically on the impact of this visit to the slum, Slavin says:

> I started thinking about my very comfortable life as a New York attorney and my own evolving spirituality. Intellectually I knew that a missioner signs up for living in a mystery and is required to give up certainty and control. *I also knew I was undergoing a conversion of sorts.* I was leaving my position of privilege and moving toward the margins of society. And through it all, my motivations were driven by seeking an answer to the question of Where is God in the middle of all this and what's so damn blessed about being poor?" (emphasis added)[12]

Slavin's experience in Kibera helps us to feel how meeting the poor can change us and leave us with unanswered questions. Jeremiah went as a "judge" sent by Yahweh, but he met broken, abused, battered, marginalized, bruised people. and he wondered about the meaning of life in the poverty he saw. It became impossible for him to utter his divine judgement. It would have been like trying "to kill a dead snake" as we say in Africa.

My wife and I recently had a similar experience. Johnny, my wife's cousin, came to visit us one afternoon. He is fifteen years old. We left him at home with other children and went to visit some friends. When we came back, we noticed that he had managed to enter our bedroom and had stolen twenty dollars before leaving. His sister Mary had been living with us for two weeks. On learning about the theft, my wife got so angry that she wanted to send Mary away immediately! I resisted, arguing that we should not punish her for what her brother had done. Unfortunately, only three days later, Mary also left our home, after having stolen two nice dresses and two pairs of shoes from other girls who were living with us. Early in the morning, my wife went to get back what Mary had stolen and, if possible, to punish Johnny.

When Johnny saw his aunt entering their house, he ran to hug her, but my wife pushed him away. Johnny knew what was going on. He immediately knelt down, with his hands up, confessing his sin, telling my wife why he stole the twenty dollars. Mary also came, even before my wife said anything, and joined Johnny on their knees. Two other younger children, also joined them, kneeling in front of my wife (probably the two youngest just imitated their elder brother and sister without knowing what was going on). Johnny spoke first: "Aunt, we have been living alone in this house after our mother left us two weeks ago.

---

12. Slavin and Salvador, *What's So Blessed*, 10–11.

She left us without food. We depend on the generosity of our neighbours. We eat only if someone has mercy on us and gives us some food (the last born in the family was only five years old). Otherwise, we go hungry, sometimes for two days." Mary added her plea: "Aunt, I love Jesus, I love Sunday School, but I cannot go because other children mock my old dress. This is why I was tempted to steal. Forgive us . . ." For three minutes, my wife could not speak, and the children were still on their knees, in silence. My wife left, in tears. To make this story short, within four hours we had bought enough food for these children, and within four days, we had contacted their mother to find out what we could do to help her and the children. Thus, while she set out with anger, judgement and condemnation, my wife was overwhelmed and moved to show compassion; she even came back with a strong sense of culpability for what had happened. It seems to me that the prophet may have had a similar experience. It is what happens often when we meet the poor and listen to and understand their stories.

Johnny and Mary had been telling us their story, but we never took it seriously or fully understood their situation until my wife visited them at home. What I am saying is that it is rarely possible to understand the true condition of the poor unless one encounters them and interacts with them directly, seeing them and how they live. We may give to the poor spontaneously when we see their condition, but such tokens, when given without understanding of what they are going through in life, do not make a lasting difference. To encounter the poor, one must commit to visiting them, to going closer to their lives, to listening to their stories, to changing the negative attitudes we have towards them. Ethiopian theologian Alemayehu Mekonnen, thinks along the same lines when he says:

> To develop empathy for Africans, one needs to walk in the slums of Africa and go through the stench and smell that makes you feel like throwing up, travel across Africa and see the hungry and emaciated bodies of young and old, the sick who have never stepped in a clinic or been treated by a physician, the young illiterate and jobless Africans with no future who are prone to criminal activities, and those who languish in the prisons of authoritarian governments. As Éla said, "We must go and rediscover Christ in the slums, in places of misery and domination, among the majority of the poor and the oppressed people. It is the Third World that allows the church to make salvation in Jesus Christ visible."[13]

---

13. Alemayehu Mekonnen, *The West and China in Africa: Civilization without Justice* (Eugene, OR: Wipf & Stock, 2015), 387.

Sadly, we live in a culture of indifference in which each person minds their own business. We drive very fast; we build strong walls not only to protect ourselves but also to prevent us from seeing the poor in the street. More than anything else, we have developed a very negative attitude towards the poor and those who are in pain. Often, we condemn them without first listening to the stories of those who are like Johnny, Mary and the poor in the streets of Jerusalem. The people in the streets and the poor in general have stories to tell.

Again, as I have already shown, a major characteristic of Jesus's ministry on earth was his close contact with people and his deep compassion for those who were poor and in pain (Luke 7:11–17). He had compassion on the multitude who were distressed and scattered like sheep without a shepherd (Matt 9:36; Mark 6:34); he had compassion on the hungry (Mark 8:21); on the blind (Matt 20:34); on the demonized, the victims of the power of unclean spirits (Mark 9:22, 25); on those with leprosy (Mark 1:40–41); on the bereaved (Luke 7:12–13); on the sinful, the lost, the spiritually dead (Luke 15:20), and on the crowds in general (Matt 14:14).

Spirituality and poverty in Africa

The argument that because of their dire conditions, the poor in Jerusalem did not know God and, that poverty appeared to hinder faith in God seems to contradict the reality in Africa today. Africa has become a Christian continent yet it is at the same time the poorest of all continents. Contrary to the argument in this chapter, it seems that in Africa, poverty and suffering open up an opportunity for the people to seek God and worship him as Sanneh argued in the quotation on page 72. This can be observed nearly everywhere on the continent. Maybe the most remarkable thing of all is that whenever Africans flee for their lives because of wars and conflicts, they move with their churches. Refugee camps are easily transformed into places of worship. Our denomination now has fourteen churches in western Uganda, at the border with DR Congo, all planted by Congolese refugees, former members of our church who fled their homes between 2001 and 2003. New churches are being planted by refugees every year in Africa. For years, we struggled with what to do for those churches in a foreign country. South Sudan would be another good example. This newest country in the world is also the one most affected by conflicts and wars, with an estimated 2.5 million of its people displaced. At the same time, South Sudan is among the top twenty countries in the world where Christianity is growing the fastest.[14]

It is also well known in sub-Saharan Africa, that starting new churches has become a flourishing business for people who cannot find employment elsewhere. Independent charismatic churches and prayer groups are mushrooming everywhere. The streets, private houses, woodlands, abandoned cinemas halls, private homes, former bars, schools, trees, papyrus mats, hilltops, and stadiums are among the places where new independent charismatic churches are planted. The poor flock to these places several times a week for prayers and worship. In many large towns, you get the impression that every street has its own church or prayer group. In 2007, for example, the Kenyan Attorney General, Amos Wako, reported that "his office was facing difficulties in processing 6,740 pending applications by various religious organizations."[15] By 2010, there were approximately 10,000 registered churches in Kenya.[16] These churches are led by individuals with big titles: apostles, archbishops, bishops, patriarchs, visionaries, evangelists, prophets, and right reverends. Some of the churches have extravagant names: God's Glory Temple, Maximum Miracle Center, Water of Life Center, the New Testament Church of God, among others. As David Z. Niringiye, a former Bishop with the Diocese of Kampala, Uganda, writes: "On a Sunday morning . . . one has the sense of being in a religious supermarket of churches, and as with choosing a supermarket, the choice of church is yours."[17]

Consequently, whenever they experience severe suffering, Africans tend to seek refuge in the church. It might look at first sight as if in Africa, worship and knowledge of God go hand in hand with poverty and suffering. As Jesse N. K. Mugambi laments:

> Contemporary Africa continues to be, perhaps, the most "religious" continent in the world, and yet its people remain the most abused of all history. How could it be that people who continue to call God

---

14. "The Top 20 Countries Where Christianity Is Growing the Fastest," in https://discipleallnations.wordpress.com/2013/08/25/the-top-20-countries-where-christianity-is-growing-the-fastest/.

15. Julius Gathogo, "The Challenge of Money and Wealth in Some East African Pentecostal Churches," in *Studia Historiae Ecclesiasticae* 37 (2), http://www.ku.ac.ke/schools/humanities/images/stories/docs/Research/challenge-of-money-and-wealth.pdf.

16. Gathogo, "Challenge of Money."

17. David Zac Niringiye, *The Church: God's Pilgrim People* (Downers Grove, IL: IVP Academic, 2015), 2.

most reverently are the ones whom God seems to neglect most vehemently? Could it be that "irreligion" is the key to success, and that religion is the key to backwardness?[18]

In other words, how can we explain the argument that poverty was a hindrance to a faithful, God-honouring life for the poor in the streets of Jerusalem whereas it seems to open the door to the poor of Africa to enter the church?

The best way to answer this question is by asking more questions: What kind of churches do we have in Africa? And which kind of Christianity is there? What happens, for example, after the refugees have prayed? Does the war stop? Do those who pray fervently change and behave differently? Does the situation of the poor change in our cities? Has the high number of churches planted in our cities resulted in a matching improvement in the lives of the people who attend them? What is the church for? Why do people pray? What do they pray for?

The often repeated saying that African Christianity is a hundred miles wide and an inch deep helps in answering many of these questions. It signals that there is something wrong with African Christianity as we experience it, despite its phenomenal growth. It is well known that Christianity in Africa is characterized by large numbers of churches but little impact, or alternatively, by maximal spread but minimal transformation of individuals and society. Some churches are actually part of the problem. Instead of promoting peace, service, and community building, they have become places of division, breeding grounds for personal interests and tribalism, and sites for massacres. In fact, many Christians in Africa keep shifting from one church to another, from one prayer group to another, in search of a long-lasting solution to their problems, which they hardly find. African Christianity has not been able to bring lasting, positive change to advance the continent and to give it a new direction of peace, progress, and hope for a better future.

What then is the problem? Cameroonian theologian Jean-Marc Éla has wrestled with this issue in most of his writings and ministry. For him, the challenge of the African church goes beyond simple Africanization or enculturation, beyond the so-called new evangelization, or even beyond developing new doctrines or adequate methodologies and strategies for

---

18. Jesse N. K. Mugambi, "Problems and Promises of the Churches in Africa," in Jesse N. K. Mugambi (ed.), *The Church and the Future in Africa: Problems and Promises* (Nairobi: All Africa Conference of Churches, 1977), 43.

intervention.[19] He argues that the problem with the African church is rooted in its conception and structure.

For a long time, the church in Africa had restricted its ministry to preaching and teaching people how to get to heaven, while neglecting the everyday lives of its members. Éla argues that the African church should not simply be a copy of Roman Catholic, Southern Baptist, or Reformed churches that are weighed down by an ecclesiastic mentality and a foreign culture. Rather, he wants to see it as a new community of believers who are able to give a structure to their community that allows them to sit, discuss and try to find concrete solutions to the real problems affecting them where they live. This is how Africans traditionally addressed problems in their villages and this is what Éla had in mind when he said,

> we must struggle against alienation forces and, at the same time, give back to people their responsibility for themselves and their bodies, teaching them to challenge anything that smacks of chance and destiny.[20]

The church in Africa must be part of the everyday lives of its members. Instead of continually accusing demons of causing poverty, it must talk about and teach its members how to organize themselves so as to fight against real issues. This requires the church in Africa to reinvent itself.

With these arguments, we join the poor in the streets of Jerusalem in saying that poverty and severe suffering are indeed hindrances to faith and to proper knowledge of Yahweh. A lot of Africans love the Lord Jesus Christ and love the church, but at least two things are preventing them from fully enjoying their relationship with God: poverty and the inability of the church to deal with the real issues facing the poor. Éla adds:

> The church in Africa is faced with a serious choice. Swept up in the mutations of African society, it finds itself before two inexorable alternatives: slip away into anachronism and become a stranger to the real questions of today's Africa or else become prophetic and daring but at a price of a revision of all its language, all of its

---

19. Emmanuel Katongole, *The Sacrifice of Africa: A Political Theology for Africa* (Grand Rapids: Eerdmans, 2010), 109.

20. Jean Marc Éla, *My Faith as an African*, trans. John Pairman Brown and Susan Perry (Eugene, OR: Wipf & Stock, 2009), 84.

forms, and all of its institutions, in order to assume the African human face.[21]

The Bible supports Éla's argument that God's vision is to create a new community of people who have been liberated from their bondage to sin to worship the living God, to foster a new identity as a witness to their liberation, and to seek solutions to whatever tries to destroy their community, their freedom, and their hope. This is what Éla calls "a different world right here, a world being gestated in the deeds of the everyday."[22] Thus, from the Bible we can take the following three examples: one from the Old Testament, the second from Jesus himself, and the third from the early church.

In Exodus, God sent Moses to urge Pharaoh to let his people go from Egypt. Exodus 5 opens with the following sentence: "Afterward Moses and Aaron went to Pharaoh and said, 'This is what the LORD, the God of Israel, says: Let my people go, so they may hold a festival to me in the wilderness.'" (Exod 5:1 NIV). The message is repeated in Exodus 5:3: "The God of the Hebrews has met with us. Now let us take a three-day journey into the wilderness to offer sacrifices to the LORD our God" (NIV).

Egypt had become an oppressor, subjecting all the Israelites to severe sufferings and utter poverty. In this extremely oppressive situation, it was almost impossible for the Israelites to properly worship their God. In Exodus, worshipping and serving God are clearly associated with liberation from oppression and from poverty. The Israelites may have had an idea about Yahweh, but like the poor in the streets of Jerusalem and Africa, they probably had a distorted view of him as a God who was unable to come to their rescue. Even if they had wanted to worship him, God, it would not have been possible because of the oppressive situation in which they found themselves in Egypt. Their experience shows that suffering and poverty are enemies of true worship of God. Moses's request to Pharaoh to release the Israelites was the beginning of the creation of a new community of God's people who, freed from slavery, would move together toward greater knowledge of God. The Israelites were to be an example of a transformed community in God that always reinvents itself and resists threats to its well-being.

The second example is taken from Luke 4:16–30. Philip Francis Esler, who has studied Luke's attitude to the poor, describes them in the following terms:

---

21. Jean Marc Éla, *African Cry*, trans. Robert J. Barr (Eugene, OR: Wipf & Stock), 134.
22. Éla, *African Cry*, 53.

The poor suffered extreme forms of economic, social and political deprivation. For them life was a very grim business. Ill-fed, housed in slums or not at all, ravaged by sickness, precluded from all access to social prestige and power over their own destinies, and having virtually no hope of improvement in their conditions, they went through life with little if any confirmation that they, as much as the tiny elite who lorded it over them, were creatures with personal dignity and respect, entitled to share in the fruits of the earth.[23]

It was in this general context, argues Esler, that Jesus pronounced his revolutionary manifesto (Luke 4:16–30) in which he clearly linked the good news with deliverance from social, economic, spiritual, and physical bondage. All the miracles that Jesus performed in Luke 4:31–41 were a demonstration that people needed to be released from their oppression (and sufferings) before they could properly know and worship God. And Jesus never separated physical and spiritual needs. Therefore, it is again clear that Jesus knew that suffering and poverty were obstacles to the knowledge of God and service to him. This is why, wherever he went, Jesus sought to deliver his people both physically and spiritually.

I wonder what would have happened to the faith of the blind, the lame, and the demon-possessed if Jesus had called them only to repentance without first healing their physical sicknesses, as we tend to do today. Would it even have been possible for them to respond to Jesus's call with the hope that they would enjoy good health in heaven, as we often ask people to do? Jesus's presence brought a new world in Jerusalem and around it, and he was inviting the poor and those who came to him to become members of this new world.

The third example is from Acts 2:45, where we read that wealthier Christians in the early church willingly put their possessions up for sale and distributed the proceeds to the needy members of the Christian community. This is an example of what a church should be like, and how the rich believers should unite to use part of their wealth to lessen the pain of the poor so that both groups can serve God together in joy and unity. This generosity among Christians also served as a testimony to unbelievers that the church was a new community marked by social justice. In other words, Luke's community in Acts demonstrates that the elimination of poverty and the alleviation of the

---

23. Philip Francis Esler, *Community and Gospel in Luke-Acts: The Social and Political Motivations of Lucan Theology* (Cambridge: Cambridge University Press, 1987), 179.

sufferings of the destitute must be a vital constituent of Christianity not just in Africa, but anywhere in the world.

The Rich Guilty of Not Knowing God (v. 5)

In the Hebrew Bible, Jeremiah 5:5 is introduced by a cohortative phrase: *Let me go off to the great men*. The cohortative ("let me go off") expresses self-encouragement, a wish, a decision, and a strong desire. After realizing that the poor do not know God because of their conditions, the prophet decides to go to the great men (*haggĕdōlîm*) of the city with the strong hope that they must know the Lord. This is why the entire verse reads: *Let me go to the noblemen (great men), and (let me) speak to them, for they know the way of Yahweh, the manners of their God*.

There are three important things to be noted here. First, the *haggĕdōlîm*, the big people, are those who occupy a position of prominence or importance. They are "the shapers of opinion, those who set the pace for the whole community,"[24] the leaders, the decision-makers. In modern terms, they are the government officials, successful politicians, those occupying higher administrative positions, diplomats, members of parliament, business people, and the like.

Second, the prophet seems to suggest that these leaders lived in a different location, since they were not to be found in the same places as the *dallîm*, the poor. This is why the prophet has to go elsewhere to meet them. The rich are thus contrasted with the poor who crowded the streets of Jerusalem. *Haggĕdōlîm* suggests the idea of rich people, living in beautiful houses, far from the noisy, smelly streets and marketplaces of Jerusalem, or of the slums in Africa today. In modern-day Africa, they would be the people living in large, fenced compounds in expensive areas with gate guards and watchdogs and round-the-clock security.

It is clear from this passage that one of the causes of poverty is the absence of human solidarity. There is a shameful division of our society based on whether we are rich or poor: while some live in the slums, others shut themselves off in their fenced compounds. Sometimes, the gap between the two communities is just some few metres of wetland or a bridge – or an electric fence and a guardhouse.

If only the wealthy could come out as a team like in Acts 2:45 and extend a hand of solidarity to the poor in the streets. Unfortunately, while the poor are

---

24. Holladay, *Jeremiah 1*, 178.

languishing in misery, the wealthy are busy working out strategies to increase their wealth and position while pushing the poor into ever-deeper destitution.

Third, the prophet assumes that the leaders know the law. He does not go to them to check whether they know the way of Yahweh their God, but simply to speak to them as just and honest people. Jeremiah assumes that they must know God's law. In fact the second line of verse 5 in the Hebrew Bible is introduced by the particular *kī* ("because," "for" they know) to mean that the prophet was certain that he would find a better situation than the one he experienced with the poor. Moreover, the pronoun *hēmmâ* (they) in the same line (in the Hebrew Bible) is emphatic and seems to constitute another indication of the confidence Jeremiah had towards the leaders. Thus, that sentence has to be translated "For/because (*kī*) they are the ones (*hēmmâ*) to know." Or "For they for sure know the way of Yahweh, the manners/justice of their God." Sadly, Jeremiah finds that the leaders too have broken the yoke; they have snapped their traces. Thompson observes that the "picture here is one of rebellion and defiance and seems to have in mind the ox, who is normally yoked to his plough and draws the plough with the aid of its traces."[25]

Why did Jeremiah assume that leaders should have known the law while the poor were somehow excusable? Because the leaders, who are rich, clearly do not have the same struggle in life as the poor. They have money, they have time, they have education, and they have opportunity to know and serve God. They do not work long hours like the poor do who come back home late, exhausted, frustrated and hungry.

There is no reasonable justification for the rich not knowing God apart from simply defying him and refusing to follow his law. Theirs is active rebellion. Those who have enough money know that wealth can give them extraordinary advantages: good housing, good education for themselves and their children, social influence, etc. However, as Jeremiah warns, there is a real danger of accumulating wealth without surrendering one's life to God, without putting God before all things, including our money and all our possessions.

Conclusion

The main argument of this chapter is that poverty is an obstacle to the Christian faith in Africa because it destroys the dignity of human beings. Severe poverty has a terrible impact on spiritual, psychological, and physical health and creates a sense of meaninglessness. It makes people withdraw not only from society

---

25. Thompson, *Jeremiah*, 238.

but also from life itself. The chapter does not discuss the multifaceted causes of poverty in Africa but only its impact on our faith in God. Africans love Jesus, but the church on the continent has not been able to help its poor members find solutions to their problems so that they can improve their lives. Éla argues that the structure of the African church today is the real obstacle to the fight against poverty. The African church as it is conceived and structured now is a copy of a foreign organization. Consequently, it does not reflect the way African communities function or should function, and it does not respond to the needs of the poor. The solution is to change this structure and allow the church to become a place where people take time not only to listen to preaching and teaching, not only to spend whole days praying, but also to think together, to identify their needs, and to seek to find ways to solve their problems as a community. The church should focus on enabling every member to do something for themselves, for their family, and for others in the community. The leaders of the church should also challenge well-off members of the community to contribute their knowledge, experience and wealth to lift up the poor.

5

The Anatomy of a Dysfunctional Community

Jeremiah 9:2–9

² Oh that I could find in the desert
    a traveller's lodging,
that I may leave my people,
    and go far away from them.
For they are all adulterers,
    a band of traitors.
³ They bend their tongue like a bow;
    it is by falsehood not faithfulness that they prevail in the land;
they proceed from one evil deed to another;
    they do not know Yahweh, the Lord's oracle.
⁴ Let each man be on a guard against his fellow,
    and put no trust in any brother;
for every brother is a deceiver
    and every friend a slanderer.
⁵ Each man deceives his neighbour;
    they never speak the truth,
they have taught their tongues to speak lies;
    they commit iniquity, they have no will to repent.
⁶ Oppression is heaped on oppression, fraud on fraud,
    they refuse to know me, Yahweh's oracle.
⁷ Therefore, thus says Yahweh of hosts:

I am going to refine and assay them;
> for what else can I do because of my people?
⁸ Their tongue is a deadly arrow,
> deceitful are the words of their mouth;
one speaks peace (amicably) to his neighbour,
> while planning an ambush in his heart.
⁹ Shall I not punish them for these things? Yahweh's oracle.
> On a nation like this,
> shall I not avenge myself?

Historical and Literary Context

Some scholars regard this passage as an editorial that was produced many years after the ministry of the prophet. However, despite the fact that it lacks clear historical clues, it is possible to discover its probable setting from a literary analysis of the passage in its context.

Jeremiah 9:2–9 belongs to a section that begins in chapter 8 and ends in chapter 10. Several units in these three chapters are poetry (8:4–23; 9:1–11, 16–21; 10:17–22) and two themes appear in all of them: (1) the destruction of Jerusalem by invaders (8:10, 13–27, 18–23; 9:9–11, 16–21; 10:17–22), and (2) the idea that Jerusalem brought destruction upon itself because of its depravation and unwillingness to come back to Yahweh (8:4–7, 8–9, 10–12, 14; 9:1–8; 10:21). Jeremiah 9:1–8 fits into the second theme.

The two themes, invasion and the reasons for invasion, establish similarity between 9:2–9 and the Foe from the North unit (4:5–6:30). There are also several similar passages in 9:2–9 and 4:5–6:30. For example, the sentence "they do not know Yahweh" is found in 9:3, 4:22 and 5:4–5. Similarly, the idea contained in the sentence "they refuse to know me" in 9:6 is similar to "they refuse to repent" in 5:3 and 8:5.

Therefore, it is not wrong to allocate 9:2–9 to the same period as the texts related to the enemy from the north, with the difference that in chapters 8 to 10, there is no hint of repentance by the people of Jerusalem, and therefore no possibility of forgiveness, as was the case in 5:1. On the contrary, 8:4–6; 9:4b; 10:19 show that people are no longer able to come back to Yahweh. This means that 9:2–9 should be located to a period later than the one referred to in 4:5–6:30. Holladay suggests that this text is best assigned to the autumn of 601 BC during the tumultuous reign of Jehoiakim,[1] but I would argue for its placement at an even later time, at the very end of Jehoiakim's reign.

---

1. Holladay, *Jeremiah 1–25*, 299.

Structure

There are two major challenges in the interpretation of this passage: (1) the disagreement among scholars about some Hebrew expressions and their meanings, and (2) the determination of who is speaking. Aspects of the first issue will be dealt with when we look at the passage in detail. Concerning the person speaking in the passage, some scholars argue that the speaker is Jeremiah, at least in the first five verses.[2] Commentators who adopt this view delete the sentence "Yahweh's oracle" in verses 3 and 7 where it occurs. This textual amendment is supported by the Septuagint. The justification is that God cannot speak and complain like a human being (the so-called "anthropocentric viewpoint of the verses"[3]). Others remove verse 8 and place it immediately after verse 3 because both passages are condemning the sin of the tongue. They also delete the whole of verse 9, considering it as a repetition of 5:9, 29. Finally, Bright considers 9:1–6 as the prophet's words and 9:7–9 as an oracle of Yahweh's judgement introduced by "therefore" (*lākēn*).

Holladay adopts the opposite view and argues that Yahweh is the one speaking (through the prophet) in all eight verses (9:2–9). This position is supported by other passages in the book of Jeremiah that contain a first-person lament by God himself preceded by a lament of Jeremiah (12:7–13 and 15:5–9). Craigie, Kelley and Drinkard support this idea and argue that,

> The concept of a God who suffers is rejected by many because it implies that he is weak and finite. The impossibility of God suffering is a central teaching in some of the great world religions and is even advocated in some Christian circles. However, the notion of a God who cannot suffer, while perhaps making theology more manageable, nevertheless leaves it placid and spiritless. If the love of God is more than an empty metaphor, then the suffering of God must also be regarded as real.[4]

The position that I adopt for interpreting this passage is that the whole passage is Yahweh's word, and that through his prophet, Yahweh is expressing his feeling as a human being would so that we can understand him. I see no convincing grounds for deleting the formula "Thus says Yahweh," and so attributing the first verse of the passage to Jeremiah simply because it seems abnormal that

---

2. Craigie, Kelley and Drinkard, *Jeremiah 1–25*, 143.
3. Craigie, Kelley and Drinkard, 143.
4. Craigie, Kelley and Drinkard, 145.

Yahweh might complain in the same way a human being would and decide to leave his people.[5] Thus, the structure of this passage will be discussed as follows:

- Verses 1–2: Yahweh's discouragement and desire to leave his people,
- Verses 3–5: the reason for Yahweh's lament: sin of the tongue and others, and
- Verses 6–8: Yahweh's lament and judgement of Judah.

A Story from Kinshasa

All the ninety-eight mainline Protestant denominations in DR Congo are grouped together in an umbrella organization known as the Church of Christ in Congo or CCC (*Église du Christ au Congo*, in French). As the leader of the Brethren Church in north-eastern Congo, I attended the 2014 national synod of the CCC in Kinshasa, the capital city. This was my first experience of working with an extremely dysfunctional organization. It took a day and a half to get the quorum needed to start the meeting because some seventy-five denominations were in conflict and most of them sent two or three competing delegations to the event. The moderator did not know which faction should be allowed in. Finally, "Christian" police officers were asked to guard the door to the main conference room. I recall a deeply disturbing scene: When the delegation of one particular episcopal denomination was called in, three different groups rushed up to the door. I saw a bishop running like a common man to try to get in ahead of the others, only to be stopped by the police because there were people behind him, shouting out insults, telling the police not to let him and his group in because he was a crook. The bishop was sweating in his beautiful gown and begging the policeman to allow him in. I really felt bad, hearing all the insults being hurled at him, things nobody could imagine.

When the meeting eventually started, I found myself appointed to a commission that was analysing the admission of fourteen new members. At least 90 percent of these applications came from splinter groups in existing denominations. One bishop proudly stated: "This is how Protestants multiply." I was distressed by his words because this kind of multiplication can be a source of tension, physical confrontations and sometimes even death. But the

---

5. Timothy Polk (*The Prophetic Persona*, 113) acknowledges the systematic ambiguity of the relationship between the word of Yahweh and that of the prophet. This can be justified by the fact that, in the book of Jeremiah, the prophet shares Yahweh's perspectives and attitudes (see other ambiguities in 9:10; 13:17a; 14:17).

bishop seemed to think that this type of growth is fine because that was how he himself became a bishop.

While on the commission, I opposed one particular request because I knew the story behind it well and felt I would be betraying the Lord if I accepted it. I managed to convince the majority of the members in the commission to see my view. But one of the top leaders of the CCC was behind this division. He had managed to divide his own denomination, and he wanted the synod to officially accept his faction as a full member of the CCC. He was using his position of privilege (he was a CCC leader and a senator) not only to divide his own denomination but also to make sure that it ceased to exist. This case had already been before the tribunal for more than ten years.

My opposition to this leader created a deep crisis and the meeting was cancelled for the entire following day because he convened a private meeting with the moderator and his close friends to circumvent the decision of our commission, which had already been shared with all the members of the CCC. I finally felt that I was wasting my time. I knew that most of the bishops around him were playing the same game and that they would not agree with me. I left the meeting and flew back home. What a waste of money and time! I was sickened by the level of the corruption and dysfunction. We had paid a lot of money to participate in the meeting, and had struggled even to get food during lunch. How can God be pleased with such a dysfunctional organization of the top church leaders of a country? How can the church reach such a level of division, corruption and dysfunction? How can we as a church claim to serve and honour God in such a situation? How can the church be salt to the nation if our conduct is the same as or worse than that of politicians? Can what I experienced in that conference explain why DR Congo is socially and politically in such bad shape?

This story opens just a small window to help us understand what is going on not only in DR Congo, but in most of our denominations in Africa. It will also help us to understand in some way, the situation in Judah during the time of Jeremiah as presented in 9:2–9 and why Judah was finally destroyed.

God Wishes to Leave Jerusalem

The situation described in verse 2 is almost unthinkable. So far, in the book of Jeremiah, the image has been of the people abandoning Yahweh and going after other gods (2:13, 17, 19; 5:7, 19) and of Yahweh pleading with his people and trying to help them come back to him. He has been looking for different ways to help them, including being ready to make concessions, so that he can forgive his people if he finds even only one person who seeks righteousness (5:1). This level of willingness to go to great lengths to forgive his people was unusual for Yahweh who is known as the God of justice. But out of love and mercy, he was ready to forgive. But now the situation of his people has become agonizing for him. His own people have pushed him to the limit. It has become impossible for him to continue with Judah. He must leave them and look for a place far away, in the desert. For the first time in the book of Jeremiah, Yahweh finally decides to walk away from his people.

By leaving his people, Yahweh is also leaving the beautiful temple they built for him in Jerusalem. But this temple has now become thoroughly corrupted; it is a den of thieves (Jer 7:11; Matt 21:13; Mark 11:17) and a place of total disorder similar to the meeting of the Church of Christ in Congo described above. Instead of the temple, Yahweh now prefers a modest accommodation for travellers (*mālôn*) in an uninhabited place or wilderness. Being in the wilderness would free Yahweh from seeing the repulsive and distasteful goings-on in Jerusalem that sicken him. As Brueggemann puts it, "there is only so much this God will tolerate. Now it is time to depart because the affronts and betrayals have become a burden too great for God."[6]

It is important to remember that the community being described here is not the nations, not unbelievers and the Gentiles who did not know God and did not have the law. What is being referred to here is a community of "believers of Yahweh," who had received the law at Sinai. It is a community surrounded by Levites, prophets, and priests. Like the delegates to the CCC meeting in Kinshasa, they were supposed to be examples to others, but failed dismally.

Before asking how they got to this point, we first need to hear how the prophet describes the situation inside this community.

Inside the Dysfunctional Community (vv. 2b–3)
The sin of adultery (v. 2b)

In verses 2b–6 and 8, Yahweh through his prophet gives a long catalogue of the social and moral depravity that causes Yahweh's discouragement. God accuses all the people of being adulterers (*měnā'ăpîm*). In Israel, adultery was condemned for both sociological and theological reasons. Sociologically, the extended family was the cornerstone of Israelite society; a threat to its stability could not be tolerated. Adultery could cause disruption in the family through divorce, perpetual tensions and separation of family members, etc.

---

6. Brueggemann, *Commentary on Jeremiah*, 94–95.

Theologically, marriage was grounded in a divine ordinance (Gen 2:24) and was regarded as a mirror of God's covenant with his people.

Given this theological understanding, the word "adulterers" (*měnā'ăpîm*) is probably used here metaphorically to describe offences against the covenant between Yahweh and Judah. In this sense, Lundbom believes that here the word is used as a general term to disparage a debased community.[7] Furthermore, this disparagement and Yahweh's pain in this passage do not come from what the people have done to Yahweh (breaking the first four commandments, if we divide the Decalogue into two parts[8]) but from what they have done to each other (that is, the breaking of the second part of the Decalogue[9]). In this sense, the word "adultery" as used here does not point at one particular form of sin, but describes a society crumbling under different kinds of *social* evil. In other words, an adulterous community is a polluted and unholy community that has lost all the characteristics it was supposed to reflect.

The social life of a community matters to Yahweh because from the beginning, God's plan has never been to create scattered individuals but to build a society, a community of people who reflect his character of peace, justice, mercy, righteousness and love. These qualities cannot be displayed or experienced when people live alone. They are to be demonstrated in a community setting. It is the same with Christianity today. The world will not be interested in our church and in knowing God unless they see a difference in the way we live as a Christian community. In this sense, true evangelism should start with the building of a transformed community.

The sin of a wicked tongue (v. 3)

Verse 3 is more specific in the accusation against the perversion in Judah: "They bend their tongue like a bow; it is by falsehood not faithfulness that they prevail in the land; they proceed from one evil deed to another." Here "tongue" is used to represent human speech. The image of using the tongue as a bow powerfully captures how destructive human speech can be when used to harm other people. The tongue can cause enormous, sometimes irreparable damage. Proverbs 16:27 compares the speech of a scoundrel to a burning fire.

---

7. Lundbom, *Jeremiah 1–20*, 538.

8. No other gods beside me, no carved images (idols), no misuse of Yahweh's name, observance of the Sabbath.

9. Honour your father and mother, do not murder, do not commit adultery, do not steal, do not give false testimony, do not covet.

Psalm 140:3 gives the image of evil people who "make their tongues as sharp as a serpent's, the poison of vipers on their lips." Paul quotes that passage to illustrate the various sins of the non-Christian world (Rom 3:13). For James, "The tongue also is a fire, a world of evil among the parts of the body. It corrupts the whole body, sets the whole course of one's life on fire, and is itself set on fire by hell" (Jas 3:6 NIV). Jesus himself pointed to the danger of our speech by stating: "by your words you will be acquitted, and by your words you will be condemned" (Matt 12:37 NIV). An African proverb makes a similar point: "A cutting word is worse than a bowstring – a cut may heal, but the cut of the tongue does not." A similar proverb in Kiswahili states *baada ya kovu na jeraha ndani* (even after it has been covered by scar tissue, the wound still hurts inside). In other words, it is not easy to forget an insult.[10] It is very hard to heal a person whose life has been destroyed by an evil tongue. Speech generates a lot of problems, division, and disagreements and can even cause bloodshed. Very often, the person who insults is incapable of self-control. Thus, another Kiswahili proverb states *Akutu kanaye hakuchagulii tusi* ("the one who insults you does not choose insults"; in other words, their goal is to try to hurt you deeply).[11]

In my culture, women who like to be rude and cause division are referred to as *mangbarasi*. I have never asked about the origin and the meaning of that word, but in our childhood, we were taught to avoid dealing with the families of such women, and to never play with their children because if something happened to them, their mothers might cause a lot of trouble and division in the village by their words. I remember one such woman in my childhood, who made the lives of people in our village miserable. She had scars on her body because she was beaten several times by people she insulted when she was drunk. Even her husband was not able to control her. I have now come to realize that evil speech indicates the spiritual life of the person who uses it in the same way the temperature of our body indicates our health. So, the flow of the words that come out of mangbarasi shows the condition of their soul. The situation is no better in the church, even sometimes in the preaching. Sometimes we hear preaching that can really harm people instead of helping them.

But the real art of destructive insult and damaging words in Africa has now been mastered by politicians, especially during elections, when candidates are campaigning and trying to build support for their position while undermining

---

10. Swahili Proverbs: *Methali za Kiswahili*, http://swahiliproverbs.afrst.illinois.edu/abuse.html.

11. Swahili Proverbs: *Methali za Kiswahili*.

their opponents. Such speech is also common among winners and losers of elections. Some scholars have argued that Ghana is one of the countries where insults and damaging words have reached an all-time high in recent political debate. So in his inaugural sermon as the third Catholic Archbishop of Kumasi (Ghana), the Most Reverend Gabriel Anokye reminded politicians about the importance of national peace-building, saying "we can see a peaceful, secure and stable country when the media boldly denounces and cuts off people who shamefully abuse, insult, curse and inflame passions on the airwaves."[12] Kwame Asamoah and his colleagues describe the situation in Ghana as follows:

> It, therefore, becomes disturbing when political leaders, Ministers of State, members of Parliament or government spokespersons act as "demons" when they use offensive language against their opponents. Such attitudes have a cascading effect on their supporters known in local parlance as "foot-soldiers" who are encouraged to use similar posture to defend their leaders.[13]

Kenya is another example of an African country where the destructive effect of insulting and damaging rhetoric has led to violence. In an unpublished paper describing the role of hate speech in post-electoral violence in the country, Susan F. Hirsch writes,

> Those who engaged in negative speech during the 2007 election violence voiced not just the well-worn and familiar stereotypes of commonly circulating ethnic jokes about lazy or lascivious politicians, but they also used cold, dehumanizing language. They called people "spots" or "weeds" that needed to be cleansed or pulled out. They referred to people as animals (e.g. mongoose) or insects . . . The use of dehumanizing epithets, as well as the refusal to speak of certain groups of people as humans, are key indicators that groups in conflict may have become locked in axiological opposition . . . The rationale implicit in the use of dehumanizing, value-laden language is: "We are the good and they are the evil.

---

12. Kwame Asamoah, Emmanuel Yeboah-Asiamah and Alex Osei-Kojo, "Demons of Transitional Democracies: Politics of Insults and Acrimony in Ghana," in *Journal of Social Science Studies* 1, no. 1 (June 2014): 52, http://dx.doi.org/10.5296/jsss.v1i1.4725.

13. Asamoah, Yeboah-Asiamah and Osei-Kojo, "Demons of Transitional Democracies," 50.

We are the people and they are the animals. We are the worthy and they are the killable."[14]

There is no doubt that hate speech is one of the causes of violence in many countries in Africa. Ghana and Kenya have been given as examples, but they are not the only ones affected. We know of the role played by the dehumanizing hate speech broadcast by *Radio Télévision Libre de Mille Collines* (RTLMC) during the genocide in Rwanda. Sometimes, the hate speech appears in graphic cartoons in newspapers and on television. There is an urgent need for combined efforts by the church and the legislators in African nations to find a way to help people understand the danger of hate speech and its consequences. Unfortunately, this has not yet become the concern of many Africans, not even in the academy.

The sin of treachery (v. 2b)

At the end of verse 2, the people of Judah are also accused of being a band of traitors or acting treacherously (*bōg'dîm*). This word comes from the verb *bāgad*, which means to cover, and when used figuratively means to act covertly. This verb occurs forty-three times in the Old Testament with reference to the following types of people: (1) those whose outward appearance masks the inner realities (Jer 12:1, 6); (2) those who keep on praising God while betraying him with their actions; (3) and those who use kind and peaceful language in conversations with others while planning to harm them in their minds. Another word for such behaviour is hypocrisy, another evil that was destroying Judah. Nigerian sociologist Layi Erinosho argues that hypocrisy or treacherous behaviour can be key to explaining the dysfunctions of international communities in the globalized world today.[15] He defines hypocrisy as "behavior which pretends to have a moral standard or an opinion that does not reflect what is actual or the true viewpoint of an individual."[16] Hypocrisy creates mistrust in a community and breaks relationships. In the specific context of Jeremiah 9:2, the word *bāgad* shows that

---

14. Susan F. Hirsch, "Putting Hate Speech in Context: Observation on Speech, Power, and Violence in Kenya." Unpublished paper, prepared for George Mason University, https://www.ushmm.org/m/pdfs/20100423-speech-power-violence-hirsch.pdf.

15. Layi Erinosho, "Sociology, Hypocrisy, and Social Order," in *African Sociological Review* 12, no. 2 (2008): 87, http://www.jstor.org/stable/24487607.

16. Erinosho, "Sociology, Hypocrisy, and Social Order," 87.

not only does the deceitfulness of life erect a barrier between God and his people . . . but the poison, corruption, and treachery it generates causes communities to disintegrate . . . Faithlessness to God inevitably leads to acts of faithlessness against members of the community.[17]

In verse 3, the list of evil deeds in Judah culminates in two antithetical words: falsehood (šeqer) and truthfulness, trustworthiness (ĕmûnâ) presented side by side: "it is by šeqer (falsehood) not ĕmûnâ (truthfulness, trustworthiness) that they prevail in the land." The prophet is accusing those who have become rich and the leaders in general of prospering not by acting justly but by acting falsely. In this passage, the paired words šeqer and ĕmûnâ go beyond individuals' daily dealings with one another and designate the whole "attitude of human beings in their global orientation: their faithfulness to the revelation and will of God (or their rejection of it) and the consequences that follow from such an attitude in the society (5:1–3)."[18]

Again, the emphasis here is on community building. For Jeremiah, human beings exist in community, which ought to be characterized by a common will and a common sense of responsibility. But Yahweh and his prophet have come to the conclusion that nobody in Judah is concerned with building a just, loyal, and harmonious community. Everybody looked for ways to increase their power, material possessions, and whatever else would make them prosperous. Because of the falsehood in which they constantly lived, the people were driven to commit a series of evils. Thus, the term šeqer (falsehood) in this passage implies the operation of a destructive power in the society. This is in contrast with the Kiswahili proverb that says *kweli ndiyo fimbo ya kukamata* (truth is the walking stick to take hold of). It means that straightforwardness or truthfulness is the best help in life because it helps to build the reputations of people, their relationships and the community.

The sentence "they proceed from an evil deed to another" (v. 3) underlines the fact that social evil in Judah had become a culture, a system that appeared to be accepted by the majority of the population. In other words, almost everyone who had become great (rich and powerful) did so through falsehood, corruption, extortion, and all kinds of social injustice. This disease of falsehood and perfidy had extended to the very heart of the social order in Judah. McKane

---

17. Wakely, בגד, in *NIDOTTE*, 1:583.
18. Laurent Wisser, *Jérémie, Critique de la Vie Sociale: La Connaissance de Dieu et la Justice Sociale dans le Livre de Jérémie* (Geneva: Labor et Fides, 1984), 24 (my translation).

writes: "the situation described by Jeremiah is one where evil is on the increase as men become more and more bold in their socially destructive enterprises."[19]

The sin of lying (vv. 4–6)

Verses 4–6 reflects social unrest at its worst. The community is totally broken down because of the sin of deception, of lying. McKane calls it "the worst kind of civil war, where mistrust has become part of the ordinary life of the community and where every social encounter has to be regarded as a possible trap."[20]

The passage begins with a word of warning. Yahweh, through his prophet, cautions the entire community of Judah that each person has to be on their guard against their "fellow," that is, their neighbour. The danger in the society is not coming from foreigners or long-standing enemies but from the people who live around them, with whom they even share some material goods. In our context we would talk about neighbours, colleagues, classmates or members of the same church, people who live in the same village or on the same street. What makes the situation worse in Judah is that the evil does not only come from neighbours but also from brothers. While the word translated "brother" could simply refer to a fellow Israelite, that would seem unnecessary since Jeremiah has already spoken of neighbours. My understanding is that Jeremiah is emphasizing the level of brokenness of Judah as a society. He is emphasizing the level of evil that has utterly destroyed relationships between close members of the same community and members even of the same family. All are condemned to live together in total mistrust. These destructive evils are coming from within, i.e. from fellow citizens, members of the same village, the same "church," even the same household.

The reasons for the warning pile up in the verses that follow (vv. 4b–6a); every brother is a deceiver (*'aqab*), every friend a slanderer (*rākîl*), they have taught their tongues to speak lies, they never speak the truth (*'emet*), they commit iniquity, oppression is heaped on oppression, and they have refused to know Yahweh. Judean society is a community collapsing under the weight of its own corruption. Some of these words are important and should be looked at more closely.

The words "every brother is a deceiver" can also be rendered "every brother will utterly trick" or "every brother is Jacob" (*'āqôb ya'qōb*). This expression is

---

19. McKane, *Jeremiah 1–25*, 200.
20. McKane, 200.

untranslatable, but the emphasis is on the verb *'aqab* (to deceive). It is found five times in the Old Testament. Three of the five uses allude directly or indirectly to Jacob's grasping Esau's heel at birth and supplanting him twice by taking first his birthright and then his blessing. Genesis 27:36 records how Esau complained that Jacob has supplanted him. In Hosea 12:3, the prophet accuses Israel of behaving like their forefather Jacob, and Jeremiah (9:4) describes the social decay of Judah as having its root in the way of Jacob. In other words, "rather than seeking each other's good, brothers sought to hinder each other for their own advancement."[21] Thus, in Jeremiah 9:4, the verb *'aqab* means to supplant, to overreach, to deceive, to hinder, or to dupe in order to take advantage. So, for Jeremiah, Jacob as a specialist in deception has been emulated by his descendants, the Judeans.

African tradition strongly condemns lying because it recognizes its disastrous consequence for the community. In the traditional setting, people lived communally in villages and there was nothing like conceiving a person simply as an individual. A person was a person in a community, in a village, in a clan, in a tribe. The sin of lying would destroy not only the person lying but also their house (family) and village. Thankfully, this understanding of the need to preserve the community is still present in many parts of Africa. About twenty-five miles from my hometown, in Lendu Bindi County, there is a village called *Kinywa mubaya*, which literally means "bad tongue/mouth." Not long ago, there was a man in that village who loved to insult people. Eventually, his bad behaviour led to the whole village and everyone in it being labelled as having the same bad character. Men are warned against marrying girls from *Kinywa mubaya*.

Kiswahili, the lingua franca of East Africa, has more than fifty proverbs condemning or warning against all forms of lying, falsehood, and deception. For example, the proverb *Afadhali kuwa na jirani mchawi kuliko mwongo* says it is better to have a wizard than a liar as a neighbour because a wizard, though dangerous, can be trusted, but a liar cannot be trusted.[22] Another Kiswahili proverb, *Asemaye uwongo husema mwenziwe*, says that a liar abuses a companion, for telling lies hurts or destroys friendly relationships.[23]

It is believed in African tradition that a liar is likely to commit other kinds of immoral acts such as stealing and killing. One often hears that "he who

---

21. Eugene Carpenter and M. A. Grisanti, עָקַב, in *NIDOTTE*, 3:504.
22. Swahili Proverbs: *Methali za Kiswahili*, http://swahiliproverbs.afrst.illinois.edu/lying.html.
23. Swahili Proverbs: *Methali za Kiswahili*.

lies will steal." Like hypocrisy and hatred, lying can ruin people's lives. There are curses that are invoked on liars in some cultures. The oracle Odu Ogunda Bede of Nigeria warns:

> The deceiver went on a twenty-year journey and never returned.
> The liar went on a thirty-month journey and never returned.[24]

It warns deceivers and liars who are going on a journey that they may not return if they kept deceiving and betraying people in the foreign land.

Another important issue that was destroying community life in Judah was slandering (*rākîl*). The word *rākîl* means slander, defamation, or gossip. Five of the six occurrences of this word in the Old Testament are used with the verb "to walk" with the meaning to go about as a huckster, deceiver or defamer (Lev 19:16; Prov 11:13; 20:19; Jer 6:28; 9:3). It is possible that this idiomatic use of the terms refers to the reputation of the *rākîl* (a defamer) who moves from one door to another to tell lies and accuse other people to get some benefits from those who pay attention to the lies.

The use of *rākîl* in this text needs to be understood in the social and cultural context of the ancient world of Jeremiah. At that time, information was transmitted from one person to another. People lived in community and needed to protect their reputation. There was neither television nor radio nor social networks one could turn to for public self-defence. A bad testimony could be a permanent hindrance in matters such as marriage, business, and eldership. The Decalogue thus considered defamation as a grave offence. Exodus 20:16 states: "You shall not give false testimony against your neighbour" (NIV). Leviticus 19:16 puts it this way: "Do not go about spreading slander among your people" (NIV) (see also Exod 23:7; Deut 19:18). Unfortunately, this law was not being observed by Jeremiah's contemporaries.

The sin of oppression (v. 5)

Finally in this passage, we find that Judean society was characterized by oppression (*tōk*). In the Old Testament, this word is used five times (Pss 10:7; 55:12; 72:14; Prov 29:13; Jer 9:5) and points to some form of social oppression in a corrupt society. In three of the five passages (Pss 10:7–15; 72:12–14; Prov 29:13), the poor are specifically mentioned, suggesting that the word describes the tyranny of political and economic exploitation of the socially

---

24. S. A. Adewale, Crime and African Traditional Religion, http://www.africaspeaks.com/reasoning/index.php?topic=2978.0;wap2.

weak in Israelite society. In other words, the rich and the powerful were using oppression to exploit the poor to make profit and remain in power.

In Africa, this exploitation and generalized corruption can take different forms. It is what Elmer A. Martens calls "megatrends of sin expressed in corporate misrepresentation, double-tongued diplomacy, excessive competition, the hoarding of power, excessive concern for self-fulfilment."[25] Those of us who travel across Africa know that in some of our countries, this corruption starts at the airport or other points of entry, is found in every single office, in private and public transportation, and in education (elementary to tertiary), health system, infrastructure projects, and transport and communications. One gets the impression that everyone is paralysed by corruption and no one can escape the system, even at home. For example, a military officer who is a Christian is pressured by his wife, who keeps asking, "Why do not you bring me expensive clothes and shoes like other officers bring their wives. Why do not you bring me money from your work like other people bring home? Do you think that you will build this country alone?" Her mindset and expectations are not unique.

The consequences of such megatrends of sin in the community include (1) high infant and adult mortality among the poor due to broken health systems while the rich access the best medical services abroad; (2) high rate of stunting or death among children due to malnutrition while the rich throw food away every day; (3) inadequate housing for the majority while the rich live in villas and buy houses abroad; (4) lack of good education for ordinary citizens while the rich send their children to study in the West; (5) persistent civil wars that decimate the families of the poor while the rich, who provoke these wars, get richer and send their families abroad for safety; (6) starvation, unemployment, migration, spread of disease; and (7) lack of good roads and means of transport and communications for the public.

Many in African countries today do not care for the progress of the community as a whole but fight only for their own interests. This way of life institutionalizes injustice and corruption, and the social system is transformed into one that protects the interests of the small cabal that controls nearly all the wealth of the country and denies the poor any significant means to overcome their poverty. This is the anatomy of a dysfunctional society that some specialists call a "failed state." Maybe Judah at the time of Jeremiah can be studied as the model of a failed state.

---

25. Elmer A. Martens, *Jeremiah*, Believers Church Bible Commentary (Scottsdale, PA: Herald, 1986), 89.

This description of life inside a dysfunctional community ends with a summary similar to the one in verse 3: "they refuse to know me, Yahweh's oracle" (v. 6). This statement always comes after a long list of sins (adulterers, traitors, deceivers, slanderers, and oppressors, etc.) that spell out what the absence of knowledge of Yahweh means. For Jeremiah, the measure in which the nation departs from Yahweh's law is the measure in which it ceases to know him. The people of Judah might maintain the externals of their religion, but their attitude to their fellow citizens reveals how far they are from the law that Yahweh has given them and shows that their claim to know God is false. For the prophet of Anathoth and all other true prophets of Yahweh, the measure of a nation's knowledge of Yahweh is the measure in which, within its borders, it stamps out the sins of humanity. Knowledge of God should not be a matter of empty rhetoric but must guide the nation's way of life. Put differently, as long as theft, fraud, adultery, slander, telling lies in the court and in the society, killing, and deception in all their forms are rampant, those who claim to know Yahweh are living in falsehood.

Attack on falsehood is a feature in Jeremiah's theology, as one notices throughout in chapter 9. True knowledge of Yahweh was supposed to empower the people of Judah to make positive changes in the society in the light of Yahweh's law. Unfortunately, the people of Judah had failed to obey God, but they still claimed Yahweh's approval as if by right. Despite abandoning the law of God, they cherished dreams of an inevitably successful and glorious future. As J. Lundblom noted, for the people of Judah, "the essential was not the claim of the people on Yahweh, but Yahweh's claim on Israel in virtue of election."[26] There was an attitude that "no matter what we do, we are secure because Yahweh has to be with us." Presuming on the certainty of Yahweh's protection was the root of Judah's dysfunction.

No Option but Judgement (9:7–9)

In Hebrew, verse 7 is introduced with the particle *lākēn* (therefore), best rendered as "as a result of." It is used to introduce judgements in the lawsuit speeches of the prophet, seeking to justify the reason for the judicial sentences. But there is a new and important element in this section that needs to be connected with that introduction. At the end of verse 7, we hear Yahweh lamenting again: "What else can I do because of my people?" This is a statement of deep disappointment. This sentence takes us back to verse 2, which describes

---

26. Quoted by Overholt, *Threat of Falsehood*, 12.

an unimaginable situation for God. So far in the book of Jeremiah, Yahweh has been trying to help his people come back to him. He has been looking for ways to help them, and is ready to make concessions, by agreeing to forgive his people if the prophet can find one person who strives for justice (5:1). But now (v. 2), because the situation has become unbearable for him, Yahweh is forced to leave his people.

Verse 7 returns to Yahweh's dilemma and pain in verse 2. The words, "what else can I do?" are not intended as a question to be answered. Yahweh is not seeking our advice. He is not wondering what should be done. The words are those of someone who is tired of his people making the same mistakes over and over again. They are the words of someone who has done his best to help, but in vain. All that remains is to punish. Mark S. Smith put it like this: "Like Jeremiah, God begins as Israel's helper, but becomes Israel's victim and therefore initiates Israel's demise. Both victims of Israel, Jeremiah and Yahweh, call for Israel's destruction."[27]

Yahweh starts this process of judgement by examining his people. This appears in the use of the verb *bḥn*. Terry L. Brensinger notices that the use of the verb *bḥn*, to examine, "captures the process through which Yahweh evaluates the spiritual condition of his people."[28] The emphasis of the evaluation or examination is on scrutiny of the heart and the mind. In other words, before any punishment, Yahweh wants to carefully examine the inner condition, the thoughts, the motives, and the wrong aspirations of his people. He wants to know exactly what is going on, the degree of responsibility of each member of the society, and then exercise a true and fair judgement. This idea seems to be confirmed by the use of another verb, *ṣrp* that means to dissolve, to purify, to purge, refine, to winnow, or to test. The verb *ṣrp* refers to melting a metal in order to purify it. In this text, the word probably anticipates the punishment to come on the nation as a way of purifying the dysfunctional society, with the hope that such punishment will succeed where all else has failed.

Verse 8 recapitulates what was said in verses 2–6, and insists on the tongue as the major problem in that society. The new and important element in this passage is hypocrisy. People greet one another with a word of peace on the lips while they are planning an ambush in their hearts. This kind of evil is worse than just telling lies or deceiving other people (v. 4). Probably this is why it is put at the very end of all other evil deeds in Judah.

---

27. Mark S. Smith, "Jeremiah 9:9 A Divine Lament," in *Vetus Testamentum* 37 (1987), 98.
28. Terry L. Brensinger, בָּחַן in *NIDOTTE*, 1:637.

Verse 9 concludes the whole passage. It is the response to the rhetorical question in verse 7: "what else can I do because of my people?" The answer is: I must punish this nation (*gôy*) for their deeds. The word *gôy* normally means "nation" or "Gentile." It is used here figuratively with the sense of a community, probably to indicate that the punishment is to be inflicted on the whole nation of Judah.[29] The last line of the section ends on a sad note as Yahweh asks himself, "Shall my soul not take vengeance?" In the whole Old Testament, the expression is only used in Jeremiah (three times). The other two passages (5:9, 29) are very similar to 9:8 and are used in the same context of the punishment of Judah. Wisser comments that it shows Yahweh as "a person passionately engaged in the history that he begun himself with his people and strongly affected by their faithlessness."[30]

The Root Problem: A Contextual Reflection

What it is that pushes a whole community into violence, stealing, corruption, living in falsehood, and pursuing limitless wealth without regard for others?

There is reason to be concerned that there is very little difference between African Christians and non-Christians these days as far as daily life is concerned. We all want to live well, have enough to eat, educate our children, have a good house, drive a car and so forth. But when you look at how people are seeking these "normal" things, why is there almost no difference between Christians and non-Christians? Christians are pursuing these things in the same ungodly ways as non-Christians.

I was once invited to preach at the opening of a new hotel built by a member of our church. I declined the invitation and went to talk to the senior pastor of our church, asking him where this brother got the large amount of money (about $2 million) needed to build such a hotel, because his everyday job gave no indication that he could be that rich. But the senior pastor was not interested in my questioning, simply because the owner of the hotel was from his ethnic group.

I can ask the same question differently: Should there be a difference between Christians and non-Christians as far as daily life is concerned? If

---

29. Thompson (*Jeremiah*, 310) suggests that the use of the term *gôy* for Israel may represent the transfer to Israel of a term which was regularly used of non-Israelite peoples. He adds that its use here suggests that Jeremiah had come to regard the people as no different in their behaviour from the *gôyim*, the people outside the covenant. This is a good insight, but it seems to me that the main idea in the passage is the designation of the entire nation as a faithless people.

30. Wisser, *Jérémie, Critique de la Vie Sociale*, 31.

yes, what would be the difference? What can help us to live in a way that shows the difference in us as Christians, so that people notice that there is something greater in us and that we live for something greater? To relate this to my experience of the CCC synod meeting in Kinshasa: What should a meeting of bishops, reverends, pastors, and other church leaders look like?

The church exists to help us become a community of difference. The first business of the church should be to help us cultivate virtue, resilience, and a character of difference, and to help us understand that what is significant about Christians is not what they do or do not do, but how they do what they do because of the hope they have of the future, because of Christ, their Master, who lived his daily life on earth in a very different way to those around him. Christians should not live like Jeremiah's contemporaries but like those who know God, who have a hope and who are on a journey to a better world marked by God's righteous rule. With this in mind, the main work of the church should be to transform people's mind sets, and move them towards creating a new community that is consistent with their conviction and what they proclaim. The Christian community should arouse envy in non-Christians. The envy should not be based on what we do as Christians, but from how we do it: with justice, love, integrity, courage, determination, and hope. These virtues should mark our everyday lives, including how we lead others, how we pastor God's people, and how we run our businesses. Christians who live in this way know that because of the difference others see in them, they are often consulted for advice, help, wisdom, and sometimes prayer by non-Christians.

Not long ago, most Africans lived in villages. One could tell the origin and culture of a people by observing their courage, their unity, the way they lived, talked, laughed or the way they farmed because the village (community) played a key part in forming the character of its people. That is why, in Africa we say: "You are lazy like the people of X village; you talk very fast like the people of Y village, or you are courageous like people of Z village." But, as with Judah, the character of many African Christians is now formed by the anti-values of the world, and we fail to make a difference in our communities. Often, this failure starts with those who are supposed to help teach and instil virtues in us including our parents, teachers, and pastors. In Judah, the failure of the nation started with the failure of priests, prophets and teachers to perform their God-given responsibilities.

Conclusion

This chapter describes how Judah as a society was ultimately destroyed from within by the force of its own corruption. This corruption was the result of not living by the standard of the law. This refusal to live by the law showed that Judah had broken the covenant, and so had ceased to be a covenant community. The moral decay in the society was the result of too many people having too little concern for others. These people of Judah failed to observe the moral and ethical norms that are necessary for the preservation of social order.

Once the covenant was broken, any claim Judah could make about knowing Yahweh was false because to know Yahweh means to follow his commandment and is an expression of high ethical earnestness. Concretely, the breaking of the covenant in Jeremiah 9:2–9 created a debased community characterized by (1) the abuse of the tongue that destroyed the community; (2) oppression of the weak in the community as a way for the powerful to prevail in the nation and to increase their wealth and their control over the nation; and (3) total deceitfulness in the community and a lack of confidence in one another.

These evils point to a total lack of concern for the building of a just community, everyone was destroying those around them and pursuing their own interests without regard for the law of God. It is the sum of these social evils that Jeremiah calls the lack of the knowledge of Yahweh.

The situation is no better in Africa because the church has not done enough to help Christians understand their calling in an irresponsible society. More specifically, the church fails to emphasize the formation of virtues. Because of the lack of godly virtues, the faith of Christians in Africa makes little difference in their daily lives and the community; they have little concern for building a community of hope. The challenge posed by this chapter is the need for the church in Africa to build the kind of community that will tell the story of God rightly in a continent whose people are divided by ethnic strife, corruption, and violence.

6

The Secret of True Greatness and Power

Jeremiah 9:23–24

²³ Thus says Yahweh:

"Let not the wise man glory in his wisdom,
and let not the powerful man glory in his power,
let not the rich man glory in his riches;
²⁴ but let him who glories glory in this:
that he has understanding and knows me,
that I am Yahweh who practices steadfast love (lovingkindness),
justice, and righteousness on earth.
For in these things I delight." Yahweh's oracle.

Historical and Literary Context

Earlier commentators thought of this passage as characteristic of the wisdom tradition in Scripture because of its many uses of wisdom vocabulary.[1] In addition, most of them did not see any connection between Jeremiah 9:23–24[2] and its immediate context. As a consequence, the general tendency among earlier Jeremiah scholars was to reject its authenticity. But modern students of Jeremiah have started recognizing that the oracle is authentic. Holladay, for example, refers to Brueggemann who goes beyond a simple passive acceptance

---

1. See the discussion in Craigie, Kelley and Drinkard, *Jeremiah 1-25*, 152.
2. MT 9:22–23.

of its authenticity to viewing the passage as a specific expression of Jeremiah's prophetic message.[3] This is important for this interpretation because it helps to locate the text historically.

In the context of chapters 8–10, it is possible to understand why Jeremiah 9:23–24 was placed where it is. Two words that often recur often in these chapters are "wise/wisdom" (8:8a, 9; 9:16b) and "know/knowledge" (8:7, 12b; 9:3b, 5b; 10:23, 25a). Although these two (groups of) words have different nuances, their frequent use in chapters 8–10 may indicate that the prophet brought them together to pose the central epistemological question that Jeremiah discerned at the end of Israelite royal history.[4] He may have sought to demonstrate that there was a problem related to the use of wisdom, wealth, and knowledge in Judah, or that a distorted knowledge of Yahweh resulted in the distorted wisdom of those administering the nation and a distorted understanding of material possessions and power.

There is also the question of whom the oracle was addressed to. All the verbs used in the passage are in the third person masculine singular (he, him, his) and so refer to an unknown individual. It seems that this statement is thus addressed to a rich, wise, and powerful person in Judah. Some see it as a general statement to the individuals who make up the whole nation of Judah. In this sense, one can argue that the oracle was addressed to every single member of the covenant community, and called on them to reconsider the way they used wealth, power, and knowledge because these three things can easily become objects of worship and can control the person who owns or wants to own them if they do not use them in obedience to Yahweh. The distortion and the worship of these three things ends up creating severe social, economic, political, and spiritual disruption in the community.

However, if we consider that in Israel and Judah, it was the responsibility of the kings (and their administration) to lead the whole community in obeying God's law, and that the message of the prophet was primarily addressed to them,[5] it becomes clear that Jeremiah 9:23–24 is a critique of the royal ideology during the days of Jeremiah's ministry. In this way, the verb "to glory" or "to boast" reminds the reader of King Jehoiakim, in particular, whose life was

---

3. W. Holladay, *Jeremiah 1*, 317.

4. Brueggemann, *Old Testament Theology*, 270–80.

5. Gary V. Smith, "Prophet," in *ISBE*, 3:993. He argues that "although some prophets delivered their messages in the temple, others spent far more time delivering God's word to the kings of Israel."

characterized by self-aggrandizement or self-glorification. Thus, the passage fits well the period of the reign of Jehoiakim, and this is how I interpret it.

Another particularity of this passage in the whole prophetic spectrum is that, while it is clearly an oracle (it begins with the formula "Thus says Yahweh" in verse 23 and ends with the phrase "Yahweh's oracle" in verse 24), it does not issue either an open condemnation or a judgement. This is why commentators such as Bernhard Duhm treat it as theologically unimportant, saying it is a "harmless insignificant saying."[6] However, it is not possible to agree with Duhm's judgement. On the contrary, a careful reading of the passage points to a serious problem that might have been happening in the nation in terms of administrative and political skills (here called "wisdom"), national defence or security systems (referred to in the text as "power"), and the accumulation of wealth in Judah's leadership. The passage is not insignificant and harmless, for in it the prophet is implicitly accusing Judah's leadership of failure by demonstrating how a distorted tradition can lead to relying on a purely human and secular system that ignores Yahweh and brings death to a nation.[7] In modern terms, this reminds of the confidence nations and individuals place on military strength, economic might, and scientific knowledge. By placing their trust in these systems, nations and their people slowly but surely forget that true success and true greatness come from God, who is the ultimate source of power, wealth, and knowledge/wisdom.

In recent decades, Africa has experienced great changes. There have been internal and external wars in many countries, the wealth of many countries has been looted by dictators, presidents have been idolized and have boasted of their power and wealth while mismanaging the economies of their nations and crushing all who oppose them. Because of the selfishness and the lack of understanding of political leaders, many African countries have been unable to make any significant economic and social progress. Many African thinkers are now calling for a "second independence" or what some are calling the "African renaissance." But what will be the foundation of this renaissance? What kind

---

6. Duhm, *Das Buch Jeremia*, 97.

7. So also Brueggemann, *Old Testament Theology*, 279. Here I disagree with both Craigie, Kelley and Drinkard (*Jeremiah 1–25*, 153), and Carroll (*Jeremiah*, 248). They both accuse Brueggemann of overstating his case when he argues that this passage represents two major views of life that are in conflict in Judah. Carroll thinks that such an understanding is misleading. I wonder if the problem with Craigie, Kelley, Drinkard and Carroll is that they underemphasize the literary matters over the historical, social, and political understandings of this passage. My African context is helping me to see that no text or saying in the Bible is produced in vacuum, and that it is a mistake to dismiss a passage as unimportant simply because our context does not help us to understand it.

of renaissance will it be? Who will conceive and apply it? Will it only be a renaissance that continues to give advantages to the powerful?

In this chapter, Jeremiah 9:23–24 will be read in the light of developments in the continent in terms of power, knowledge, and wealth. By criticizing the leaders of Judah for their lack of the knowledge of Yahweh, Jeremiah was helping his hearers know why the country would finally be destroyed. The prophet's message is as pertinent for Africa today as it was for Judah at that time.

Structure

The internal structure of this passage is clear. The sentence is divided into two parts. Verse 23 is introduced by the messenger formula: "Thus says Yahweh." The formula is followed by a negative appreciation of human boasts of wisdom, power and riches. Verse 24 presents the proper grounds for human boasting by showing what really constitutes the source of true greatness. This passage ends with another messenger formula.

Interpretation

This chapter analyses the relationship between knowledge of Yahweh and the grounds for true power and true glorification both for individuals and the community (society). More specifically, it discusses three things in which people or nations of this world trust and glory: knowledge, power, and wealth. The prophet Jeremiah offers an alternative to this view, saying that there is only one thing in which human beings and nations should glory: knowledge of Yahweh. It is this knowledge, says the man from Anathoth that should guide our use of knowledge, power, and wealth if we want to build a just community that is obedient to Yahweh's vision. Otherwise, the misuse of these three things will lead to suffering, destruction, and even death of people and nations.

In the context of Africa, the interpretation of this passage will have a particular focus on the subject of the failure of leadership, which in our continent is characterized by a selfish and idolatrous use of knowledge, power, and wealth as opposed to the godly way of understanding them and their proper use for the building of nations.

False Concept of National Greatness (v. 23)

The passage opens with the ordinary prophetic messenger formula "Thus says Yahweh." The key word in the passage is the verb "to boast" (*hălāl*) (jussive masculine, third person, singular in *hithpael*), which means to praise, glory, boast, exult. In verse 23, this verb is used three times, all of them in negative form. In all three occurrences, the verb *hălāl* is used in *hithpael*, and therefore, has the meaning "to praise oneself, pride oneself" (i.e. to brag, boast). All three of these uses of *hălāl* are put into relationship with what Holladay calls three traditional human pursuits: wisdom, power and riches[8] that the prophet is here condemning.

Wisdom and leadership

First, the prophet condemns boasting about one's wisdom. The Old Testament in general recognizes human wisdom, while strictly presenting it not as a fruit of human effort but as a gift from Yahweh (Gen 41:39; 1 Kgs 5:9–14; 10:7; Dan 1:4; Prov 1:2–7; 13:14).[9] The Old Testament also makes clear that to those who are wise in their own eyes (Prov 3:7; 26:5, 12, 16; 28:11; Isa 5:21), the door of true wisdom will remain closed. As an African proverb says: "If you are filled with pride, then you will have no room for wisdom."

In the context of prophetic literature, wisdom is sometimes associated with the critique of leadership in general, and of Israel/Judah's leadership in particular. Thus, in the book of Isaiah, particularly in the context of the critique of Judah's leadership (chs. 3–5) Isaiah 5:21 condemns the leaders who think they are wise and consider themselves to be clever. Likewise, Yahweh rejects the priests' claim to possess wisdom in Jeremiah 8:8–10 because their lying pen has turned their wisdom into falseness. In Isaiah 31:2, the reference to Yahweh's wisdom treats with irony the claim to wisdom of the Jerusalem leadership: "the tactical shrewdness of those who go down to Egypt for help and rely on horses instead of on Yahweh."[10] In Isaiah 10:12–13, Yahweh promises to punish the king of Assyria for the pride (boasting) and arrogance, especially for saying: "By my own power and wisdom I have won these wars." Finally, in Isaiah 29:14 Yahweh promises to frustrate the wisdom of wise men so that they might be

---

8. Holladay, *Jeremiah 1*, 317.

9. The issue concerning the place of wisdom in Old Testament theology is complex and we still have to wait for some time before reaching a scholarly consensus. However, my concern in this section and the whole chapter is about the place of wisdom, not in scholarly debate but in daily social and institutional practice. In this perspective, see George E. Mendenhall, "The Shady Side of Wisdom: The Date and Purpose of Genesis 3," in Howard W. Bream et al. (eds.), *A Light unto My Path: Old Testament Studies in Honor of Jacob M. Myers* (Philadelphia: Temple University Press, 1974), 318–32.

10. Muller, חָכַם, in *TDOT*, 4:384.

obliged to hide their political insights in the face of the terrible coming events. According to von Rad, in this last text (Isa 29:14), "Isaiah sees, in conjunction with political catastrophes, a darkness falling with which human abilities at understanding will no longer be able to cope."[11]

If the word "wisdom" (here associated with "power" and "wealth") in Jeremiah 9:23 refers to Judean leadership, as I think it does, my argument is that this wisdom has the following mixed and broad meanings: the capacity to understand, manage and control political and social affairs of the nation; the necessary skill to maintain national security in the face of threats of all kinds (internal and external); the cleverness to manipulate and reduce everything under the control of the king; and the maintenance of the national status quo or/and well-being by purely human management without any reference to Yahweh, etc. This wisdom can be equated to what we know today as leadership management techniques or skills, international cooperation or the management of political and administrative affairs, etc.

This text gives no clear reason for the rejection of the boasting in this kind of wisdom (skill). Claus Westermann would qualify this critique as a "judgement speech without a reason."[12] And for the modern reader, it seems odd that the prophet is condemning a mastery of leadership skill that works well and is beneficial in many societies. But it was not so in Israel (Judah). Whenever human wisdom gave human beings a sense of security, whenever it became a set of skills for manipulating others: wherever it tempted them to boast, to oppress other members of the community, or by-pass Yahweh's law, as it surely did with most kings in Israel and Judah, such wisdom became idolatry, a self-serving tool, and revolt against Yahweh. This is probably what happened to King Solomon when he became more concerned with building an international reputation for his mastery of such wisdom than with spending his energy on right leadership according to Yahweh's word. In fact, we can now start questioning the hidden reason that pushed Solomon to compose his many wisdom sayings and songs (1 Kgs 4:29–34; 1 Kgs 10:1–13).[13] If we consider

---

11. Gerhard von Rad, *Wisdom in Israel* (London: SCM, 1972), 104.

12. Claus Westermann, *Basic Forms*, 161.

13. I am aware that many scholars consider 1 Kings 4:29–34; 10:1–13 as an exaggeration and legendary. However, my argument does not proceed from a correlation between literary evidence and historical evidence. My understanding is that the text is not produced in a vacuum and that there are reasons to associate Solomon with wisdom teaching. Brueggemann (*Social Reading of the Old Testament*, 261) is one of the few who saw this correlation between Solomon and wisdom teachings. He concludes his study on this correlation by stating: "Solomon is remembered as a patron of a self-serving theodicy settlement that permitted power, wealth,

the fact that his apparent political success (apparently guided by his wisdom) collapsed with the division of the monarchy immediately after his death, we will discover that wisdom might have been one of the tools used for keeping the status quo and oppressing the people.[14] Brueggemann rightly noticed that the modes of knowledge operating in wisdom instruction "tend to buttress the status quo as an order that is to be maintained and not disrupted."[15] His further argument is that "proverb wisdom in any family or clan tends to assume the legitimacy and durability of present power arrangements."[16] Thus, the much praised Solomonic wisdom might reveal more than a God-given knowledge, especially since it was used in the royal court setting where the ideology of the monarchy was in action to justify and maintain (oppressive) power.

The lesson we learn here is that even a God-given wisdom can be distorted and abused if it is used for other purposes than promoting justice, serving the needy and the well-being of the community. In Israel, true or godly wisdom had to be strictly guided by the law and used for the promotion of a great and discerning people characterized by the intimate relationship the covenant created between God and this people (Deut 4:5–6). Consequently, godly wisdom came from following God's commandment and not from any individual greatness, manipulation, or academic or secular qualification. In the same way, in 1 Corinthians 3, Paul contrasts worldly and godly wisdom and condemns those in the congregation who pride themselves on being wise "by the standard of this age" (NIV). According to Paul, and rightly so, worldly wisdom creates pride (boasting) and division and destroys the community. This is exactly what happened in Judah from the time of King Solomon up to the destruction of the kingdom.

Most people in Africa are convinced that politics is a culture of lies. Politicians are known as liars, demagogues. This might justify the reticence of the church to encourage Christians to engage actively in politics. *Ipso facto*, the faith of a Christian who joins politics is sometimes viewed with suspicion if not outrightly rejected. The situation is changing slowly, but this conviction, that Christian belief and politics do not go together, is still very strong in most of our churches. One of the reasons for this negative view of African politics is the

---

and wisdom in disproportionate measure. Thus, he was a patron of a theopolitical enterprise that did have emancipator dimensions but that in the end was also ideological."

14. There is a clear contradiction between Solomon's most praised wisdom and the oppression of his subjects that was the main reason for the schism of the kingdom.

15. Brueggemann, *Social Reading of the Old Testament*, 257.

16. Brueggemann, 257.

manipulation it is associated with, which in my view is an example of worldly, corrupted wisdom. This wisdom can take different forms that will be difficult to summarize in this work. I will give just two examples of manipulated, twisted wisdom in African leadership.

The first and most widespread one is the politicization of ethnic identities for private (political) interests by politicians in the continent. This is where some politicians attempt to gain support and build solidarity by creating divisions between ethnic groups so that they can secure the support of some groups (usually the most influential in a country) to help them gain power. Many countries in Africa are characterized by strong competition for political power and economic resources, and in many cases, these contests have turned into ethnic rivalry because of the politicization of tribal identities. A good example of such politicization is the transformation of South Africa's Inkatha Movement from a cultural association into a political organization. What was intended to be movement advocating for equal representation of communities in South Africa (to avoid majority rule by one group over others) was turned into a platform for promoting ethnic identities and loyalties in both the private and the public sphere. Sadly, this is not the only such example in the continent. Many of our political leaders use "cultural slogans, lies, demagogy to arouse emotions of the people in order to make them accept what they do not even understand."[17] Such leaders distil lies upon lies to reformulate ethnic loyalties to suit their political agendas. They persuade their people by proclaiming "themselves as representatives of the ethnic group while at the same time promoting their own interests."[18] They combine twisted wisdom and demagoguery to cheat people and set them against other citizens. This use of twisted wisdom to politicize ethnic identities has become one of the major causes of ethno-political violence on the continent. We will do well to remember that it was a similar kind of political manipulation that caused the division of Israel immediately after the death of King Solomon the "wise."

The other example is almost the opposite of the first, in that fear of the politicization of ethnicity is used to reject democracy, claiming that the freedom democracy brings can "unleash ethnic rivalries whose embers are forever

---

17. Aquiline Tarimo, "Politicization of Ethnic Identities," The Common Good in Kenya, Markkula Center for Applied Ethics at Santa Clara University, https://www.scu.edu/ethics/focus-areas/more/resources/the-common-good-in-kenya/.

18. Tarimo, "Politicization of Ethnic Identities," https://www.scu.edu/ethics/focus-areas/more/resources/the-common-good-in-kenya/.

smouldering in Africa and destroy the fragile unity of African countries."[19] This is partly true, if one considers the current situation of the continent as demonstrated in the first example. Unfortunately, leaders who make these claims also do it to maintain themselves in power for as long as possible (and sometimes for life), not in the interests of promoting justice. This is the case with the current Cameroonian president Paul Biya, who is now 88 years old and has been leading the country for the last thirty-nine years; the Ugandan President Yoweri Kaguta Museveni who has been to power since 1986; the 79-year-old Alassane Ouattara who managed to twist the constitution to cling to power; Denis Sassou Nguesso of the Republic of Congo who staged a referendum in 2015 to remove a 70-year age limit and a ban on presidents serving more than two terms. This list is not exhaustive and it is clear that many African leaders have not learned the advantages of stepping down from their leadership positions. This would have allowed some of them to become much better mentors to young politicians. Regular transfers of power could have given citizens hope that new and better policies and programmes would be adopted. It could also have overturned numerous political, social, and economic impacts of uninterrupted strangleholds on power in the continent.

These examples of manipulated wisdom both in Israel and Africa show that in the ancient world, as well as in our own, wisdom can be used calculatingly not only to serve the interest of the few but also to produce chaos and death in the community. This is in fact how one can explain the division and the destruction of the kingdom of Israel, and the situation in most African countries today.

I have already mentioned that many Israelite (Judeans) kings relied on the wisdom of false prophets who would tell the kings exactly what they wanted to hear and not what Yahweh wanted from them concerning right leadership. Reliance on false prophets was one of the important factors that led the kings of Israel and Judah astray. Jeremiah 37:17–21, for example, reports how King Zedekiah turned to the true prophet of Yahweh for advice only when it was too late to receive true wisdom from Yahweh, and when the deceptive channels of the national intelligentsia had been found inadequate. At that point, the prophet turned to Zedekiah and asked him an ironic but very important question in verse 19: "Where are your prophets [intelligentsia] who prophesied to you, 'The king of Babylon will not attack you or this land'?" (NIV). Jeremiah's attack on false prophets was actually an attack on false wisdom in Judah.

---

19. Claude Ake, "What Is the Problem of Ethnicity in Africa?," Journals/pdfs/transformation/tran022/tran022002.pdf.

Power and leadership

In the Bible, the concept of power is primarily associated with God himself.[20] However, whenever "power" is used of a person, animal, or thing, it designates the kind of power that goes beyond ordinary strength and is able to accomplish great feats (e.g. Gen 10:8; Pss 45:3; 89:19). Edward Laarman notices that while many Old Testament passages express admiration for human power, they also criticize it because it is sometimes used either to obscure reliance on God's power or to oppress the powerless.[21] The book of 2 Samuel in particular shows that power in its various forms belongs to the kings (10:7; 16:6; 17:8; 20:7; 23:9–22). Thus, power in this passage in Jeremiah might include not only physical strength but also and primarily military and political supremacy.[22]

On the basis of the above understanding of the concept of power in the Old Testament, Jeremiah 9:23–24 can be interpreted in two ways. First, if we consider the critique in verse 23 as addressed to the administrative leadership, power refers to the capacity of the royal/presidential establishment "to work its will by human power before which none may issue a challenge."[23] In this context, power can also be used to protect the king, his administration, the system he creates and his relatives by crushing all the opposition voices, including Yahweh's voice through his prophet. This is what happened to the prophet Jeremiah under both Jehoiakim (Jer 36) and Zedekiah (Jer 37–38). And this is what is happening in most of our countries in Africa when those who denounce the abuse of power by the ruling class are crushed. Used this way, power becomes an idol that can destroy faith in Yahweh. Such power leads to the dislocation of the society because it loses touch with its real source.

Second, if we consider this critique of the use of power in reference to the defence system of the nation (Judah), the phrase "and let not the powerful man glory in his power" can be understood as a system of national security rooted in a powerful army, the accumulation of the best and most sophisticated armaments (whatever that meant in Jeremiah's time, but we know what it

---

20. P. H. Menoud, "Power," in *IDB*, 3:855. He points out that all power of every kind is derived from God and that while God grants autonomy to human beings in their respective realms, his own prerogative remains uncompromised.

21. Edward Laarman, "Power, Might," in *ISBE*, 3:927. See also Andrew Kirk, *Liberation Theology: An Evangelical View from the Third World* (Atlanta: John Knox, 1979), 209.

22. Holladay, *Jeremiah 1*, 317. See also Robert Jamieson, A. R. Fausset and David Brown, "Jeremiah," in *Commentary Critical and Explanatory on the Whole Bible*, https://www.biblestudytools.com/commentaries/jamieson-fausset-brown/. They understand power in this text as military prowess.

23. Brueggemann, *Old Testament Theology*, 287.

means today),²⁴ and alliances with other nations. In this way, Israel's wars ceased to be Yahweh's wars. People could no longer say that Yahweh was the one fighting for them; they were able to prevail through their own effort.²⁵ These false claims and a false sense of security were blinding the people of Judah and distancing them from trusting in Yahweh. Von Rad summarizes the whole matter well:

> Again and again in Israel, one encounters a passionate attack on any form of false security and that kind of self-glorification in which a man can badly misjudge himself. Thus, for example, before a battle, Yahweh takes precautions that the Israelites should not "vaunt themselves" (Judg 7:2). In Deut. 9:1–6, there is a whole war-sermon in which the Israelites are warned not to attribute the guidance of Yahweh to their own goodness and righteousness. Can, then, the axe vaunt itself over him who wields it (Isa. 10:15)? Thus, it is not the quantitative limitations of human capabilities which forbid self-confidence and self-glorification; it is, rather, something which can be explained only in theological terms: self-glorification cannot be combined with trust in Yahweh.²⁶

Consequently, according to Jeremiah and many other prophets of Israel, for Yahweh to have a say in our affairs, this falsehood or what I am calling the idolatry of power must first be delegitimized. What was true for ancient Israel, is also true for us today.

The issue of trust in military power has become a serious one in many African nations during our own days, with many consequences: many countries have used such power to become abusers and oppressors of their own citizens

---

24. Military superiority generally creates arrogant boasting and haughty pride (Isa 10:12–13; 14:13–14).

25. I find 2 Chronicles 35:20–27 (2 Kgs 23:29–30) a good example of how Judah might have abandoned the habit of consulting Yahweh before going to war. Ironically, in our text (2 Chr 35:20–27) it was Pharaoh Necho (a non-Israelite king) who insisted that God had spoken to him and had allowed him to go and fight against the enemy, and that King Josiah was making a mistake by trying to stop someone who had been allowed by God. This response could have sent Josiah back to consult Yahweh. King Josiah's death opened the window to the shift in the confidence Judean leadership placed on Yahweh in the last years of the kingdom. Not consulting Yahweh before engaging in the war against Necho is also a good explanation of Josiah's death as scholars struggle to understand how a good king like him could have been allowed to die. This suggestion goes against Wittenberg's somehow simplistic argument that in the case of Josiah, we must distinguish between knowledge of Yahweh and a prosperous life. In other words, a just and compassionate government is good in God's eyes, even if its outcome (Josiah's death) is bad in the eyes of men ("Exegetical Problems of Jer 22:15 and 16," in *OTWSA*, 24 [1982], 110–119).

26. Von Rad, *Wisdom in Israel*, 102.

and other weaker nations. They have also become arrogant and defiant and have forgotten that Yahweh will judge them for the way they are using this power.

According to a recent report by the European Union Institute for Security, wars in Africa have "killed more than 7 million people and created about 19 million refugees since 1960 – not to mention the huge losses in terms of infrastructure and economic opportunities."[27] One of the dangerous aspects of African armies is the existence of armies within armies; that is "an independent, counter-balancing force, committed to the protection of one person: the President. Very often, these elite military units benefit both from better training and equipment, and higher economic and social payoffs."[28] Members of these elite units have strong ethnic ties with the president and frequently play a decisive role in the various coups and countercoups on the continent. In Mali for example, there were almost 1,217 Red Berets to protect the former President Amadou Toumani Touré; in Burkina Faso, former President Blaise Compaoré was protected by the feared *Régiment de Sécurité Présidentielle* composed of 1,300 well-trained, equipped and paid soldiers mostly from his own ethnic group. In Mauritania, President Ould Abdel Aziz was the commander of the Autonomous Presidential Security Battalion (BASEP) for more than fifteen years before using the same BASEP to seize power. Joseph Kabila, the former president of DR Congo, had between 10,000 and 15,000 soldiers (*Gardes Republicaines*) working to protect him alone. These private armies often blind presidents, leading them to assume that they have become so powerful that they can defy the constitution and ignore the grievances of the citizens.

This scenario also reminds us of former Zairean President Mobutu's system of self-protection with its many special units and security organizations, including the DSP,[29] SNIP,[30] and *Garde Civile*. All these units vied for identical duties: the protection of the dictator's regime.

> Despite the sheer size of the country, most of these elites were kept close to Kinshasa, rather than patrolling the borders. Their positioning reflected their role, the Zairean army was not aimed

---

27. David Chuter and Florence Gaub, *Understanding African Armies*, EU Institute of Security Studies, April 2016, https://www.iss.europa.eu/sites/default/files/EUISSFiles/Report_27.pdf.

28. Chuter and Gaub, *Understanding African Armies*, https://www.iss.europa.eu/sites/default/files/EUISSFiles/Report_27.pdf.

29. DSP (*Division Spéciale Présidentielle*: Special Presidential Division)

30. SNIP (*Service National d'Intelligence et de Protection*: Service for Action and Military Intelligence).

at resisting external attack. It was an internal security machines whose sole *raison d'être* was protecting the president.[31]

It was estimated that in case of a coup d'état or assassination attempt on President Mobutu, he would die only after at least ten thousand people who were working day and night to protect him were killed. But Mobutu died in solitude, in exile, far from his army and all the people he had employed to protect him. Blaise Compaoré is also currently living in exile in Ivory Coast, far from his 1,300 *Régiment de Sécurité Présidentielle*. He too will probably die in exile, if not in prison. This is the lesson we learn from those who are addicted to power. Yahweh will certainly judge us for accumulating, relying on, and misusing worldly power.

Wealth and leadership

Yahweh condemns boasting about riches. Brueggemann insightfully notices that in the Old Testament, riches are primarily a royal prerogative (1 Kgs 3:11, 13; 2 Chr 1:12; Dan 11:2; Esth 1:41; 5:11); and that they are an identifying mark of a good king (David: 1 Chr 29:12, 28; Solomon: 1 Kgs 10:23; 2 Chr 9:22; Jehoshaphat: 2 Chr 17:5; 18:1; Hezekiah: 2 Chr 32:27).[32]

From this perspective, it becomes clear that among the reasons Yahweh condemned Judah were that its leaders were using their position (power) to get rich, using their wealth to abuse the powerless, and were becoming arrogant and defiant because of their wealth. As Thompson puts it, "they [had] forgotten Yahweh in the midst of concentrating on their own achievements and activities."[33]

In most African countries, becoming president or being appointed to a position in the government is synonymous with getting rich. Our political leaders get rich fast mainly by embezzlement. Corruption has always been a major problem in Africa, and it is the greatest cause of both the misery and the instability of the continent because it alienates citizens from their rulers. Samuel Atuobi argues that "more often than not, corruption has played a key role in fomenting and prolonging . . . conflicts by serving as the basis

---

31. Michela Wrong, *In the Footsteps of Mr. Kurtz*, 252.
32. Brueggemann, *Old Testament Theology*, 286–87.
33. Thompson, *Book of Jeremiah*, 318.

for grievance against political leaders and violent political changes."³⁴ George Kinoti has rightly pointed out that one of the causes of Africa's economic and social wretchedness is the misuse of public institutions by African leaders whose aspiration is only to become rich:

> There is the problem of misuse of public institutions and embezzlement of public funds. In many African countries, government is quite plainly in the hands of crooks . . . men are ready to do anything including killing others and causing civil war, to get into position from where they can eat.³⁵

This corruption at the higher levels of a country can take several forms. It includes kickbacks to win large public procurement contracts, embezzlement of public funds, "ghost names" on the civil payroll, and bribes paid by multinationals to top officials to obtain contracts that will not benefit the nation.³⁶ Back in 1961, Franz Fanon noticed that in Africa "scandals are numerous, ministers grow rich, their wives doll themselves up, the members of parliament feather their nests and there is not a soul down to the simple policeman or the customs officer who does not join in the great procession of corruption."³⁷

In a letter to Mobutu, Zairean Catholic bishops once openly criticized the plundering of national resources:

> The national bank, the parastatal institutions and the whole portfolio of the state satisfy political demands and function as the cash desk of the state-party, left at the disposal of individuals, especially the authorities of the country . . . each one fetching as much money as he pleases.³⁸

Apart from the fact of impoverishing the nation, there is another dimension of the danger of longing for material possessions, especially by those who have power in the nation. The burning desire for becoming rich bears in itself the seed of covetousness and murder. The story of Naboth and King Ahab in 1

---

34. Samuel M. Atuobi, "Corruption and State Instability in West Africa: An Examination of Policy Option," http://www. kaiptcorg/Publications/Occasional-Papers/Documents/no_21.aspx.

35. Kinoti, *Hope for Africa*, 38.

36. See also Atuobi, "Corruption and State Instability in West Africa."

37. Cited in Atuobi.

38. Hizkias Assefa and George Wachira (eds.), *Peacemaking and Democratization in Africa: Theoretical Perspectives and Church Initiatives* (Nairobi: East African Educational Publishers, 1996), 134.

Kings 21 is a good illustration of how poor people in Israel/Judah might have lost their lives under the monarchy's abuse of power. The same happens in our societies because powerful people want to take our lands and our other possessions. Ambrose of Milan (339–97) vividly describes the plight of all the Naboths in our nations:

> The story of Naboth is an ancient one, but an everyday experience. What rich man does not daily set his heart on other people's goods? What millionaire is not engaged in tearing the poor man from his tiny holding and driving him empty-handed from the borders of his family allotment? Who is satisfied with what he has? What rich man's heart is not fired by the prospect of acquiring his neighbour's property? There was more than one Ahab born. An Ahab is born every day, alas! And Ahab will never die in this age . . . A Naboth is cut down every day; every day a poor man is killed.[39]

Thus, from Solomon onward, wisdom, power and riches were the basis of Israelites self-boasting (glory).[40] This boasting characterized the monarchy in particular, with its concentration of power and its tendency to want to become like the surrounding nations, forgetting that Israel's life was initiated and sustained by Yahweh. They forgot that self-boasting in human wisdom, power, and riches was an attempt to get away with God to make room for the pride of human beings in their wickedness. This was the problem brought about by human kingship. Self-boasting in human achievement, in wealth, and in power shows how Israel's royal consciousness understood its way of maintaining its security and the pretended well-being of the nation. Unfortunately, this was a mistake and the nation did come to an end, and the Judeans' worldly and wicked way of leadership was proven wrong.

What is currently happening in Africa is somewhat similar to what happened in Judah during the monarchy, when "the paganization" of the monarchy caused the abandonment of the way of Yahweh and replaced it with the way of human beings. Brueggemann puts it this way:

---

39. Taken from Oliver O'Donovan and Joan Lockwood O'Donovan (eds.), *From Irenaeus to Grotius: A Sourcebook in Christian Political Thought* (Cambridge: Cambridge University Press, 1999), 75–76. The story of Naboth also reminds one of Isaiah 5:8–30 where the prophet condemns the powerful who end up buying all the land and all the good things in the country, leaving poor people hopeless and eventually homeless.

40. Bruce C. Birch et al., *A Theological Introduction to the Old Testament* (Nashville: Abingdon, 1999), 249. He argues that Solomon led Israel to a place of prominence among the nations, both in terms of wealth and political influence, but that his policies laid the foundation for the kingdom's collapse and undermined concern for the Yahwistic covenant tradition.

> Mendenhall, most critically, has characterized this history as "the paganization of Israel." Bureaucracy, harem, standing army, tax districts, and temple are not only institutions that concretize a social vision. They are ways by which pagan, that is, non-covenantal, patterns of life were adapted from Israel's neighbors. This radical adaptation caused the abandonment of a certain vision of history, the loss of a covenant notion of God and humanity, and a forgetting of the messianic vision the monarchy was intended to guarantee.[41]

To sum up this section, I have argued that there are only two alternatives for any government or leadership: To follow the way of Yahweh, of justice, of understanding the high position as that of service; or to deviate and follow the way of corruption, self-service, and self-glorification characterized, in our context, by human wisdom, power and the ungodly search for wealth. In the case of Israel, God's desire for godly leadership among his people explains why he gave the law before the beginning of the monarchy, and then sent the prophets (during the time of the monarchy) to enforce the awareness of the law and the covenant that were being neglected and so to protect the nation against selfish and idolatrous political practices.

Wisdom, national wealth and power must be used for the good of the community and their use should be centred on the need to promote and defend the life of the people against enemies of life in the society. These enemies include idolatry, social injustice, poverty, and foreign nations.

True National Greatness (v. 24)

Verse 24 is introduced by the particle *ki 'îm*, which is rendered by "but" in most English translations. However, the disjunctive conjunction *ki 'îm* in this sentence does not only express the idea of opposition (the first element opposed to the second), but it also introduces an inner fundamental opening for a new behaviour, a change of mentality, a new understanding of matters, and a new way of doing things (see other examples of its use in Prov 23:17–18; Deut 10:12–13; Mic 6:8; Jer 31:29–30; 2 Kgs 17:35–36, 38–39).

In addition, this disjunctive conjunction introduces the same verb *hălāl* (*hitphael*, jussive) in verse 23. But this time, the verb is in the affirmative and directed not toward the self but toward Yahweh. Elsewhere in the Old

---

41. Brueggemann, *Old Testament Theology*, 274.

Testament, when the boasting is addressed away from self and directed toward God, it is called praise (Pss 34:3; 64:11; Jer 4:2). So in verse 23, not boasting about the self is the equivalent of boasting in (or praising) Yahweh. In other words, as we read in the passage itself, the new idea introduced by the particle *ki 'im* used with the verb *hălāl* and Yahweh as its complement is that the sole ground for human boasting is "to have understanding (*sa 'kal '*) and to know Yahweh."

The verb to have understanding (*sa 'kal '*) is often used in wisdom literature and describes the attitude of those who listen to[42] and practice the instructions of the wise. Their knowledge, which is born from listening, is understood as a gift from God (Ps 32:8; Neh 9:20), and is accompanied by God's presence and help (1 Sam 18:14; 2 Kgs 18:7). A knowledge born from listening to Yahweh gives life (Prov 21:16; 16:22); it is understood as an act of seeking God (Pss 14:2; 53:3), of fearing him (Ps 111:10), and of trusting him (Prov 16:20). When applied to leadership, it means guiding the nation under Yahweh's leadership. This understanding is sometimes associated with discerning how Yahweh has intervened in human history and the impossibility of idols doing the same (Pss 64:10; 106:7; Isa 41:20; 44:18).

To listen to Yahweh, to understand what he wants and to apply it in his leadership is the substance of the knowledge of Yahweh. This is what God wanted of Israelite kings, and it is what he wants of all the kings/presidents of the world. I can make this argument about all the leaders (kings, presidents, rulers) of the world because the Old Testament describes Yahweh not only as the God of Israel but also as the key character and decisive agent in the public process of the whole history of humanity, as we shall see at the end of this section. In other words, Yahweh is the real maker and definer of what happens in the visible world of public power everywhere in the world.[43]

Unfortunately, most of the kings in Israel/Judah ended up thinking that their power could sustain them despite their endless self-aggrandizement and brutalizing self-indulgence. For example, Jeremiah depicts King Jehoiakim as a model of the king who would not listen to Yahweh and who believed that

---

42. Writing from a leadership perspective, John C. Maxwell and Jim Dorman (*Becoming a Person of Influence: How to Positively Impact the Lives of Others* [Nashville: Thomas Nelson, 1997], 80–84) list the following values of listening: it shows respect, it builds relationships, it increases knowledge, it generates ideas, it builds loyalty. This description is of listening at the level of interpersonal human relationships, but it is also important for a leader to learn how to listen to Yahweh so that they can increase their knowledge and become wise.

43. For the relationship between Yahweh and non-Israelite leadership, see Brueggemann, *Theology of the Old Testament*, 492–525. For more details, see also William A. Dyrness, *The Earth Is God's: A Theology of American Culture* (Maryknoll, NY: Orbis, 1997).

Yahweh's word had nothing to do with him. In Jeremiah 36, Jehoiakim not only refuses to listen to Yahweh's word (v. 24) but he also tears apart the scroll and burns it! He does so in the mistaken belief that his well-being, prosperity, and security and that of the nation are maintained by his own abilities (and those of his close collaborators). He typifies the refusal of the Israelite kings to listen to Yahweh that finally brought the debacle of 587 BC, when the temple, the monarchy, and the city of Jerusalem fell into the hand of enemies, and the people were taken into exile.

In addition to the combination with the verb "to have understanding," the concept of the knowledge of Yahweh in Jeremiah 9:24 is also associated with two other important elements: the formula "I am Yahweh," and the group of three key terms "lovingkindness/steadfast love" (*ḥesed*), "justice" (*mišpāṭ*) and "righteousness" (*ṣĕdāqâ*).

The expression, "I am Yahweh" is the formula by which Yahweh introduces himself. It is believed to have its *Sitz im Leben* in the discourses of Exodus 3 and 6 where Yahweh presented himself to Moses by revealing his name. In the context of these two texts (Exod 3, 6), Yahweh introduces himself to Moses in the formula "I am Yahweh" as the one who is present to act, especially to deliver the suffering Israelite community in Egypt under Pharaoh. Yahweh's introduction to Moses as a deliverer articulates Yahweh's resolute decision to intervene determinedly against every oppressive, alienating situation and power that distorts a life of well-being. This means that Yahweh is more than a match for the powers of oppression, whether sociopolitical or cosmic.

In this sense, many Old Testament scholars have recognized that Yahweh is a salvific name, and that to know him as Yahweh and the God of Abraham, Isaac and Jacob (that is the God who acts in history to fulfil his promise, to rescue the oppressed and to punish the oppressor)[44] is to understand that this God will not tolerate injustice of any kind in any society. This same formula is repeated at the beginning of the Decalogue as a reminder to the people not only about the saving act of Yahweh (Exod 20:2; Deut 5:6), but also about the place that Yahweh should have in Israelite society.

The repetition of the formula "I am Yahweh" in Psalms 50:7; 81:10 combines both the mention of the commandments and the saving acts of Yahweh in the history of Israel. Thus, the function of the formula "I am Yahweh" in these passages was to call the Israelites to faith, to trust in Yahweh. In the same way, it is probable that the use of this formula in Jeremiah 9:24 was to call the

---

44. Elmer A. Martens, *God's Design: A Focus on Old Testament Theology* (Grand Rapids, MI: Baker, 1981), 1981, 15–17.

Israelites back to their traditional faith as set in the covenant. Faith in Yahweh would help the Israelite leadership to remain humble (by remembering how God has been helping them all the time that they were helpless). It would also help them to put their trust in Yahweh who is the true source of their power, wisdom (Deut. 4:6) and riches. Finally, remembering Yahweh as the deliverer would also help the Israelite leadership to keep in mind that God hates injustice in the society and punishes whoever practices it. These are most common meanings attached to the formula "I am Yahweh" in the Old Testament. In this sense, the self-boasting condemned in verse 23 is the misplaced trust and godless self-commendation that seeks to usurp the achievements of Yahweh among his people. When applied to politics or leadership management, it can describe the self-aggrandizing methods used by leaders of countries without regard for Yahweh's law or his will. This is one example of what it means to not know Yahweh.

The second element that helps us to understand the concept of the knowledge of Yahweh is the group of three words: "lovingkindness/steadfast love" (*ḥesed*), "justice" (*mišpāṭ*) and "righteousness or virtue" (*ṣĕdāqâ*) which describe Yahweh's activity in favour of humankind. This triad is the object of the verb "to do, to practice, to perform," in the sentence: "I am Yahweh *who practices* (who does) steadfast love (lovingkindness), justice, and righteousness on earth."

The Hebrew word *ḥesed* is difficult to translate into English. Carroll actually thinks that the word is virtually untranslatable.[45] D. A. Baer and R. P. Gordon define it as "faithfulness, steadfast love, or more generally kindness."[46] Their argument is that, in the Old Testament, *ḥesed* is frequently used of the attitudes and behaviour of humans towards one another, and "more frequently (ratio 3:1), to describe the disposition and beneficent actions of God towards the faithful, Israel his people, and humanity in general."[47] They also quote Glueck who argued that *ḥesed* is based on covenantal relationship with his people, and that it is the essence of the covenantal relationship between Yahweh and Israel. It should only be noted that in the case of Israel and Yahweh, while *ḥesed* does contain the idea of mutual demands, service and fear, it does not necessarily depend on Israel's faithfulness. In other words, though the root of *ḥesed* is in the covenant, Israel's experience of it depended on the eternal faithfulness of Yahweh alone.

---

45. Carroll, *Jeremiah*, 247.
46. D. A. Baer and R. P. Gordon, חסד, in *NIDOTTE*, 2:210.
47. Baer and Gordon, 2:210.

Hence, in the Old Testament, we find several uses of the word *hesed* with the idea of Yahweh's interventions to save people from disaster or oppression. These uses are particularly with regard to the patriarchs (Gen 24:12, 14, 27; 32:11); the Israelites in Egypt and in the desert (Exod 15:13; Ps 136:10, 16); and the Israelites again during the time of the occupation of Canaan (Ps 136:21); or during attacks by neighbouring nations (Pss 136:16–20; 118). The word is also used in the promise to David and his descendants of an enduring dynasty (2 Sam 7:15; 22:51; 1 Kgs 3:6; Ps 89:25–29). Briefly, in general, the concept of *hesed* is related to Yahweh's aptitude to rescue those in destitution (Pss 31:8; 32:10; 44:27; 52:10; 59:11; 66:20; 69:14, 17; 85:8; 107:8, 15, 21, 31).

From the above examples and in reference to communal/national life, it will not be an exaggeration to define *hesed* as a reaching down to help prompted by love toward the needy in general. Yahweh is the best example of this stooping down to help and inexplicable generosity because he is capable of kind, gracious, invigorating, rehabilitating, sustaining, and liberating actions towards those who need such actions. In the context of a nation, or a government, similar actions by leaders are what I would call a "practical politics" that aim at working for those who are in need, at helping the helpless, at listening to the cry of those who are crushed, and educating the nation toward love for one another. Morgan is among the few scholars who have understood well the transformative power of *hesed* in a nation when every member of the community practices it, but more particularly when it is done by the leadership:

> If we climb to the heights and imagine a nation wherein lovingkindness shall abound, and be the inspiration of life, we cannot escape from the conviction that such a nation would be strong indeed. Lovingkindness strengthens the things that remain, gathers all waste material and transmutes it into true wealth. Within the life of any nation, by the ministry of that lovingkindness, which is a stoop prompted by love toward all lack, in pity, patience and power, the true strength will be realized.[48]

God alone knows how many African leaders practice lovingkindness and are aware that the strength of their nation does not come from political power but from Yahweh's blessings because leaders bend down and meet those who are crushed by oppression and by their daily struggle for life. An African proverb reminds us that "happiness is not perfected until it is shared," especially

---

48. Morgan, *Studies in the Prophecy of Jeremiah*, 69.

with those in need. This was the attitude of Jesus and the whole programme of his ministry on earth according to Luke 4. But in most of our countries, instead of serving the needy, our leaders are working for their own benefit and that of their close relatives.

It seems to me that this is also where the challenge is most acute for the church in Africa. Lovingkindness must be practised first in the church, which is meant to model God's *ḥesed*. But very often, church leaders are the first to be egotistic, to hunger for a luxurious life and forget that they are in the service of others. They forget that God's call requires a denial of self for the service of others. Far too many church leaders in Africa use their positions for making profit. Philippe Kabongo-Mbaya quotes J. F. Bayart who, in his book, *Religion et Modernité Politique en Afrique*, criticized Congolese Catholic bishops for living in luxury while the great majority of common believers were living in abject poverty:

> The Mercedes-Benz car has become the episcopal vehicle par excellence, attributed to church leaders and elders and making them elites in the prominent places within the postcolonial state. In 1970, the Catholic bishop of Lisala shared this privilege with only two other dignitaries: the commissioner for territorial administration and a rich merchant.[49]

Has this situation changed today? I do not think so. It has even become worse, especially in Protestant denominations, as my experience in Kinshasa has demonstrated (chapter 5). True *ḥesed* cannot co-exist with the desire for personal aggrandizement. It was Jose Miranda who made clear that "knowledge of God is attentiveness to the needs of brothers and sisters."[50] In other words, knowledge of God is observed through the practice of *ḥesed* in the society.

The two other words *mišpāṭ* (justice) and *ṣĕdāqâ* (righteousness, virtue) are used to express Yahweh's intervention in order to maintain the integrity of the covenant people by protecting them against external attacks (Judg 5:11; Deut 33:20; Mic 7:9–20; Pss 9:4–7; 48:5–12; 89:14–19), and against internal oppression (Deut 10:18; Isa 11:4–9; 28:6–7; Pss 7:12; 10:18; 43:1; 72:1–4; 99:4; 103:6; 140:13; 145:7, 17; 146:7; Job 36:6; Prov 29:26; Jer 12:1; 11:20; 23:6; 33:16; 22:11–13; 50:7). For a nation, to practice justice and righteousness is to discover Yahweh's direction for leadership. In other words, righteousness and justice

---

49. Philippe Kabongo-Mbaya, "Churches and the Struggle for Democracy in Zaire," in Hizkias Assefa and George Wachira (eds), *Peacemaking and Democratisation in Africa* (Nairobi: East African Educational Publishers, 1996), 138.

50. Quoted by Brueggemann, *Social Reading of the Old Testament*, 48.

are conformity to Yahweh in action because in him, there is "no iniquity, no crookedness."[51]

Understanding, righteousness, lovingkindness, and justice are divine leadership qualities. They do not cover all aspects of Yahweh's leadership, but they show Yahweh's way of dealing with human society. This is why, in verse 24, all these words are the object of a single verb meaning "to do, to practice, to perform." In other words, Yahweh practices righteousness, lovingkindness, and justice. What defines a good leader is not their words, nor what they say themselves about what they can do, but what they actually do. To know Yahweh does not refer to theoretical knowledge about Yahweh. Rather, the concept has to do with how that knowledge is applied to practical (political) leadership of the nation or the church. Here the verb "to do, to practice, to perform" is a key word because Yahweh is defined in the text not by who he is but by what he does in and for Israel and in the whole world. In other words, Yahweh is not known through speculation or theory but always through acts of social intervention and inversion that make possible human life in a situation where human existence has been threatened.

To do what Yahweh does or to lead as Yahweh leads the nation is to know him. It is only when one knows him that he can boast. However, this boasting will not be about ourselves (i.e. our achievement, our wealth, our power, our knowledge) but about the true leader who is influencing the action of human leadership. This plainly reminds us of Paul, who could say: "Follow my example, as I follow the example of Christ" (1 Cor 11:1 NIV) and "I will boast all the more gladly about my weaknesses, so that Christ's power may rest on me" (2 Cor 12:9b NIV). In the same way, Jeremiah 9:23–24 should have become the call of Judah's kings, priests and prophets, urging the whole nation: "Follow our example, as we follow Yahweh in what he does," that is, in modelling righteousness, lovingkindness, and justice in the nation.

Unfortunately, they failed to lead as Yahweh wanted. This is why verse 24 ends with Yahweh's affirmation: "For in these things I delight." In other words, Yahweh is the one who does these very things for all humanity: he has power beyond measure, but he uses it for our benefit; he has wisdom beyond our understanding, but he uses it to lead the universe; he has wealth beyond our imagination, but he uses it for the sake of the humankind. For a human leader, to do what Yahweh does is to truly know him.

Finally, in the book of Jeremiah, the concepts "lovingkindness/steadfast love" (*ḥesed*), "justice" (*mišpāṭ*) and "righteousness, virtue" (*ṣĕdāqâ*) go beyond

---

51. Morgan, *Studies in the Prophecy of Jeremiah*, 69.

the boundary of the covenant people to the whole world. This is the idea contained in verse 24: "I am Yahweh who practices "lovingkindness/steadfast love" (*ḥesed*), "justice" (*mišpāṭ*) and "righteousness, virtue" (*ṣĕdāqâ*) on earth (*bā'āreṣ*). The use of this single word (*bā'āreṣ*) is important because it helps us realize that Yahweh's lovingkindness, justice, and righteousness does not apply only to Israel/Judah, but to the whole world because the agent who does these things is God himself, not the personal and impersonal powers of this world that we sometimes think of as causes.

Conclusion

Jeremiah 9:23–24 should be viewed as a summary of two opposed ideologies that characterized Judean society towards the end of its existence. On the one hand, verse 23 describes those who possessed authority in the nation (symbolized by wisdom, power, and wealth) but did not understand its true nature, and therefore did not understand how to use it. They were using their authority without reference to the source of that authority. What mattered for them was the exigencies of the situation and their own benefit, not Yahweh's will. They had forgotten that Yahweh is the owner and giver of all power, wisdom, and wealth who intends these things to be used for the benefit of the entire community.

Every nation has something in which it glories or takes pride – for example, its military power, economic might, or knowledge (technological know-how, education system, etc.). But the prophet Jeremiah was in open conflict with all these systems in Judah because they had become a source of human pride. Yahweh had, in particular, warned against Israel's kings taking pride in military power (Deut 17:14–20). The danger of relying on military power was primarily (political) idolatry, that is, the abandonment of the covenant and trust in Yahweh.

Jeremiah 9:23–24 shows that wisdom, power and knowledge can be distorted and become either idols that people worship or a calculation of interest that is used to take advantage of others, and Yahweh disappears as a critical principle. In other words, true wisdom, power, and knowledge disappear when people manage to make credible the practice of foolishness, the mistaken sense that they are autonomous and determine the measure of their own life. When this happens, people no longer use wisdom, power, and wealth for Yahweh's purpose (by practising lovingkindness, justice, and righteousness); instead they become wise in their own eyes and self-referential. The wisdom, power, and wealth that God intended to be used for the good of his people become a source of self-deluding autonomy and a terrible revolt against Yahweh. They become idols, a self-serving, self-deceiving ideology. Ideology and idolatry always want to compel us to bow down to the work of our hands, to our knowledge and might, to our achievement, to our wealth, to our ethnic group, and to our family so that we may worship them. This is true not only for a nation, but also for any society, any ethnic group, any institution, and any individual.

7

The Use and Abuse of Political Power

Jeremiah 22:13–19

¹³ Woe to him who builds his house by unrighteousness,
    and his upper room without justice;
who makes his neighbour work for nothing,
    and does not pay him his wages;
¹⁴ who says, "I will build for myself a large house
    with spacious upper rooms,"
and cuts out windows for it,
    panelling it with cedar,
    and painting it with vermilion (bright red).
¹⁵ Do you reign
    because you compete in cedar?
Your father, did not he eat and drink
    and do justice and righteousness
    and it was well for him.
¹⁶ He judged the cause of the poor and needy;
    then it was well.
Is not this to know me?
    Word of Yahweh.
¹⁷ But your eyes and your heart
    are on nothing else except on your dishonest gain,
and on shedding innocent blood,
    and on practising oppression and extortion.

¹⁸ Therefore, thus says Yahweh concerning Jehoiakim, son of Josiah, king of Judah:

"They will not lament for him,
    Ah, my brother! or Ah my sister!
They will not lament for him,
    Ah! lord! Or Ah! majesty!
¹⁹ He will be buried with the burial of an ass,
    dragged off and thrown out outside the gates of Jerusalem."

Historical and Literary Contexts

Jeremiah 21:11–23:8 contains various sayings that were probably uttered over a considerable span of time and have been grouped together because of their relationship to the theme stated in the heading (21:1): "The Royal House of Judah."[1] They are almost equally divided between poetry and prose. The specific poem we are looking at here has one clue to help the reader set a precise date for it: the name of King Jehoiakim.

Most scholars divide this poem into two parts: (vv. 13–17 – accusation, and vv. 18–19 – judgement). However, here we will be considering it in three parts: The abuse of power (vv. 13–15a, 17), the right use of power (vv. 15b–16), and the announcement of judgement (vv. 18–19).

The Monarchy in Israel

This passage offers a case study of the consequences of proper use or abuse of political power by comparing two kings: one good and one bad. Jeremiah explains the consequences they will each face for how they exercise leadership. There will be blessings for the good and judgement for the bad.

To properly interpret this passage, it is necessary for us to understand the purpose and role of the monarchy in Israel and to establish the criteria against which the use of power will be analysed in this chapter. The reason for this is that there is widespread disagreement among theologians on Yahweh's attitude toward Israelite human kingship.

To properly study or evaluate the monarchy in Israel two central questions must be answered: Should Israel have asked for a king and did God intend there

---

1. Bright, *Jeremiah*, 144.

to be a king in Israel at all? Roberts summarizes the three leading positions in ancient scholarship on the subject:

> In ancient debate some voices claimed that the mere request for a human king was tantamount to a rejection of God, to a rebellion against divine rule (Judg. 8:22-23; 1 Sam. 8:7; 12:12, 17-20). Others, arguing less theologically but equally opposed to the monarchy, saw kingship as a totally unnecessary and unproductive drain on the resources of a healthy society (Judg. 9:7-15; 1 Sam. 10:27). Still others, the ancient promonarchists, viewed kingship as God's gift that finally brought order to an irresponsibly chaotic society in which formerly "every man did what was right in his own eyes" (Judg. 17:6; 21:25; cf. 18:1; 19:1).[2]

The issue continues to divide modern scholars as well. On one hand, there are those who argue that from the beginning to the end, human kingship was what God wanted for Israel; others think that kingship had never been God's intention for Israel and that by developing it on the model of pagan states, the Israelites introduced paganization into the political and social history of Israel with fateful and lasting consequences.[3] A third group of scholars agrees with this second view but adds that, though God never intended Israel to have a human king, he adopted Israel's decision and then sought to adapt it to fit his covenant.[4] The task of this chapter is not to discuss these different positions. Rather, it is to evaluate the use of power by two of the last kings of Judah. However, a good evaluation requires a clear understanding of the criteria from which to evaluate. This is why, as far as the different positions about attitudes towards kingship are concerned, I concur with scholars who say that God adopted and then adapted human kingship in Israel. This view helps us to understand that human leadership is a serious responsibility because it has the potential to build and to destroy. Successful leadership must refer to something greater or better than itself. The notion of autonomous leadership is simply a delusion.

In Deuteronomy 17:14-20 and 1 Samuel 8:1-18, Yahweh sets out strict and precise regulations for human kings who essentially rule under him. In

---

2. J. J. M. Roberts, "In Defense of the Monarchy: The Contribution of Israelite Kingship to Biblical Theology," in Patrick D. Miller, Paul D. Hanson and S. Dean McBride (eds.), *Ancient Israelite Religion* (Philadelphia: Fortress, 1987), 377.

3. George E. Mendenhall, "The Monarchy," *Interpretation* 29 (1975): 155.

4. See Chester Wood, "With Justice for All: The Task of the People of God: A Biblical Theology," unpublished class notes (Nairobi Evangelical Graduate School of Theology), 1998.

Deuteronomy 17:14–20, there are at least six limitations on the kingship: the king must be selected by God (v. 15a); he must not be a foreigner (v. 15b); he must not acquire great numbers of horses (v. 16a); he must not take many wives (v. 17a), he must not accumulate large amounts of silver and gold (v. 17b); and when he has taken the throne, he must write for himself a copy of the law and obey it (vv. 18, 19).[5]

Two more requirements are found in the passage: the king should not consider himself better than other Israelites and he should not turn aside from the law (v. 20a). These restrictions would make the Israelite monarchy unique compared to the monarchies of neighbouring nations. In Mesopotamia, for example, kings were considered to have descended from heaven and were, therefore, very different from the common people.[6] But the Israelite king was a brother among (and not above) his fellow Israelites; he was to obey the law and trust in God for his leadership; he was forbidden from becoming a great military, political or economic leader because doing so could mislead him into thinking that he was autonomous, ruling by his own power. The king had no absolute power; rather, he was commissioned to lead under Yahweh himself.

The result of following these limitations or instructions would be that the king and his descendants would not be threatened from either inside or outside Israel (v. 20b). Theirs would be a stable kingship that would ensure a stable nation. Success in leadership (which involved both victory over enemies and the continuation of the dynasty) depended directly on whether a king accepted this view of himself as leading under Yahweh or not. The success or failure of a king had direct consequences for the nation as a whole.

---

5. Many scholars do not agree on the date of this passage in general, and on the date of verses 18–19 in particular. Marcus Dodd et al. (*Exposition of the Bible: Genesis–Ruth* [Hartford, CT: S. S. Scranton, 1908], 573) have a lengthy discussion on Deuteronomy 17:14–20. They give several reasons for believing that the passage is of late origin. Two of those reasons are that (1) the passage suggests that the book of the law would already be available to the king, and yet during the time of Moses it was impossible to think about such a book; (2) the sending of Israelites to Egypt in order to buy horses was a reality during the time of Solomon, not before. But J. A. Thompson (*Deuteronomy: An Introduction and Commentary* [Tyndale Old Testament Commentary, Leicester: IVP, 1974], 204) argues that "there is no reason why Moses should not have been aware of the extremes to which human monarchs could go in the exercise of their autocratic rule, for he had the example of the king of Egypt." See also Jack Ford and A. R. G. Deasley (*Deuteronomy*, 563) who state that the passage fits the time of Moses on the eve of entering the land as it fits no other time. I have a more traditional view and agree with Thompson that the passage fits well the time of Moses and that, in his sovereignty, God may have inspired Moses to instruct the Israelites on the possible danger ahead of them.

6. On the nature of kingship in Mesopotamia, see the detailed study by Perdue, *Wisdom and Cult* (Missoula: Scholars, 1977).

In 1 Samuel 8, the question of the establishment of kingship in Israel is posed with great vitality. According to this passage, the request for the establishment of the monarchy in Israel was precipitated on the one hand by the age of Samuel, the prophet and the judge of Israel, and on the other hand by the pursuit of selfish gain by his two sons (8:1–5).[7] The request was the result of a crisis situation. Many scholars also think that the real issue that motivated the elders of Israel to ask for a king was the constant threat by neighbouring nations. But while considering external threats (or historical context), it is also important to keep in mind that 1 Samuel 8 comes immediately after the passage that relates, with great details, the mighty victory of Israel, under Samuel, over the Philistines (1 Samuel 7).[8]

What stands out clearly in the passage is that Israel's problem was not external but internal, more specifically the people's relationship with Yahweh and with one another. Moreover, the strong reaction of Samuel against the establishment of kingship in Israel reveals that he knew that a human king would not be able to solve Israel's problems but would only worsen them. Interestingly, Samuel's warning about the danger of the monarchy was not based on historical arguments but on social and religious grounds.

First was the religious danger of the monarchy (1 Sam 8:6–8). God's response to Samuel concerning the request of the people (vv. 6–8) makes it clear that Israel had a theological rather than a political or historical problem, as it might appear at first. The crisis in the passage is that the establishment of the monarchy is a rejection of Yahweh himself. Brueggemann rightly points out that this rejection is not something new but a characteristic of Israel's history, for the whole history of Israel is one of forsaking Yahweh and going after other

---

7. See also the following articles: Lyle M. Eslinger, *Kingship of God in Crisis: A Close Reading of 1 Samuel 1–12* (Sheffield: JSOT, 1985), 251–82. M. Weinfeld, "Judge and Officer in Ancient Israel and in the Ancient Near East," *Israel Oriental Studies* 7 (1977): 65–88. I. Mendelsohn, "On Corvée Labor in Ancient Canaan and Israel," in *Bulletin of the American Schools of Oriental Research* 167 (October 1962): 31–35.

8. It is possible that the threat of the Philistines and the other neighbours of Israel was renewed after the victory related in 1 Samuel 7, just as Walter Brueggemann sees it (*First and Second Samuel* [Louisville, KY: John Knox, 1990], 61). When commenting on 1 Samuel 8:1–3, he writes: "It is a long time between chapters 7 and 8. Samuel is suddenly old." But in my opinion, the long time between the two chapters cannot justify saying that Israel is now unable to cope with the situation and that the solution is to have a human king. The issue is that of faithfulness of Israel to Yahweh: whenever the people were faithful, God intervened to help them, and whenever they became unfaithful, God abandoned them. I would, therefore, say that the request for a human king is another example of the unfaithfulness of Israel to Yahweh. So, the gap between chapter 7 and 8 as Brueggemann notes is narrowed by the narrator of 1 Samuel who puts the two texts side by side. This is not accidental. He wants to communicate a clear message that Yahweh's faithfulness is available for the nation if they care.

gods.⁹ The request for a human king "is one more step in that continuing performance of mistrust."¹⁰ It marks the climax (or the beginning of the climax) of disobedience to Yahweh, since "the issue of monarchy in Yahweh's speech is perceived as Israel's unwillingness to have Yahweh as the source and ruler of life."¹¹ This is what Eslinger calls the covenantal sin of Israel.¹²

Second was the social danger of the monarchy (1 Sam 8:9–20). Yahweh makes it clear to Israel that their request for a king will bring a serious distortion in the society in the form of structural change from a balanced clan-based economic system to a centralized, unbalanced temple-based system. Yahweh accepts the request and commands Samuel to show the people the "ways of the king," that is, the kind of social justice a human king will introduce into the society and its consequence for the whole nation. The governing word in the passage is the verb "to take." The king is the one who takes or who confiscates what belongs to the people, and Samuel goes on to list what the king will take: he will take their sons for military purposes (vv. 11–12), their daughters to serve in the newly emerging royal class and its routines (v. 13), the best of their fields and vineyards and olive orchards (v. 14), one-tenth of their grain and of their vineyards (v. 15), their slaves, cattle and donkeys (vv. 16–17a).

The first consequence of human kingship is that the people will become slaves of their king. The Israelites knew from experience what it meant to be slaves, as they themselves were slaves of Pharaoh in Egypt. The second consequence is that the people will cry out for relief from their king because the king would make them miserable. Samuel is trying to demonstrate to the people that whatever they think of a king, life under the monarchy will turn to their disadvantage. The third consequence is that Yahweh will not answer the people when they cry out for relief from the monarchy. Cry–answer is a "central construct and practice in Israel's faith (Exod 2:23–25)."¹³ Throughout the Bible, we see how Yahweh intervened as the result of people's cry for help (Exod 3:7; Isa 65:24). But by substituting God with a human king, Israel was forfeiting the possibility of God answering their prayers for help.

---

9. Brueggemann, *First and Second Samuel*, 63.
10. Brueggemann, 63.
11. Brueggemann, 63.
12. Eslinger, *Kingship of God in Crisis*, 264.
13. Brueggemann, *First and Second Samuel*, 64.

The Abuse of Power: Jehoiakim (vv. 13–19)

God's ideal for kingship in Israel forces us to think about the perils of human leadership, more particularly, the failure of human leadership that is common in Africa. As I am writing these words, demonstrators are being killed in the streets of Kinshasa, DR Congo, because they are demanding presidential elections before the end of 2016.[14] It is unfortunate that very few of these people demonstrating in the streets remember that DR Congo has had two elections in the last 10 years, but that nothing has changed in the country. Some things have in fact become worse. Change is unlikely to come after the upcoming elections, and citizens will go back to the streets to agitate for new elections. I strongly argue that Africa's problem is not democracy as we conceive it today or as it is imposed on us by the West. Our problem in Africa is not even elections or lack of them. Our problem is the wickedness of our leadership, a leadership that neither fears God nor understands its duty as that of leading citizens under a higher and greater authority. The leadership situation in the continent is unlikely to change soon, and not before Africans change how they think about leadership and seek the right kind of leaders, who are desperately needed. The stability of a society depends on the quality of its leaders.

The building mania of African presidents

"The matter has caused a lot of frustration and confusion, for which I apologize," said Jacob Zuma, the 74-year-old former South African president in a TV address on 1 April 2016.[15] He was apologizing for the $23 million of public money spent to upgrade one of his houses in rural Nkandla, KwaZulu-Natal Province.

Elsewhere, the *Sunday Times* (UK) reported on 20 June 2008 that "a mansion worth £15 million in one of Paris's most elegant districts has become the latest of 33 luxury properties bought in France by President Omar Bongo Ondimba of Gabon."[16] A leak from a French investigation that started in

---

14. These street demonstrations took place on 19–20 September 2016. According to official sources, 54 people were killed. Three more demonstrations took place on 31 December 2017, 2 and 25 February 2018.
15. "South Africa's Jacob Zuma 'sorry' over Nkandla Scandal," *BBC News*, 1 April 2016, http://www.bbc.com/news/world-africa-35943941.
16. "Omar Bongo," *Wikipedia*, https://en.wikipedia.org/wiki/Omar_Bongo.

February 2012 revealed that Omar Bongo's family might own up to thirty-nine luxury apartments or houses in the French capital alone.[17]

Teodorin Nguema Obiang, the 41 year-old son of President Teodoro Obiang Nguema Mbasogo of Equatorial Guinea, who also served as vice-president of the republic in his father's government, is reported to possess two lavish homes in Cape Town, South Africa; an unknown number of homes in Buenos Aires, London, and in the wealthy 16th arrondissement of Paris; a mansion in Malibu, and another one in California that reportedly costs over $30 million, etc.[18]

President Sassou Nguesso of the Republic of Congo is reported by the UK newspaper the *Independent* to have twenty-four properties in Paris alone according to documents leaked from the French investigation. In addition, Sassou and Bongo's families are said to have two hundred French bank accounts.[19]

Building mania is only one of the many facets of the abuse of power by African leaders. It seems that becoming a president in Africa is synonymous with living an extravagant life and forgetting the poor citizens, most of them living on less than $2 per day. How can a leader or their family live in thirty-nine houses that are thousands of kilometres away? And this is without considering the many other buildings they own in their own countries. This situation is compounded by the fact that many government ministers and governors emulate their national leaders and acquire many buildings too. These examples help us understand Yahweh's fury against King Jehoiakim of Judah, who, on a small scale, behaved like one of these African presidents.

Woe to the king who builds by injustice!

The "Woe" (v. 13) that begins this poem is usually used to denounce unjust practices that disrupt the social order of the community.[20] This woe introduces

---

17. John Lichfield, "The Parisian Treasures of African Tyrants: French Government May Seize Mansions and Luxury Cars of Corrupt Regimes," 13 July 2013, http://www.independent.co.uk/news/world/europe/the-parisian-treasures-of-african-tyrants-french-government-may-seize-mansions-and-luxury-cars-of-8706535.html.

18. Mfonobong Nsehe, "An African Dictator's Son and His Very Lavish Toys," 7 July 2011, http://www.forbes.com/sites/mfonobongnsehe/2011/07/07/an-african-dictators-son-and-his-very-lavish-toys/#1e879f044913.

19. Lichfield, "The Parisian Treasures of African Tyrants," 13 July 2013, http://www.independent.co.uk/news/world/europe/the-parisian-treasures-of-african-tyrants-french-government-may-seize-mansions-and-luxury-cars-of-8706535.html.

20. Carroll, *Jeremiah*, 426–27.

a series of accusations against King Jehoiakim because of his disdain for righteousness and justice; but the name of the king is not given until verse 18. There are three charges against him, all connected with building projects: he builds his house "by unrighteousness," his upper room "without justice," and makes his neighbours "work for nothing" or without paying them their wages.

The first charge in verse 13 is that the king builds his house by unrighteousness. There are two important observations to make at this point. First, it might appear that the condemnation is not on the building itself but on the way the building project was carried out. In other words, the king was using unrighteous means to build his palace. But a problem with this view is that the king likely did not need to build a new sumptuous palace because one had been built by Solomon (2 Kgs 7:1–12) where, apparently, all the kings after him lived.[21] Moreover, Jehoiakim was a vassal of Egypt and as such, he had the terrible burden of raising the tribute demanded by Pharaoh. The only way he could raise these revenues was by taxation of his people (2 Kgs 23:35). It is, therefore, difficult to imagine that under the yoke of Egypt, and later of Babylon, the small-minded king could think about starting a luxurious building project and add yet another burden to his people. The project could not be carried on without harming people already impoverished by heavy taxation. We can, therefore, understand why the prophet opens the accusation against Jehoiakim with a woe denouncing his actions.

The second charge is that he builds his upper room without justice. The upper room here refers to the building obsession of Jehoiakim: he was not building a small house but had started a large building enterprise. Martens writes: "it is tempting to equate an elaborate complex of buildings found by archeologists south of Jerusalem with Jehoiakim's palace."[22] He adds that the "imposing wide house with large chambers was surrounded by a citadel extending over five acres."[23] Craigie, Kelley and Drinkard underscore this point, pointing out that what the king was building was not the house of just a wealthy man but one that was elaborate, both in its dimensions (large, with spacious, windowed upper rooms) and in its decor (panelled with cedar).[24]

In verse 14, we find two important additional details: first, the passage describes the king saying: "I will build for myself." This declaration shows the

---

21. See also Ovid R. Sellers "Palace," in *IDB*, 3:620. He notices that, presumably, subsequent kings of Judah occupied Solomon's palace.
22. Martens, *Jeremiah*, 147.
23. Martens, 147.
24. Craigie, Kelley and Drinkard, *Jeremiah*, 310–11.

intention of the king: his desire to have more houses, just like many African leaders! The project was not in the interests of Judah; it was his personal interest with a negative impact on the whole nation. He wanted a kind of private mansion for the king so that he could have two or more mansions like those of other Near Eastern monarchs of his day, or like those of some African presidents today. Feinberg is right to comment on Jehoiakim's habit: "the building mania, common among oriental monarchs, [had] seized him."[25] For Jehoiakim, to be a king meant becoming very rich, and one way to show that wealth was by having several palaces. This goes against Deuteronomy 17:17b, which prohibited Israelite kings from accumulating personal wealth at the expense of their subjects.

If Jeremiah vigorously condemned Jehoiakim for building just one palace, I wonder what would have been said about our African presidents? We too know that the problem is not just the act of building; it is also the cost of maintaining these buildings and feeding the many relatives, wives, and children living in them. Those costs weigh heavily on poor countries like Judah and on our countries.

The third charge is that Jehoiakim is making his neighbours work for nothing, without paying them wages (v. 13). The king is forcing his people to work on building project as slaves, so breaking the law that forbade an Israelite from withholding their neighbours' salary. Leviticus 19:13 states: "Do not hold back the wages of a hired worker overnight" (NIV). There is a similar law in Deuteronomy 24:14–15. Failure to pay daily wages to workers would deprive them of the money they needed to buy food for their families for the evening meal and for the following day. But Jehoiakim was not only delaying payment of wages; he was not paying them at all! In other words, he made his people his slaves. We are reminded of Samuel's warning to the Israelites that the king they wanted would take everything from them and would make some of them his slaves (1 Sam 8:17), which is exactly what Jehoiakim, and many other kings did. Similarly, many Africans have been enslaved by their leaders. That is why there is a saying that "we came to this world to accompany others," implying that the speaker is inferior and is only there to serve those in authority. Often, the actions of African leaders have reduced citizens to slaves, who work and pay taxes that benefit only the rich and the powerful.

This discussion takes us back to the role of the kingship in Israel. What was the role or the responsibility of the Israelite king toward the people and toward Yahweh? In other words, and in the context of this passage, was the

---

25. Feinberg, *Jeremiah*, 157.

king allowed to use his power to enslave his subjects for his personal projects? He was not. The king had two responsibilities: to ensure loyalty to the covenant and to promote the well-being or *shalom* of the people. To quote McKane,

> It is his responsibility to ensure that the weaker members of the community do in fact, and not merely in theory, enjoy equality before the law ... This is a concern to preserve an effective reciprocity of rights in the community despite differences of station, power and wealth among the individuals who constitute it. He must be vigilant that these rights are not infringed by new departures against which older forms of safeguards will not avail, and always alive to what is necessary to preserve them. It is the will to implement whatever is required to achieve these ends which constitutes "knowledge of Yahweh."[26]

King Jehoiakim's type of thinking ("I will build for myself") with all the negative effects it had on the people, had no place in Yahweh's plan for the Israelite king.

The detailed description of the king's private house (note the repetition of the phrase "upper rooms") with big windows, a house panelled with cedar and painted with bright red or vermilion (v. 14) raises the following questions: Why does the prophet mention all these details? Why were other building projects, such as Solomon's, not condemned with such strong words? Where did the vassal-king obtain funds for such a spacious building? The answer to the last question is simply that the labour for his building project cost him nothing because his subjects were forced to work without pay. The details given by the prophet in the passage drive home the cost of this huge building and its impact on the economy of the nation. It appears that Jehoiakim was a thoroughly spoiled and self-indulgent young despot.[27]

The essence of kingship

The climax of the accusation against King Jehoiakim begins in verse 15 with its important question: "Do you reign because you compete in cedar?"[28] This question takes us back again to the role of the Israelite king, especially to his

---

26. McKane, *Jeremiah*, 531.
27. Thompson, *The Book of Jeremiah*, 479.
28. Scholars differ on the translation of this passage. Bright (*Jeremiah*, 137) writes that the text of verses 15 and 16 is somewhat confused, that the translation in some places is conjectural, and that the LXX differs widely from the MT. His translation of the passage resembles that of Thompson: "That makes you a king – outdoing everyone in cedar?"

use of power. Thus, Jehoiakim could have been asked: "Why do you reign? Or why are you a king? How do you understand your kingship?" Jehoiakim's answer, according to the passage, would be: "I reign because I outdo everybody in my use of cedar; I reign because I have the best houses in Judah; I reign because I am the richest person in the nation; I reign because everybody in the nation fears me; I reign because my soldiers can arrest (and kill) anybody; I reign because I have power." This is probably how Jehoiakim understood the monarchy. For him, being a king was synonymous with accumulating material possessions, being the most feared person, and ruling unchallenged.

There are a lot of similarities between Judah and Africa today as far as leadership is concerned. In Africa, rather than seeing politics as public service to the nation and the poor; most of our leaders consider it an avenue for enriching themselves and building up their careers. They confuse leadership positions with private family businesses and want their children to take over after their retirement or death. In countries such as Gabon, Togo, and DR Congo, presidents have been succeeded by their sons or are aggressively preparing their children as heirs. In East Africa, the media and opposition parties in Uganda accuse President Museveni, who has been in power since 1986, of grooming one of his sons to replace him. In West Africa, many Senegalese believed that Karim Wade, nicknamed "the minister of earth and sky" because of his extensive political portfolio (Minister of State for International Cooperation, Regional Development, Air Transport, and Infrastructure) was intended to inherit the presidency from his father, Abdoulaye Wade, but the plan failed. The attempt, whether successful or not, to bequeath political power from father to son in undemocratic ways is a clear demonstration of how our politicians conceive of their leadership.

In verse 15 Jeremiah compares Jehoiakim with his father King Josiah, the good king of Judah. We can imagine Jeremiah asking Josiah the same question: "Why do you reign, Josiah?" His answer would be: "I reign to do the will of God; that is by doing justice and righteousness, and by pleading the cause of the poor and the needy." For Josiah, to reign meant to serve Yahweh and his people and to abide by the covenant.

A Kenyan proverb says: "To lead is not to run roughshod over people." But for Jehoiakim, leading meant serving himself and being served by the people. Jeremiah declares in the second part of verse 16 that what Josiah did proved he knew Yahweh: "Is not this to know me?" In other words, the deeds of each of the two kings were dependent on whether they knew the true source of their leadership or not. Josiah knew God; he knew that to reign was to serve Yahweh. As a result, he used his power properly by defending the cause of the powerless.

This was God's will for the covenant-king. But in verse 17, the prophet tells us that as a result of not knowing Yahweh, Jehoiakim had his eyes and heart set only on dishonest gain, shedding innocent blood, and practising oppression and extortion. It is important to briefly analyse each of the three accusations.

First, the king is accused of having his eyes and heart set on dishonest gain. Dishonest gain is the translation of the word *beṣaʻ* which means gain or bribe (and the pursuit of gain through greed). It is used in conjunction with the perversion of justice. In this sense, the gain is to be understood as unjust (Prov 28:16; Hab 2:9), selfish (Ps 119:36; Prov 15:27; Jer 6:13), or even sinful (Isa 57:17).[29] God made it clear that the Israelite king or any other leader must first of all be one who shows righteousness and who judges justly (Exod 18:13–27).

The book of Samuel indicates that the people of Israel revolted against the sons of Samuel because their heart turned aside after gain (1 Sam 8:3). McCann rightly notes that turning aside after gain is the opposite of walking in the way of righteousness, according to the will of Yahweh (Ps 119:36; Isa 33:15; 56:11; 57:17; Jer 8:10).[30] The person who walks in their own way has little regard for God or for fellow humans. This was certainly the case of Jehoiakim, whom the prophet contrasts with Josiah the godly king who knew Yahweh and who, consequently, did not pursue unjust gain.

Second, Jehoiakim's heart and eyes were on shedding innocent blood. The word for blood (*dam*) used in this passage refers to bloodshed in the context of murder or warfare. By using this word, the prophet may intend to show that obsession and warped ambition drove Jehoiakim to repressive and cruel actions. Actually, cruelty and obsession with power always go together. Those who dare to oppose dictators know their fate well. For example, those who oppose President Paul Kagame of Rwanda endure the politics of silence, fear, and terror. Clive Gabay and Sophie Harman of the University of London cite two examples: The tortured body of André Kagwa Rwiseka, vice-chairman of the Democratic Green Party and a vocal opponent of Paul Kagame's regime, was found in a marsh outside Butare a month before the 2010 elections; Patrick Karegeya, Kagame's former intelligence chief turned dissident and exile, was found murdered in his hotel in South Africa. The authors conclude that Rwanda remains an unsafe place for vocal opponents of Kagame's regime.[31] Rwanda

---

29. J. Clinton McCann Jr., בצע, in *NIDOTTE*, 1:695.

30. J. Clinton McCann Jr., בצע, in *NIDOTTE*, 1:696.

31. Clive Gabay and Sophie Harman, "Rwanda: The Politics of Success, Silence and Genocide Leverage," http://www.qmul.ac.uk/media/news/items/ hss/128742.html.

may indeed at present be the most unsafe country in Africa as far as political cruelty is concerned, but it is wrong to think that it is the only one.

Third, Jehoiakim is accused of practising oppression and extortion. The word *hā'ōšeq* in this sentence means "to oppress," "to wrong," or "to extort." When related to Israel, the word frequently describes various forms of social injustice by which the rich oppressed the poor in Israel. As we have already mentioned, the responsibility of the king was to protect the oppressed from their oppressors; but when the king himself, as in this case, practices the oppression, the oppressed become helpless. This is why the Bible is clear that the act of oppression of the poor is an act against God himself (Prov 14:31).

The Right Use of Power: Josiah (vv. 15b–16)

Jeremiah takes King Josiah as the model of a good leader and indicates that if Jehoiakim wants a predecessor to emulate, he can try his father. The prophet briefly enumerates the elements that constitute the right leadership of Josiah: he ate and drank, he did justice and righteousness, and he pleaded the cause of the poor and the needy.

The exact implication of the first two verbs (to eat and drink) is difficult to understand and scholars interpret the passage in different ways. For Cornill, Bright and Thompson, it means that Josiah lived well and still managed to adhere to the covenant. According to Duhm and Condamin, the passage means that Josiah lived simply and was concerned rather to adhere to the covenant. Volz thinks that what the passage underlines is the juxtaposition of eating, drinking and doing justice; in other words, Josiah accepted the responsibility of being the head of his people in both his daily habits and in the royal maintenance of the covenant.[32] The passage may also mean that doing what was socially equitable and desiring to maintain it came as easily to Josiah as the natural activities of eating and drinking.[33] Finally, Feinberg says that "he (Josiah) enjoyed the normal comforts of life but never made ostentation his goal. He knew how to enjoy life without extorting or oppressing his people. He was no ascetic but did not make it his ambition to rival Solomon in building."[34]

What is clear in all these interpretations is that there is a relationship between eating and drinking on the one hand and doing justice on the other. I understand eating and drinking as representing the comfort in which the king

---

32. Holladay, *Jeremiah 1*, 596.
33. McKane, *Jeremiah 1–25*, 530.
34. Feinberg, *Jeremiah*, 157.

lived. When this comfort is exaggerated, it brings suffering and poverty on the people who produce (or are forced to produce) it for their king. In other words, the king's comfort does not exist in a vacuum, it has to originate somewhere (normally from the common people). Thus, it is clear that in Jeremiah 22:15b, the prophet is contrasting the well-balanced life of the "good king" and that of Jehoiakim who lived too sumptuously at the expense of the common people. In other words, Josiah had enough food and drink (not too much) that did not affect the economic condition of the people of the land because he cared both for his palace (as a king) and for his subjects. This is probably what eating, drinking, and at the same time, doing justice (*mišpāṭ*) and "righteousness" (*ṣĕdāqâ*) mean.

The result of eating and drinking and at the same time doing justice and righteousness is that "it was well" or "it went well." Holladay suggests that the word "well" must be construed as a perfect verb "it went well," and that it has the most general application, suggesting not only that life was "pleasing" to Josiah in eating and drinking but that things went well for him as head of the covenant people.[35] This is clearly the fulfilment of the promise given in Jeremiah 22:4 that the result of the king's obedience to the law would be continued blessings on the monarch. It is also a reminder of the result of the king's obedience to the six limitations on Israelite monarchs in Deuteronomy 17. "It was well with him" means that the king was blessed by Yahweh because his reign was guided by the law.

In verse 16, the prophet states that doing justice and righteousness concretely involves pleading the cause of the poor and the needy. In the light of the beginning of the monarchy and its development in Israel, the primary task of the covenant-king was, above all else, to maintain justice within the community and justice with God. The so-called "royal psalms" contain teachings about the protection of the powerless. For example, Psalm 72:1, 2, 4, 12 suggests that the king was commissioned to judge the people in righteousness, and above all, to be the advocate for and supporter of the weak and oppressed. This is what Josiah did, according to Jeremiah. The result was that "it was well," which is repeated twice in the passage. Many commentators rightly notice the difference between "it was well for him" in verse 15, and "it was well" in verse 16. Craigie, Kelley and Drinkard write that "the lack of the prepositional phrase 'to him' following 'good' ["it was well" in verse 15] may indicate a broader scope for good. Perhaps the implication is that the whole nation enjoyed the good brought about by the justice and righteousness of

---

35. Holladay, *Jeremiah 1*, 596.

the king."³⁶ This also remind us of the words of Psalm 72:3 which show the life of the Israelite nation under a righteous king. Commenting on this psalm, Kraus writes,

> Life, bounteous harvest, good fortune and blessing in boundless measure – these are the expectations connected with Yahweh's presence with his king, and they are not to be thought of as due to the immanent power of a "divine monarchy." Thus the petitions and hopes that look toward שלום (shalom), in the most comprehensive sense of the word, are closely connected with the monarchy in Jerusalem.³⁷

At the end of verse 16, Yahweh, through his prophet, asks a rhetorical question: "Is not that to know me?" This is the central theme of the chapter, if not of the whole book of Jeremiah, or even in the entire prophetic corpus. How well we know Yahweh determines how we live or, in the case of the king, how well he knows God determines how he leads his country. According to Jeremiah, helping the poor, the needy and doing justice are dependent on the king's relationship with God. But what is to know Yahweh? Craigie, Kelley and Drinkard rightly state that "the verb *yad* 'to know' implies much more than knowledge in the sense of information. It implies relationship, to know Yahweh is to have a relationship with him . . . that is based on covenant and keeping covenant."³⁸ Botterweck states that knowing Yahweh refers to a practical, religio-ethical relationship.³⁹ In his commentary on Hosea 4:1, McComskey says

> the knowledge of God, of which Hosea speaks in this verse, is not theological knowledge only, but knowledge of Yahweh's directive will. The nation is to be destroyed for the lack of this knowledge (Hos 4:6). The fact that the knowledge of God is in parallel with *ḥesed* (lovingkindness) in Hosea 6:6 indicates that knowledge of God involves an understanding of the ethical sphere in which God's people must live if they have to experience Yahweh's love and bounty.⁴⁰

---

36. Craigie, Kelley and Drinkard, *Jeremiah*, 311.
37. Hans-Joachim Kraus, *Theology of the Psalms*, trans. Keith Crim (Minneapolis, MN: Fortress, 1992), 120.
38. Craigie, Kelley and Drinkard, *Jeremiah*, 311.
39. Botterweck, ידע, in *TDOTT*, 5:469.
40. Thomas McComiskey, "Hosea," in Thomas E. McComiskey (ed.), *An Exegetical & Expository Commentary: The Minor Prophets* (Grand Rapids, MI: Baker, 1992), 56.

The opposite is that leaders who do not know Yahweh sin against him; they are ungodly, treacherous, oppressors, and murderers. It becomes clear, therefore, that Josiah did justice and righteousness because he knew Yahweh; that is, he properly understood his commission as a covenant-king to lead the covenant people. The result was that it went well or, to use the language of the Psalter, there was *shalom* both for the king and for the nation. In Jeremiah 22:16, the prophet is demonstrating what can happen when Yahweh's presence is with the king as a result of obedience to the covenant. In fact, 2 Kings 23:25 speaks of Josiah's obedience as the best example of kingship in Israel. The text reads: "Neither before nor after Josiah was there a king like him who turned to the LORD as he did – with all his heart and with all his soul and with all his strength, in accordance with all the Law of Moses" (NIV).

The book of 2 Kings (22:1–23:30) contains many passages testifying to King Josiah's good leadership, with the climax of his reign being the renewal of the covenant between the people of Judah and Yahweh (23:3–20). This renewal reaches its climax with the celebration of the Passover. Hobbs has convincingly demonstrated that it is not right to think that there was no Passover celebration before Josiah's reformation, but the significance of Josiah's Passover was that it was celebrated according to the demands of the Book of the Law that was found in the temple.[41]

In terms of Samuel's warning (1 Sam 8:1–18), Josiah demonstrated that he was not an oppressor who would take ("taking" was the key word in Samuel's warning) his people's properties as other kings did. On the contrary, Josiah and his officials are described as the ones who gave or contributed to the people's welfare for the good celebration of Passover. This was exceptional in the entire history of Israel. 2 Chronicles 35:7–10 reads:

> Josiah *provided* for all the lay people who were there a total of thirty thousand lambs and goats for the Passover offerings, and also three thousand cattle – all from the king's own possessions. His officials also *contributed voluntarily* to the people and the priests and Levites. Hilkiah, Zechariah and Jehiel, the officials in charge of God's temple, *gave* the priests twenty-six hundred Passover offerings and three hundred cattle. Also Konaniah along with Shemaiah and Nethanel, his brothers, and Hashabiah, Jeiel and Jozabad, the leaders of the Levites, *provided* five thousand

---

41. T. R. Hobbs, *2 Kings*, vol. 13, Word Biblical Commentary (Nashville, TN: Thomas Nelson, 1986), 337.

Passover offerings and five hundred head of cattle for the Levites. The service was arranged and the priests stood in their places with the Levites in their divisions as the king had ordered. (NIV emphasis added)

Most of the kings mentioned in the Bible are described as tyrants, oppressors (robbers) of the poor (Isa 58:3; Jer 6:6; 2 Kgs 21:16; Ezek 22:29), and perverters of justice (Amos 5:7–13; Isa 3:12–15). But Josiah and his officials are seen here as helpers of poor people, most of whom were probably unable to afford animals for sacrifices at the Passover. To use Samuel's language, Josiah and his officials were "givers," not "takers." Moreover, the text states that the officials "contributed voluntarily," that is without being forced to give by the king, by circumstance, or for any political reason. In other words, they feared Yahweh whom they had come to know and whom they were willing to serve. Once more, from this passage, we can understand why Jeremiah emphasized that it went well for King Josiah and for the whole nation, and that there was no king like him in Israel.

In conclusion, it is right to say that Josiah understood his authority or power in the context of the covenant; that is as a king who had to reign strictly under the power of God by following the limitations imposed upon the Israelite monarchy.

Judgement on Jehoiakim (vv. 18–19)

The judgement on King Jehoiakim is introduced by the preposition "therefore" (*lākēn*), which connects the accusations in verses 13–17 with the judgement pronounced in verses 18–19. This connection implies that the truthfulness of the accusations is the reason for the judgement. The formula, "Thus says Yahweh" follows immediately after the transitional word to assure an awareness that the judgement is not being spoken by a mere messenger but is from the one who sent the messenger: Yahweh himself.[42]

Another important element that appears at the beginning of the judgement is the identification of the one who is being accused and judged: "Jehoiakim, the son of Josiah, king of Judah." From verse 13 to 17, the prophet has been using different pronouns to identify Jehoiakim.[43] But in verse 18, he calls him by name "to make unmistakable the one to whom the harsh judgement is

---

42. Craigie, Kelley and Drinkard, *Jeremiah 1–25*, 312.

43. In verse 13, Jeremiah uses two pronouns: "him" and "who" to identify Jehoiakim. In verse 14, he is identified by "who," "I" and "me." In verse 15 and 17, the king is addressed as "you."

spoken."[44] The judgement itself concerns his death and it has two aspects: he will die without being mourned and he will be given the burial of a donkey.

The first judgement is that Jehoiakim's death will not be mourned. According to E. Jacob, at that time lamentation and other funerary rites were as imperative a duty as burial, and their absence was considered a grave misfortune.[45] The sentence "They will not lament for him," repeated twice in the same verse, shows the emphasis the prophet is putting on the dishonour of the king at his death because of his heavy-handed oppression. Jehoiakim, who was thinking of himself as the greatest and the best man in the land, will die without honour. There is another contrast between Josiah and his son at this level. In 2 Chronicles 35:24b–25, it is written that all Judah and Jerusalem mourned for Josiah, that Jeremiah uttered a lament for him, and that all the male and female singers commemorated him in the laments.

Mourning is also an important ritual in African culture, maybe the most important, because Africans respect and fear death and will set aside other matters including conflict to mourn the departed, give support to the bereaved, and help the affected family to cope with their loss. Ceremonies associated with mourning also offer a unique opportunity for the family to come together and find solutions to challenges and issues affecting them. Mourning periods vary across cultures and also depend on whether the person who died was a child, an adult or a leader. In the modern Africa, with the imposing presence of Christianity, when death is announced, church leaders, neighbours, and the community at large set aside their activities to reach out to the affected family. The body is sometimes moved to the local church until the time of the burial. If the burial cannot take place on the same day, a wake is organized during which preaching and singing go on until the burial. After the burial, close relatives stay at the home for least one more day. One cannot conceive of death in Africa without family and friends gathering to mourn the departed, except in cases of mass killing during war or an epidemic.

The second judgement is that Jehoiakim will have the burial of a donkey (v. 19). How was a donkey buried? In Israel, according to Charles H. Dyer, when a donkey died in the city, it was simply dragged away from the spot where it died and thrown outside the gates,[46] and then dumped in a field to become prey for dogs and vultures. Burial, however, was the norm for humans from

---

44. Craigie, Kelley and Drinkard, *Jeremiah 1–25*, 312.
45. E. Jacob, "Mourning," in *IDB*, 3:452.
46. Charles H. Dyer, "Jeremiah," in John F. Walvoord and Roy B. Zuck (eds.), *The Bible Knowledge Commentary: Old Testament* (Colorado Springs, CO: Chariot Victor, 1985), 1157.

the days of the earliest patriarchs onwards (Gen 23:4; 25:9; Deut 10:6; 34:6), and for a corpse to remain unburied or to be exhumed subsequent to burial, and thus become food for beasts of prey as announced by Jeremiah, was the climax of indignity or judgement.[47] In Jehoiakim's case, it is important to note the contrast between his grandiose way of life and his dishonourable death as predicted by the prophet.[48] And it seems that this is the point the prophet is trying to emphasize in this passage.

In traditional Africa, correct burial ensured that the deceased was put to rest respectfully, and that their spirit would travel peacefully to take their place in the new community of the living dead. It was believed that if the deceased was not buried appropriately, their ghost would be unable to cross the "border" between the living and the living dead. The ghost would wander in the land of the living and might cause harm. In Africa, there are many stories of people encountering the deceased near rivers, forests, and farms, etc.

The belief in the need to hold rituals to ensure the dead have a smooth transition to the next world is still commonplace. It can be seen even among Christians who organize prayer ceremonies for the deceased many days or years after their death, even though this practice is forbidden by most churches. Even though it is not clearly explained, the reason for these ceremonies or prayers is to assure that the deceased are resting in peace and are not "unhappy." These beliefs and practices show the high value Africans place on mourning and burial rituals, especially when the deceased had a leadership position and responsibilities in the community.

---

47. J. Barton Payne, "Burial," in *ISBE*, 1:556.

48. The question of how Jehoiakim died, and therefore, how the curse came to pass is still dividing scholars. The problem is that 2 Kings 24:6 states that Jehoiakim slept with his fathers, and nothing is said on how he was buried. The formula, "he slept with his fathers," can be said to have been used for normal burial. There is a further prediction in Jeremiah 36:30 that the corpse of Jehoiakim would lie unburied. Holladay (*Jeremiah 1*, 598) quotes Weiser who suggests that the verse should be taken to mean that Nebuchadrezzar, at the conquest of Jerusalem, had the grave of his faithless vassal violated. But Holladay disagrees saying that disinterment is not at issue here, and that Jeremiah speaks of lack of burial. Unfortunately, Holladay's solution to the issue poses a more difficult problem; he says that "in any event the power of the present verse is in its utterance, not in its literal fulfilment." To me, the suggestion given by S. J. Schultz ("Jehoiakim," in *ISBE*, 2:977) is a more acceptable explanation. For him, since neither of the historical accounts reports the circumstances of Jehoiakim's death, nor mentions even his burial, the conclusion that this defiant king was killed in battle seems warranted. His conclusion is that in wartime, it was impossible to provide an honourable burial. I agree with this argument as I have already stated that it is impossible, even in the African context, for there to be normal mourning and burial for those who die in mass killing in wars [as might have happened for a defeated king and his army] or from epidemic diseases. That war would prevent people from mourning and burying a king normally is understandable. It is also difficult to know how the king was treated by the enemy before being killed.

History repeats itself in different ways. While it is nearly impossible for us to know how the corrupt King Jehoiakim's life ended, we know how the lives of many dictators in Africa end. President Mobutu died in exile in Rabat, far from his palaces and wealth in DR Congo and far from the people who applauded him for most of his life. In fact, there is a similarity between how Mobutu died without honour and the prophet's prediction of Jehoiakim's end:

> In September 1997, less than four months after fleeing Kinshasa, Mobutu died. Far from his beloved forests and vast river, a sick leopard fading away in the arid dryness of Morocco, he had lived just long enough to see his achievements discredited, his reputation besmirched, his name vilified. There was a quiet funeral in Rabat's Christian cemetery. Ngbanda, who flew in for the event, was amid the group of former aides, personal doctors and bodyguards who stood at the grave after the family had withdrawn. Stricken by a sense of collective guilt, military and civilian alike sobbed aloud, begging their late master for forgiveness.[49]

Michela Wrong makes the following comment on Mobutu's end:

> Nothing could have been more merciless than this interment in exile. In an African society only recently touched by urbanization, where the spirits of the dead vie with the living for respect, burial outside the land of one's ancestors is worse than unnatural. For the man who had created the very nation of Zaire, with all its warts and blemishes, it could never constitute a laying to rest.[50]

Josiah, Jehoiakim and Mobutu are perfect examples of the real and contrasting consequences of good and bad leadership. Yahweh exalts those who use power to serve the people. They may not suffer the burial of donkeys like Jehoiakim or Mobutu. Take the example of South Africa's Nelson Mandela, a leader who sacrificed his life to serve the nation. His funeral on 15 December 2015 after ten days of national mourning was very unlike Mobutu's, as we can gather from a CNN report:

> Before making their way to the grave site, mourners attended a service in a tent set up at the family compound. They wept, sang and danced in what has become a familiar celebration of his life. Mandela's coffin, draped in his country's flag, lay atop black and

---

49. Wrong, *In the Footsteps of Mr Kurtz*, 280.
50. Wrong, 280.

white cattle skins in front of a crescent of 95 candles, each marking a year of his life.

As the national anthem "Nkosi Sikelel' iAfrika" or "God Bless Africa" drifted over the village, a giant picture of Mandela looked down with a smile. Mourners placed their fists on their chests, some with tears streaming down their faces. "Today marks the end of an extraordinary journey that began 95 years ago," Zuma said during the ceremony. "It is the end of 95 glorious years of a freedom fighter . . . a beacon of hope to all those fighting for a just and equitable world order."

Then president thanked Mandela's family for sharing him with the world and said his memory will live on: "We shall not say goodbye, for you are not gone," Zuma said. "You'll live forever in our hearts and minds." About 4,500 people gathered in the tent.[51]

If there is one important lesson we can learn from both Jehoiakim and Mobutu's deaths, it is that Yahweh judges the rulers who misuse the position and power given to them. God is not dead in Africa as many of our leaders think. He has the last word in every human life. African presidents and political leaders have a clear choice to make. They might not have read the story of King Josiah and his son, but they all know the two representative African stories, the story of Mobutu and Mandela, and they now know to what extravagance, corruption and dictatorship ultimately lead.

Conclusion

According to Jeremiah, Israel's social and political ordering was authorized by Yahweh's sovereignty through his law and was not a reflection of the will of political rulers. Thus, and this is important for any society, the power of the state as the creation of Yahweh is culturally bound to the norms of the word of God. In this way, any ruler reigns not above the Creator and his law but under the sovereignty of Yahweh.[52] Therefore, it is important that every king/president or leader recognizes that the power they possess has been delegated to them by the one who has absolute power, Yahweh, and that they must use

---

51. Faith Karimi and Marie-Louise Gumuchian, "Nelson Mandela Buried, Ending Journey that Transformed South Africa," *CNN*, 15 December 2013, http://www.cnn.com/2013/12/15/ world/africa/nelson-mandela-qunu-funeral/.

52. See Stuart Fowler, *The State in the Light of the Scripture* (Potchefstroom: Potchefstroom University, 1988), 10.

it according to his will. This is what Josiah did and what both Jehoiakim and Mobutu failed to do.

Africa needs its own prophets to teach this truth. And this is the responsibility of the church. The church should not only teach, but also live in a way that models to others the reality of the true power that lies beyond what we see in the world. For the church to fulfil this duty, it must first deal with the much criticized abuse of power within its leadership and members.

We must also evaluate the concept of democracy, which is presented as the cure for bad governance and the solution to Africa's political and leadership problems. As previously noted in chapter 7, my view is that democracy as is practised in the West is not necessarily the solution to African problems because it often represents yet another imposition of Western experience and culture on African societies. The idea of democracy should not be accepted without reflection. Democracy sometimes produces overzealous populist leaders who do not always deliver the many things they promise during their campaigns. We all know that "hope and change we can believe in," "stronger together," "making America great again," etc. are just slogans. In the name of democracy, many African countries have been wasting a lot of money organizing fake elections whose results are known before the election is held. India, despite being called the largest democracy in the world, still suffers from widespread poverty, a high rate of illiteracy, social and economic disparity, and a deep-rooted culture of political corruption. When people do not see improvements in leadership, they lose confidence in democracy. There is strong malaise that is expressed in complaints and low voter turnout in some democratic countries.

Another problem with democracy is that it sometimes gives too much freedom, which can produce serious moral decay. For example, a democracy that focuses on exposing the sins of the leaders publicly and parading them in the media begging for pardon is not a model that Africans should copy. A democracy that allows people to demonstrate half-naked in the streets to defend their right to be gay, to carry out abortions, or their beliefs in racial supremacy should not be accepted in Africa. I understand democracy as a society in which people freely sustain a social order in which there is justice, compassion, respect for human dignity, and reverence for the sanctity of life. In other words, in democratic nations, there should always be a tension between freedom and order. Freedom without limits creates chaos. This also means that a free society is a moral achievement and that it should be sustained by strong training in character.

Democracy should be redefined and reconceived as a system for putting in place right and godly leadership and promoting stability in leadership, rather than as a system where leaders compete to win the most votes and heap insults on their opponents, leaving societies more divided than before and the citizens angry and fearful, as we have seen happen in recent elections in the USA. There is need to invent a new method of governance in Africa that is rooted in our good social mores and inspired by God's word, without which the democratic processes that we have embraced without much reflection will continue to be a fiasco. This kind of democracy will need to avoid the temptation of creating leaders who are puppets of foreign powers, with their legitimacy defined by people outside the continent. The embodiment of a good leader in the Bible is one who fears God, who is humble, and who is aware that his or her position is to be used to serve the nation. True democracy should help our leaders to work for a strong morality, strong family and social values, justice for the poor, and a strong sense of responsibility.

8

Weak Leadership and the Dismantling of Judah

Jeremiah 24:4–7

⁴Then the word of Yahweh came to me saying: ⁵"Thus says Yahweh, the God of Israel: Like these good figs, so I will consider as good the exiles from Judah, whom I have sent away from this place to the land of Chaldeans. ⁶And I will set my eyes upon them for good, and I will bring them back to this land. I will build them up, and not tear them down; I will plant them, not uproot them. ⁷I will give them a heart to know me because I am Yahweh; and they will be my people and I will be their God, for they will return to me with their whole heart."

Historical and Literary Context

There are two opposing scholarly positions concerning the authenticity of Jeremiah 24:4–7. Some, like R. P. Carroll, regard it as belonging to a late, second edition of Deuteronomy written during and after the Babylonian exile. They argue that the passage has a close relationship with Deuteronomy 30:1–10 and represents an attitude that would have been dominant at a later time, when only the Jews who had gone into exile in Babylon and later returned to their land were regarded as true Israelites.[1] Others like Thomas M. Raitt maintain that this text is indisputably by Jeremiah. He links it with what he calls six pivotal prose oracles of deliverance (24:4-7; 29:4-7, 10-14; 31:31-34; 32:6-15, 36-41, 42-44; 33:6-9) and argues that, first, these passages taken together represent the mind of Jeremiah concerning Judah's future after it has gone into exile; second, there is a strong probability that they are from a single source; and third, this source is Jeremiah and his first circle of faithful disciples.[2]

At this point, I will respond only to the first argument (related to the close relationship of this passage with Deuteronomy 30:1-10) of those who claim that the passage is not by Jeremiah, since the second (the fact that the passage contains an attitude that would have been dominant at later times) will be dealt with in the rest of this chapter. As far as the relationship between Jeremiah 24:4-7 and Deuteronomy 30:1-10 is concerned, my understanding is that while there are many similarities between these texts, there are also significant differences between them. For example, in Deuteronomy 30:1-2, Yahweh's redemption is strictly conditional on the repentance of the people, while in Jeremiah 24:4-7, the repentance (expressed by the verb "return") comes only at the end, after Yahweh has already promised to restore the people to their land, after they have rebuilt it, and after he has given them a heart to know him. In other words, the stress on repentance in Deuteronomy is overshadowed by the divine mercy in Jeremiah. And this is theologically very important. For this reason, I adopt the more conservative view that this passage comes from the prophet himself.[3]

Concerning the date of this oracle, many scholars argue that 24:4-7 is to be located during the reign of Zedekiah, after the Babylonians deported Jehoiakin and a good number of the people of Judah in 596 BC, as Jeremiah 24:1 clearly indicates. This is the position adopted in the present interpretation.

---

1. Other scholars give other reasons for rejecting this passage as coming from Jeremiah. For example, Hyatt (*The Deuteronomic Edition of Jeremiah*, 84) rejects the contrasting treatment of the exiles (promised deliverance in vv. 5-7), and those who escaped the deportation (promised severe judgement in vv. 8-10). For Hyatt, it is impossible to think of the deportees as good people and those who remained in the land as bad.

2. Raitt, *A Theology of Exile: Judgment/Deliverance in Jeremiah and Ezekiel* (Philadelphia, PA: Fortress, 1977), 112.

3. See also J. G. McConville, *Judgment and Promise: An Interpretation of the Book of Jeremiah* (Leicester, UK: Apollos, 1993), 11-26.

Structure

The internal structure of chapter 24 is clear. Holladay describes the passage as "a more elaborate example of a vision report than either 1:11–12 or 1:13–16."[4] It begins with the announcement of the vision: v. 1a ("Yahweh showed me"), followed by a transition: v. 1b ("and behold"). Then comes the vision sequence (1c–10):

- The image (vv. 1d–2 [two baskets of figs in front of the temple])
- Yahweh's question to the prophet (v. 3a)
- The prophet's answer (v. 3b)
- Yahweh's oracle (vv. 4–10)
- Introduction to the oracle (v. 4)
- The meaning of good figs (vv. 5–7)
- The meaning of bad figs (vv. 8–10)

The Vision

Since this interpretation will only deal with the last part of the vision, it is important to give a summary of the whole vision. In verses 1–3, Jeremiah reports a vision he received from Yahweh. The time of the vision is clearly indicated in verse 1. It was immediately "after Jehoiachin son of Jehoiakim king of Judah and the officials, the skilled workers and the artisans of Judah were carried into exile from Jerusalem to Babylon by Nebuchadrezzar king of Babylon" (NIV). This was during the 597 BC Babylonian invasion. In the vision, Yahweh showed his prophet two baskets in front of the temple that were filled with figs. One basket had good figs, and the other bad figs, so bad that they could not be eaten. Yahweh then gives the interpretation of the vision, telling his prophet that the good figs represent the people of Judah who had just been exiled to Babylon, implying that those who remained in Jerusalem were the bad figs.

Verse 4 serves as a link between the details of the vision in verses 1–3 and its interpretation in verses 5–10. Craigie, Kelley and Drinkard note that the passage is similar to 16:1 and that it serves "to move from the vision to the oracle interpreting that vision."[5]

---

4. Holladay, *Jeremiah 1*, 656.
5. Craigie, Kelley and Drinkard, *Jeremiah 1-25*, 358.

Good and Bad Figs (vv. 5–7)

This section opens with an ordinary messenger formula: "Thus says Yahweh, the God of Israel." Many commentators consider this formula inapposite, and Holladay suggests that it should be deleted.[6] Their argument is that in this passage, Yahweh is disclosing his will to the prophet through a private visionary experience for the benefit of the prophet alone, "and not a message which he is charged to communicate."[7] In other words, a messenger formula usually introduces Yahweh's message to the people (through the prophet) but not a private message to a prophet like in this text.

This is a misunderstanding of the passage. The prophet is first of all an instrument for transmitting Yahweh's will to the people, and as such it is hard to think that the whole message in this passage was simply given for his own edification. The historical context of this passage suggests that the vision and the oracle in chapter 24 are directed to the last king of Judah (Zedekiah) and his people through the prophet. So I see no reason why the opening formula should be removed.

The message introduced by this messenger formula begins in verse 5b. It explains the two kinds of figs – very good figs and very bad figs – seen in the vision recorded in verses 1–3. Here we will be concerned with the very good figs, referred to in verse 5 simply as "good figs" (vv. 5b–7). However, the analysis will also pay attention to the bad figs since one cannot understand what the prophet says about the good figs without knowing what he thinks of the bad ones. The following questions will guide this analysis: Who are the good (and bad) figs? Why are they good (and others bad)? What is Yahweh's plan for the good figs? What does he think about the bad ones? And why? Finally, what lessons can we learn in Africa from this vision?

Our first concern is in the identity of the good figs. Verse 5b says that they are the exiles from Judah, whom Yahweh has sent away to the land of the Chaldeans. Almost all commentators agree that this passage as referring to the first deportation of 597 BC. The book of 2 Kings 24:8–17 records that after the death of Jehoiakim, his eighteen-year-old son, Jehoiakin became king over Judah, and that he reigned for only three months before being deported by Nebuchadrezzar, king of Babylon. The queen mother, Jehoiakin's advisers, and other nobles and officials were also deported with the young king. Jeremiah 24:1 adds that Judah's skilled workers and artisans were also among the deportees. The rationale behind this deportation was probably both economic

---

6. Holladay, *Jeremiah 1*, 658.
7. McKane, *Jeremiah 1–25*, 608.

and political. Economically, the Babylonian king wanted to take advantage of the skills of the Judeans who would now be under his direct control. Politically, he may have hoped that the removal of the upper echelons of Judean society would bring an end to the rebellions in Judah against Babylon.

The second issue concerns the meaning of this prophecy. In other words, why should deported Judeans be called good and those left in the country be labelled as bad? Many Jeremiah scholars have recognized that this statement was issued to correct the misunderstanding of the people left in Jerusalem following the exile of 597 BC. They were thinking of "themselves as the ones blessed and the exiles as the ones under judgement."[8] This wrong theology was being promoted by false prophets who claimed that with the deportation of Jehoiakin, Yahweh's anger with the nation was over and consequently, the country was safe. False prophets would also have reminded the people of Judah of Yahweh's miraculous deliverance from the threat of Sennacherib king of Assyria during the time of King Hezekiah (Isa 36–37).[9]

To claim that Yahweh's anger against Judah was over and that he would soon deliver his nation from their enemies was actually another form of rebellion against Babylon. Who, then, were these people rebelling against the king of Babylon since we know that one of the goals of the deportation was to quell revolt in Jerusalem, and that it was uncommon for poor people (such as those who remained in Jerusalem after the first deportation) to mount a rebellion against a powerful foreign king?

Leon Wood argues that not all the members of the upper class were taken into exile. Many of them escaped when Jehoiakin was being taken away. This is how he summarizes the situation in Jerusalem after the 597 BC deportation and during the reign of Zedekiah:

> A strong anti-Babylonian group in Jerusalem brought pressure for the revolt and urged Zedekiah to look again to Egypt for help. A new coalition was being formed of Edom, Ammon, and Phoenicia (Jer 27:1b–3); and this Jerusalem group wished Judah to join. False prophets aided their cause in declaring that God had already broken the yoke of Babylon and that within two years Judah's captives would return home to Jerusalem (Jer 28:2–4). In opposition, Jeremiah denounced this manner of speaking, declaring it false and urging continued acceptance of Babylonian

---

8. Craigie, Kelley and Drinkard, *Jeremiah 1–25*, 358.

9. Wisser, *Jérémie, Critique de la Vie Sociale*, 228. This is also Brueggemann's reading of the text (*Commentary on Jeremiah*, 218).

lordship (Jer 27:1–22). Two other developments outside Judah helped fan revolutionary flames in Zedekiah's fourth year: Psammetichus II succeeded Necho in Egypt, and a minor rebellion was staged in Babylon itself.[10]

National Crisis and the Role of the Leader

Zedekiah, the new king, was among the elites who were actively trying to rebel against Babylon. He was the son of Josiah, one of the greatest leaders in Judah's history, who had become king at a time when the nation was on the brink of destruction but had managed to turn it around to become a strong nation. The secret of his success was the fear of Yahweh. He actually turned the whole nation back to the fear of Yahweh, the God of the covenant.

But Zedekiah was not like this father. He was a weak and fearful leader who was guided by the populace instead of being led by the stipulations of the covenant. He was unable to listen to Yahweh and to take the decisions that would have saved Judah.

Jeremiah presents him as a weak and fearful leader. For example, when Jeremiah advised him to surrender to the Babylonians in order to save himself and the city, he said that he was afraid of the Jews who had already surrendered to the Babylonians (Jer 38:19). These were probably Zedekiah's fellow citizens who listened to Jeremiah's message and decided to obey Yahweh's word. It is important to remember that at this time Jeremiah was urging the inhabitants of Jerusalem, including the king and his officials, to stop fighting against Babylon and surrender to Nebuchadrezzar. Zedekiah and other pro-Egyptian leaders in Jerusalem had likely issued threats against those who would surrender to the enemy. Those who did surrender, did so at their own risk. Now Zedekiah feared that if he gave himself up, the king of Babylon would hand him to these people who would mock him for doing the same thing he had forbidden them to do.

Earlier, after Jeremiah had announced harsh judgement on those still remaining in the city, the princes of Jerusalem went to see Zedekiah and said to him: "This man [Jeremiah] should be put to death. He is discouraging the soldiers who are left in the city, as well as all the people, by the things he is saying to them. This man is not seeking the good of these people but their ruin" (Jer 38:4 NIV). Zedekiah, who had just consulted the prophet privately, knew that Jeremiah was speaking Yahweh's will for the nation (Jer 37:17). Yet

---

10. Leon Wood, *A Survey of Israel's History* (London: Pickering & Inglis, 1970), 375.

he lacked the courage to oppose his evil officials. In chapter 38:5, he tells them, "He is in your hands... The king can do nothing to oppose you" (NIV), a statement that makes it clear that the real power in Jerusalem was with these officials who had little respect for their king. Jeremiah was subsequently thrown into a cistern.

What is clear is that the end of Judah as a nation was largely the result of poor leadership. Zedekiah, the last king of Judah, was a weak and confused leader with no real power. His officials influenced him to make bad choices, to go against Jeremiah's prophecy, and therefore against Yahweh's will. We can conclude that Zedekiah's actions led to a power vacuum in Jerusalem that precipitated a national crisis that was to end in the overthrow of Judah. Is there any lesson Africa can learn from this kind of leadership?

Power Vacuums in African Leadership
The Akazu and the Rwandan genocide

The year 1991 saw the birth of an unofficial organization in Rwanda called *Akazu* or "little house." It was a network of extremists whose architect was President Habyarimana's wife, Agathe. The masterminds of this network were herself, her brothers, half-brothers, and some close clan and political allies. It exercised a strong influence over the president even though he often said he was not part of it and did not agree with some of its ideas. After he reluctantly agreed to implement the Arusha Peace Accord with the Rwanda Patriotic Front (RPF) in 1993 and 1994 under African and international pressure, the Akazu became increasingly violent and suspicious, deeply distracting the president from guiding the nation in a time of crisis. Members of the Akazu feared losing their influence because Habyarimana would not have total control of the nation after sharing power with the Tutsi and other Hutu who were not part of their network. This encouraged members of Akazu to join forces with those who were promoting the extremist Hutu Power ideology. Many people believe that the seeds of the Rwandan genocide were sown by the hardening of the Akazu's point of view and their embrace of Hutu Power.

The full story of Rwandan genocide is not yet known among scholars, politicians and researchers, and the truth must continue to wait. However, there can be no doubt that Habyarimana was under increasing pressure from the international community, the RPF, his own officials, and his wife. This created a dysfunctional system that could not help him make the right decisions at critical moments. His assassination in 1994 led to a power vacuum whose ultimate result was the horrific genocide of that year. And I am afraid that this story of disaster is not yet closed in Rwanda unless those in power today start listening to other dissenting voices and acknowledging their increasing frustration.

Laurent-Désiré Kabila and his Rwandese allies

In his war against Mobutu's regime (1996-97), Laurent-Désiré Kabila was heavily helped by Rwanda and Uganda. After he proclaimed himself president of DR Congo on 17 May 1997, he was forced to appoint a number of ministers who were foreigners (Rwandese). A serious incident was broadcast over foreign radio stations a few weeks after Kabila was sworn in as president: Etienne Tshisekedi, the respected Congolese opposition leader whom most Congolese expected would be appointed prime minister in Kabila's government, asked to see the president to discuss some important issues of national interest. But he was unable to meet the president because a group of top officials, who spoke Kinyarwanda, were protecting the new president and preventing him from meeting with Congolese political and religious leaders.

It is clear that between 1997 and 1998, Kabila had no real power and DR Congo was being ruled by foreigners. Such a leader could not make any significant decisions to help the nation. This group of foreign officials largely explains why Kabila could not make any meaningful progress in the reconstruction of DR Congo. It also explains his very short reign because his allies could not let him work for his country.

Confusion in leadership breaks down a nation. Particularly during a time of national crisis, there is a need to have a good, wise, and strong leader who carefully scrutinizes the situation, listens to different voices and knows how to filter relevant information and make the right decisions to save the nation from the chaos.

From the discussion above, it becomes clear that the bad figs referred to in Jeremiah 24:4-7 were the elites left in Jerusalem, who continued with the hope that they would use the temple as their refuge, that their king and the intelligentsia would work a miracle to defend them and the people against a new attack by Babylon. They carried on with their usual disobedience, relying on false securities and hoping to come up with new plans to help them survive by avoiding God's plan: punishment through exile. Unfortunately, King Zedekiah succumbed to this view and never led his people to obey God. Therefore, my argument is that it was this thinking in those who remained in Jerusalem after the 597 BC disasters, which was grounded in falsehood, that Yahweh was rejecting. For him, the people who had gone into exile were those through whom he would carry out a new divine plan.

Promises to the Exiles
I will set my eyes upon you (v. 6)

In verse 6, God gives a series of promises to the exiles. First, he promises that he will set his eyes upon them for good. Setting one's eye upon something can mean anything from simply neutral observation (Gen 44:21) to looking at something favourably or with hostility. In this passage, the verb is clearly used with the second meaning: to look favourably at the exiles. After punishment, the exiles would become objects and beneficiaries of God's gracious intervention.

Second, God promises to bring the people back to their land. This promise to bring home the exiles was perhaps the most important to the deportees who were living in utter despair when this prophecy was voiced. In our African context, the story of Moulid Iftin Hujale, a refugee from Somalia living in Dadaab camp in northern Kenya might help us to understand the feeling of Judean refugees and exiles:

> I am embarrassed when I'm forced to introduce myself as "a Somali refugee living in Kenya." I am no longer in Somalia and yet I am not a Kenyan citizen; so where do I belong? Am I going to be a refugee forever? I feel I am lost in between . . . I was only ten years old when we first arrived in Dadaab from Somalia in late 1997. My family did not flee when the civil war erupted in 1991. We didn't leave until our father died. The beautiful coastal town of Kismayo in which I was born turned into a battlefield. And there was no option but to escape. My siblings and I were separated from our mother in our struggle to escape the heartbreaking and indiscriminate civil violence . . . The journey was full of horror, exacerbated by ugly images that we came across, like families who were left along the road because they were too exhausted to go on. I still have bad memories about it . . . *But when we first arrived there, we didn't realize that the camp would unfortunately become our permanent home* (my emphasis).[11]

It is at a time like this, when one finds oneself in a foreign land as a refugee; when hope is gone; when all dependence on possessions, the familiar, and the self is gone; when nobody in the world seems to understand your situation; when sometimes death is preferred to life; and when people keep mocking you as a poor and miserable foreigner that we have no option but to rely on God and

---

11. "A Refugee's Story," *The New Humanitarian*, 18 August 2011, http://www.irinnews.org/report/93527/kenya-somalia-refugees-story.

his word starts to become meaningful in our lives. And it is in this context that we need to read the promise to the good figs that are in exile in Babylon. They were not good because of their current situation but because, though people looked down on them, God's eyes were on them. It is encouraging for some of us to realize that Yahweh allowed his chosen people to be deported, and that it was only after this judgement that he promised to intervene and create a new community from among those who were exiled. This is a message of hope for Africans who live in agony because of wars and their many consequences. God is saying that suffering will not have the last word for his people.

Another promise to the exiles is expressed in a group of four verbs in verse 6: "I will build them up, and I will not tear them down; I will plant them, and I will not uproot them." The language here is reminiscent of Jeremiah's call narrative in 1:10 (see also 12:14–17; 18:7–9; 31:27–28). These verbs contain the double themes of judgement and restoration, "which according to Jeremiah's call were to be at the heart of his preaching."[12] In Jeremiah 24:6–7, the emphasis is on the rebuilding (not the tearing down and the uprooting). But according to this passage and the whole context of the exile, this community must be rebuilt on a new basis: a new understanding of Yahweh and a new relationship in the society. Yahweh's work begins where human beings fail. Here he intervenes at a crucial moment, when all hope and all sources of self-security have been totally nullified. It is a time of utter despair, and Yahweh has to work newness where no human being can see any possible way out.

I will give you a heart to know me (v. 7a)

This promise of newness is well described in verse 7, where God promises to give the exiles a heart to know him. He adds that the exiles will be *his* people and that he will be *their* God, for they will return to him with their *whole* heart. There are at least five questions that can guide the interpretation of this verse: What is the meaning of the sentence "I will give them a heart to know me" followed by "because I am Yahweh"? What does it mean to know Yahweh in this new context? Again, what is the relationship between this sentence and verses 5–6? What is the significance of the formula "they will be my people and I will be their God?" Is the subordinate adverbial clause "for they will return to me with their whole heart" the condition for the reunification of the people with Yahweh or is it the condition for the entire restoration process?

---

12. Thompson, *Jeremiah*, 508.

In the sentence "I will give them a heart to know me," the verb "give" clearly shows that Yahweh is the actor, the giver of the heart to the deportees. In the Hebrew vision of the world, the heart is the centre of will and action. According to A. Johnson, "it is here that a man's real character finds its most ready expression."[13] On many occasions, Jeremiah condemns the people's failure as the acts of their heart: "Your own behaviour and your own actions have brought all this upon you. This misery of yours is bitter indeed; it has reached your very heart" (4:18); "this people have a rebellious and stubborn heart" (5:23); "Judah's sin is engraved with an iron tool, it is carved with a diamond point, on the tablets of their heart" (17:1).[14]

Commenting on these passages, Raitt argues that these sayings are a measure of how far Jeremiah has moved toward seeing Judah's problem as intrinsic and not merely extrinsic. Raitt adds that this view is based on a radical understanding of sin, and that it requires a radical conception of salvation. However, my understanding of the use of "heart" in these passages slightly differs from Raitt's. I see a shift in the use of the word "heart" in Jeremiah. The prophet seems to say that evil is not coming *from* the heart (the centre of will and actions as Raitt claims), rather it is *reaching* the heart (e.g. 4:18; 17:1). In other words, in the book of Jeremiah, the heart becomes the destination rather than the source of evil.

Jeremiah seems to depict a kind of society where corruption has become endemic and contagious, spreading throughout the whole society and reaching and corrupting all the members of the community. This is social sin, not just an individual's sins. The heart is here seen as a store where all the dust (spiritual and social evil) keeps accumulating. The picture is of a system that has worked its way to corrupt the entire society to such an extent that evil or sin is no longer a matter of individual misconduct but has become an institutionalized reality spreading across the nation and reducing everyone to its service. In other words, evil has become a system, a standard operating procedure, an accepted behaviour one can hardly escape. One either accepts this system and lives in this corruption or resists it and suffers or even dies. It is a society that has lost its sense of direction, a society built on corruption and totally paralysed and alienated by this same corruption. Such a society has lost any sense of its worth and is characterized only by triviality. As a consequence it produces only mediocrity and confusion because all submit to the tyranny of greed, of

---

13. A. Johnson, *The Vitality of the Individual in the Thought of Ancient Israel* (Cardiff: University of Wales Press, 1949), 84.

14. See also 3:17; 4:14; 7:24; 11:8; 17:9; 18:12; 22:17.

the accumulation of wealth and material possessions, of self-aggrandizement, and so on. Such a society lacks the strength and capacity to build its own future because its members are constantly fighting each other for their own selfish interests. In modern terms, it is a society in which trustworthiness and civic duty have ceased to be the norm that should characterize the community or nation.

These words should remind us of Jeremiah's description of Judean society in 5:1–6; 9:1–8; 22:13–19, in which he describes this exact situation where everyone has become a deceiver, a slanderer, or an oppressor, and where the leaders are fighting for their own egoistical interests. Said differently, Judeans have devalued themselves. Indeed, social sin can reduce a whole community to ruin. From this perspective, one understands the relevance of exile as a punishment for the ruling class. Yahweh has to "clean up" those who were creating and striving to maintain the evil system that was corrupting and destroying the entire nation. Unfortunately, when the upper class is punished, the poor will also suffer.

In Africa, I would say that a similarly corrupting system was characteristic of Congolese society under President Mobutu, whereby *"tout le monde devient corrupteur et corrompue* [sic]" (everyone becomes corrupting and corrupted).[15] David J. Gould describes this evil of corruption in the Congolese society in these words: "Corruption becomes the expected behavior, to the point where the civil servant not on the take is ridiculed by his family and subject to intimidation by those just above and beneath him on the chain."[16]

Gould also gives a good illustration of how evil can become contagious. He mentions a young Congolese university graduate who was employed as an economic affairs inspector, and who confided to him how his superiors showed him the way to be making $2,000 a month in illegal bribes although his official salary was only $120 monthly. The condition he was given, however, was that he would be offering substantial kickbacks to them.[17] This is an excellent illustration of how evil can be transmitted from one person to another, or of how people can be contaminated by the evil in their society.

Any who refuse to participate in this corruption become de facto enemies of their colleagues below and above them. This kind of corruption is not

---

15. David J. Gould, "Patron and Clients: The Role of the Military in Zairian Politics," in Isaac James Mowoe, *The Performance of Soldiers as Governors: African Politics and the African Military* (Washington: University Press of America, 1980), 486.

16. Gould, "Patron and Clients," 486.

17. Gould, 486.

marginal but is part of everyday life in most African nations. When it reaches such depths, it contributes to the weakening of public and private institutions and to instability of countries. This is probably how Jeremiah understood the situation in his own nation.

Summarizing the factors contributing to this kind of corruption in Africa, Kempe R. Hope writes:

> The factors contributing to corruption are somewhat like opportunistic diseases which thrive in weak immune systems. The weak immune system, in this case, stems from the fact that ethical leadership and, therefore, public accountability and integrity are seriously lacking. The ascendancy of the patrimonial state through the exercise of state power, the expanded role of state activity through centralized economic decision-making, economic retardation and elusive development which have led to poverty and lower standards of living, the lack of the rule of law which hampers institutions from acting in the public interest, and socio-cultural norms which regulate and influence relationships among members of the society and those individuals with power and clout, are all phenomena which have uniquely contributed, and continue to contribute, to the cancer of corruption on the African continent.[18]

To return to Jeremiah, Yahweh's giving of a new heart demonstrates his will to completely transform his people (as a community). The punishment alone (in terms of exile) hardly seems adequate to help Jeremiah's compatriots understand what has gone so deeply wrong in their society. By their own effort, the paralysed people of Judah would not be able to restore their relationship with one another, let alone with Yahweh.

In the context of the Near Eastern societies, vassals (ordinary people) did not have the power to re-establish a broken covenant with their lords. So what was needed was a new kind of action to help them re-establish that relationship. This is an important insight for a theology of reconstruction or renaissance. What is totally new in Jeremiah 24:4–7 is that this new action is to be the initiative of Yahweh alone, who is described as *enabling* his people to become more obedient to him and do his will. To be obedient to Yahweh

---

18. Kempe R. Hope, Snr, *From Crisis to Renewal: Development Policy and Management in Africa* (Leiden: Brill, 2012), 111.

and to do his will is "to know Yahweh." This knowledge is what Yahweh found missing in Zedekiah, in most of the kings in Judah, and in the people of Judah.

I emphasised the word *enabling* above to underline the change in the prophetic message. So far, the prophet has been urging the people to know Yahweh; now Yahweh is willing to intervene to help his rebellious people to know him. In other words, in 24:7, "to know Yahweh" becomes God's initiative, and the people's repentance is no longer the condition for the restoration of the relationship between them and Yahweh. This new initiative consisted of God giving his people a new heart to obey him. Commenting on this change in Yahweh's requirement, Raitt says,

> The weight of evidence seems to be that this is a new hope, a new level of God's promised saving activity. There are many types of expression about the heart in the Old Testament, but this is the first time that God promises to transform the heart of his whole people as part of a new and unconditioned scheme of salvation.[19]

The full result of a transformed heart is the acknowledgement by the deportees of Yahweh as their God. This is probably what is expressed in the phrase "that I am Yahweh." The problem with this portion of the sentence is whether the Hebrew word *kî* (because/for) in the passage: "because I am Yahweh" (*kî 'ănî yhwh*) should be translated by "that" or by "for/because." Holladay dismisses the sentence as a later addition to the text. But the context of the sentence that underlines Yahweh's authority and Judah's obedient subjugation seems to favour the second translation. Thus, the fuller sentence would be read like this: "I will give them a heart to know me, for/because I am Yahweh." In this sentence, Yahweh must be known (i.e. obeyed) by his people not "that he is God" (the people of Judah did know Yahweh theoretically as their God), but "because he is God" who must be revered and feared. Some good illustrations of this argument are Leviticus 20:7: "Consecrate yourselves and be holy, because I am Yahweh, your God." And Leviticus 25:17: "and you shall fear your God, for/because I am Yahweh your God." In these two passages, the phrase "I am Yahweh your God" does not simply give information on Yahweh but underlines his authority and the necessary subjugation on the part of human beings (the Israelites) if a relationship is to be maintained between the two parties. In the context of Ancient Near Eastern treaties, Yahweh must be acknowledged as the master (or because he is the master), be given due respect, and be obeyed. In this way, covenant must also be understood as an

---

19. Raitt, *Theology of Exile*, 177.

obligation on the vassal's side. Finally, though Ezekiel 11:19–20; 36:26, 28 do not have a similar sentence construction with "because/for I am Yahweh your God," they do emphasize the giving of a new heart in order that the people of Judah might fear/know the Lord.

I conclude this section by highlighting with Unterman that there is a dynamic meaning of the concept "to know Yahweh" in this verse. Though the gift of a new heart, resulting in the knowledge of Yahweh, is solely God's initiative, the content of that knowledge of Yahweh has not changed. In other words, "knowledge of Yahweh" will not become "a passive recognition but, rather, a concrete activity, the people's obedience to Yahweh's commandments."[20] Said differently, God will give a new heart to his people to know him, and the people will become able to respond appropriately to Yahweh in obedience by acknowledging him as Lord and by obeying his law. Thus, the passage shows a dynamic interaction between Yahweh's action and people's response to him in total obedience. This is what to know Yahweh means or will mean when the promise will be fulfilled.

You will be my people and I will be your God (v. 7b)

Another important element in verse 7 is the promise found in the coordinate clause, "and they will be my people and I will be their God." Apart from this passage and 31:31–34, this formula and its variations are used in five other passages in Jeremiah (7:23; 11:4; 30:22; 31:1; 32:38) and in many other books of the Old Testament: Exodus 6:7; Leviticus 26:12; Deuteronomy 29:12; Genesis 17:7–8; and Ezekiel 11:20; 14:11; 36:28; 37:23, 27; etc.

It is surprising to realize that most contemporary Jeremiah scholars overlook this passage and its importance in Jeremiah's message of hope. Holladay,[21] M. Weinfeld,[22] and R. Smend,[23] for example, simply state that this formula is taken from legal terminology used in marriage and adoption ceremonies. One good attempt to deal with this sentence comes from Raitt. For him, this formula stands for the re-election of Israel and for perfect communion with Yahweh. He holds that the first (Mosaic) covenant was imperfect and full

---

20. Jeremiah Unterman, *From Repentance to Redemption: Jeremiah's Thought in Transition* (Sheffield: JSOT Press, 1987), 80.

21. Holladay, *Jeremiah 1*, 262.

22. M. Weinfeld, *Deuteronomy and the Deuteronomic School* (Oxford: Oxford University Press, 1972), 79–81.

23. R. Smend, *Die Bunesformel* (Zurich: EVZ, 1963), 26–27.

of anxiety. There was always a risk of breaking it and creating tension between God and Israel. But the promise here moves beyond the first covenant, it is "the accomplishment of that perfect communion between God and man which was always the ultimate goal of the inward part of covenant."[24] This is a totally new kind of relationship between Yahweh and his people.

The newness of this covenant is discussed at length in the final chapter of this book. But there is something important in this passage that must be underlined. It looks forward to a new beginning in the relationship between Yahweh and his people. The new beginning is full of assurance and certainty. In other words, God chose to re-establish a relationship with his people, not because they deserved his favour, not because they had earned anything, not even because they were able to do any good thing to please him, but simply in his own sovereignty. This is an act of totally unmerited grace. This message of this passage is reiterated in Ezekiel 37, which describes a valley of dry bones that represented Israel during the deportation. Ezekiel saw a vision of Israel's death and lifelessness caused by sin. But in the vision God tells him to proclaim his word to the dry bones, and God creates a new thing from the dead nation and chooses to work with them again. What a hope for the people in exile!

The same proclamation can be made to the people of Africa. They need to hear that God does not look at a socially, politically, spiritually, and economically dead country in the same way as the people of this world do. Yahweh always sees good even in dead things like the dry bones. With God, there is always the possibility of newness in every relationship and every difficult circumstance. How this understanding should open the eyes of African Christians to realize that Yahweh has a plan for his creation in Africa and that there is always hope, even where people perceive only death!

However, I would not fully agree with Raitt when he says this verse speaks of the re-election of Israel. Comparing this message with the image in Ezekiel 37, I see this verse as representing a renewal or restoration of a relationship with the same people (who were somehow dead because of their disobedience) but who now are totally transformed by Yahweh himself. The inner transformation of the heart will result in an ideal relationship, without anxiety and mistrust when both sides fulfil all the conditions of the covenant.

The last element in verse 7 is the causal subordinate clause "for they will return to me with their whole heart." Here again, the most difficult element of the passage is the particle *kî* (because/for). Craigie, Kelley and Drinkard are adamant that the *kî* should be rendered by the conditional "if," so the sentence

---

24. Raitt, *Theology of Exile*, 198.

becomes "if they return to me with their whole heart." Their reason for the rejection of *kî* as causal ("for/because") is that

> such a statement seems to run counter to Jeremiah's theological understanding and would represent an unconditional promise of God. It is much more likely that the clause should be understood as conditional: "if they will return to me with all their heart." The strong disjunctive accent just before this phrase (*athnah*) lends support to the conditional nature of the phrase. Further, this condition serves as the focal point of the entire verse and oracle, rather than just the last half of this verse. One hearing the oracle would be led to assume that the statements in vv. 5–7 are all unconditional until reaching this last phrase. But this conditional phrase governs the whole oracle. The blessings God promises are contingent upon repentance (שוב, here translated "return") by the people.[25]

The two scholarly positions (*kî* as causal or *kî* as conditional) are in tension with no resolution in sight. This is a very important issue, and I will come back to my interpretation of it when we look at Jeremiah 31 in chapter 10 of this book. At this point, however, I will simply argue that Craigie, Kelley and Drinkard have failed to understand what is going on in the passage. The people of Judah have sinned and they cannot by themselves come back to Yahweh. That is why they have been severely judged. But the divine promise in the passage clearly means that God now turns his face towards his people, he comes to them to enable them to return to him, which will create the basis for a new future for them. To follow the logic of the passage, it would be contradictory to ask the people to do the same thing they have constantly failed to do in the past without helping them to do otherwise. This is why the verb "enable" is important here because, as I said earlier, I do not claim that the return of the people to Yahweh will be a passive process on their side, but that God will help them to act rightly in their relationship with both him and one another.

The problem with Craigie, Kelley and Drinkard is that they are thinking in terms of theological patterns in the book of Jeremiah. But we need to emphasize that the new idea in this passage does not come from Jeremiah but from Yahweh, and the decision to enable his people does not belong to the prophet but to Yahweh himself. Maybe the concept of grace (i.e. of how Yahweh sent his Messiah and his Holy Spirit to enable us to know him better and become his

---

25. Craigie, Kelley and Drinkard, *Jeremiah 1–25*, 360.

children) might help here. The Bible states that we were God's enemies when he decided to act in our favour (Rom 5:6–11). In other words, Yahweh did not wait until we turned to him before sending his Messiah. This goes beyond the type of Cartesian logic that was probably guiding the interpretation of this passage by the three scholars. Having said that, I will again insist that the work of the Holy Spirit in the believer does not mean that they remain passive. What it clearly means is that without the help of Jesus Christ we would have been unable to please God and without the Holy Spirit, we would have been unable to achieve any spiritual progress. But, at the same time, God's word insists that believers must walk (note the action) in righteousness.

You will return to me with your whole heart (v. 7c)

The last point to underline in this passage is the corporate use of the word "heart": "And I will give them a heart to know me . . . and they will return to me with their whole heart." In Jeremiah 24:4–7, the heart is used in relation to the people of Judah as a community, but not in relation to individuals (though we know that a community is formed by individuals). This might suggest that how we live our faith in relationship with others in our society matters more to Yahweh than our expression of faith as individuals. In other words, God's giving of the new heart is not for the sake of individual, personal holiness but for the sake of a righteous life in the community. In the same way, Israel is seen as a community of faith that shows to the world the character of Yahweh himself. The mandate of the church is similar, which is to stand as a community of love, justice, forgiveness, and care, to testify of Yahweh's character to the world.

The implication of this understanding of faith might be a challenge to so-called "evangelical" Christians today who put much emphasis on the individualistic and egocentric character of faith and holiness as a way to get ready for heaven. By doing this, we neglect the social dimension of the Christian faith and fail to look at our nation as one community that needs communal transformation. Faith that is not lived in community is irrelevant.

Conclusion

Jeremiah 24:4–7 opens our eyes to the damage that social sin can do to a whole community when evil becomes a system and not just an individual sin. This is why the prophet accuses the entire community of not knowing Yahweh. As a response to this social sin in Judah, Yahweh cleans up the community by sending the ruling class (who conceive and maintain this system) into exile. In doing so, God "destabilizes" the whole system that has destroyed the covenantal community's life.

However, after the punishment, the emphasis on the knowledge of Yahweh is no longer based on the people's efforts as in other parts of the book of Jeremiah. Now, the knowledge of Yahweh in Judah is based on Yahweh's grace and initiative. This is a new element in the book of Jeremiah that is discussed in the next two chapters. In the same way, repentance is no longer a condition for the right relationship with Yahweh but a consequence of the divine intervention and initiative, enabling his people to discover and repent of their wickedness.

This divine initiative enabling the people to know Yahweh does not mean that the Israelites will remain passive. The gift of a new heart will draw them closer to the Lord and help them to maintain a right relationship with their God. By maintaining a right relationship with Yahweh, they will also live rightly with one another in the community. The prophet consistently insists that the new heart will be given to Israel as a community and not just to scattered individuals so that the transformation that starts with individuals might affect the whole society of Israel. It is important for the church in Africa to emphasize this communal dimension of our salvation. Proper understanding of this truth would help reorient us as individual Africans and the communities and nations in which we live.

In the context of Africa, this passage also shows that there is hope beyond all human despair and even after God's judgement. Whatever others may think of our continent, Yahweh looks at it differently because he can give life to dead nations in the same way he did to exiled Israel in Jeremiah 24 and Ezekiel 37. Consequently, Christians in Africa must continually envision new hope for the continent and be encouraged that God gives hope to those in despair. But the main challenge that faces the growing church in Africa is the formulation of an appropriate theology that addresses the issues of social sin and its consequences for the continent. It seems that there is indeed a problem of social sin at ethnic, regional, national, and continental levels. The right theology for the continent would look for ways to make the seed of the newness of the gospel effectively grow in the religious, social, political, and economic life of Africans. In this way, the church can effectively use the gospel as a force for change and transformation.

9

Seek the Peace of Babylon: Constructive Presence in Exile

Jeremiah 29:4–9

⁴ Thus says Yahweh of hosts, the God of Israel, to all the exiles whom I have sent into exile from Jerusalem to Babylon: ⁵ Build houses and live in them; plant gardens and eat what they produce. ⁶ Take wives and have sons and daughters; take wives for your sons, and give your daughters in marriage, that they may bear sons and daughters; multiply there, and do not decrease. ⁷ But seek the welfare of the city where I have sent you into exile, and pray to Yahweh on its behalf, for in its welfare you will find your welfare. ⁸ For thus says Yahweh of hosts, the God of Israel: Do not let the prophets and the diviners who are among you deceive you, and do not listen to the dreams that they dream, ⁹ for it is a lie that they are prophesying to you in my name; I did not send them, says Yahweh.

Historical and Literary Context

There is no indication of a precise date for this letter, but it is clear from verses 1 and 2 that the setting of the correspondence is in the days immediately following the downfall of Judah in 597 BC. The culmination of this downfall was the carrying away of the elite of Judah. One would expect that the people of Judah and their leaders would learn from these painful events. Unfortunately, they became more and more divided. This division was both religious and political and could be observed both among the exiles and those who remained in the land. The main issue that divided the nation was this: Should the people in exile submit to Babylon, whose army was still threatening the nation or revolt against it by seeking help from Egypt and the neighbouring smaller nations?[1] It is in this context that Yahweh sent his prophet to give clear guidance.

The historical context of chapter 29 can thus be summarized in the following four points:

- Jeremiah received information that false prophets in Babylon were agitating the exiles by telling them that Yahweh their God would act quickly against Babylon and that they would return home soon (29:24–32). As a consequence of these false prophecies, the exiles were becoming hesitant to make any effort to accept their situation, adjust to their new surroundings for a long stay and be a constructive presence in Babylon. In this sense, Jeremiah's letter can be called a pastoral letter giving direction to the exiles during a time of uncertainty and crisis.
- For the people who remained in the land, this was a time of unrest in the region and King Zedekiah of Judah was under pressure to break with Babylon. This pressure was from both inside and outside.
- There was a period of unrest all over the Babylonian Empire. In 596–595 BC, Elam attempted to attack Babylon but was repelled (see Jer 49:34–39). A year after this attack (which was Nebuchadrezzar's tenth year), the king of Babylon had to quickly put down a rebellion in the capital itself, in which some of the deported Jews seemed to have been involved. Nebuchadrezzar executed at least two of them (29:21–23). All these events seem to have made Nebuchadrezzar vulnerable and opened the door to surrounding nations to hope for a change in the region.[2]
- The fact that Jeremiah's letter was sent by official envoys from Zedekiah to Nebuchadrezzar (29:3) fits well with a date of 594 BC, when Zedekiah may have been obliged to report on recent events in Judah and to reaffirm his loyalty. This also means that at the

---

1. It is important to note that this division runs throughout the book of Jeremiah, but that it becomes more apparent from chapter 26 and continues until after the total destruction of Jerusalem during the reign of Zedekiah.

2. A good summary of Nebuchadrezzar's reign can be found in William S. LaSor, "Nebuchadnezzar," in Geoffrey W. Bromiley (ed.), *The International Standard Bible Encyclopedia* (Grand Rapids, MI: Eerdmans, 1986), 506–509.

beginning of this rebellion against Babylon, Zedekiah might not have joined the conspiracy. However, it is clear from chapter 39 that the political restlessness continued to mount, reaching its peak in 588 BC when a new Egyptian pharaoh, Apris (called Hophra in 44:30) came to the throne (589–570 BC),[3] and probably forced Zedekiah to change his mind.

Structure

Jeremiah 29 is a complex and confusing document.[4] Its analysis presents severe difficulties.[5] John Hill rightly recognizes that the limits of the letter are difficult to define.[6] Dennis Bratcher notices that most scholarly attention has been directed toward identifying an original core of the chapter and the interpretative redactional additions.[7] In this process, some have even suggested that the entire section of chapters 27–29 is an independent tradition within the surrounding material.[8]

The chapter is introduced as the "written document" (*hassēper*) that Jeremiah sent from Jerusalem to Babylon (v. 1). It was a letter written on papyrus, rolled into a scroll, and sealed.[9] It was more than an ordinary letter, however. For example, the messenger formula ("Thus says Yahweh") typical of prophetic speech begins every unit addressed to the exiles (vv. 4, 8, 10, 16, 17, 21, 25, 31, 32). This is why some describe this chapter as a "prophetic booklet"[10] sent to the exiles in Babylon.

---

3. Bernhard W. Anderson, *The Living World of the Old Testament* (London: Longmans, 1967), 346.

4. Jean Hadey, "Jérémie 29: Demain n'est pas Hier...," in *Lire et Dire: Etudes Exégétiques en vue de la Prédication* 64 (2005): 5. Hadey qualifies the text of Jeremiah 29 as accumulated and disorganized oracles that challenge all search for coherence: "*Le livre de Jérémie se présente comme une accumulation assez désordonnée d'oracles et de récits, qui défie encore toute recherche de cohérence d'ensemble.*"

5. William L. Holladay, *Jeremiah 2*, Hermeneia (Minneapolis: Fortress Press, 1989), 134.

6. John Hill, *Foe or Friend? The Figure of Babylon in the Book of Jeremiah MT* (Leiden: Brill, 1999), 145.

7. Dennis Bratcher, "Jeremiah 29:4–7," in *The Voice: Biblical and Theological Resources for Growing Christians*, 2009; n.p., http://www.textweek.com/prophets/jer1.htm.

8. Bratcher, "Jeremiah 29:4–7," n. p.

9. Lundbom, *Jeremiah 21–36*, 348.

10. Gerald L. Keown, Pamela J. Scalise and Thomas G. Smothers, *Jeremiah 26–52* (Dallas, TX: Word, 1995), 65.

Despite all the challenges presented by the text, a careful reading can reveal that the chapter is composed of several parts, probably including some interpretative redactional additions:

- The king's messengers carry Jeremiah's letter to the exiles in Babylon (vv. 1–9).
- The audience of Jeremiah's message is expanded in verses 10–23 to both the exiles and those who remain in the land (v. 16), explaining to them that there is a future for the exiles (vv. 11–14), but that this hope must be deferred for seventy years (v. 10), after which they will be brought back home.
- In the meantime, there is an announcement of Yahweh's anger against the people who remain in the land and who continue to reject Yahweh's messengers (vv. 15–19).
- This is followed by an announcement of Yahweh's anger against Zedekiah and Ahab who also continue to mislead the exiles (vv. 21–23).
- Shemaiah, one of the exiles, reacts to Jeremiah's letter by sending another letter to Zephaniah, the priest in Jerusalem, asking him to rebuke Jeremiah and put him in the stocks (vv. 25–28).
- Zephaniah the priest reads Shemaiah's letter to Jeremiah, but it seems that he did not take any action against the prophet (v. 29).
- Yahweh then commands Jeremiah to deliver an oracle against Shemaiah (vv. 24, 30–32).

In what follows I will be looking primarily at verses 4 to 9 as embodying the basic theme of the "written document." It can be summarized this way: "Settle down and live peacefully in Babylon; pray for the peace of the city and make a constructive presence in that foreign land where I have sent you" (vv. 4–7). At the same time, do not listen to optimistic prophets who raise false hopes (vv. 8–9).

Shalom (peace)

The word *shalom* (peace) is one of the key concepts in the book of Jeremiah. The prophet from Anathoth uses it twenty-six times.[11] Many of these uses are related either to false prophets' oracles or to a false concept of peace in the

---

11. If one considers all the doublets, the word *shalom* is used 31 times in the book of Jeremiah.

community.¹² To give a few examples, in 14:13, Jeremiah complains about false prophets who were saying to the people: "You shall not see the sword, nor shall there be famine, but enduring *shalom* I will give you in this place." In 4:10, he directly complains to God who has allowed false prophets to continue telling lies about peace while devastation was approaching: "Lord Yahweh, surely you have totally deceived this people, and Jerusalem too, in saying you shall have *shalom* when a sword is pricking their throat." Finally, in 6:14 Jeremiah utters a strong complaint: "They have healed my people's wound superficially, saying: '*shalom, shalom*' but there is no *shalom*." It seems that the concept *shalom* might have been one of the distinguishing marks of Jeremiah's prophetic opponents.

From these examples, it is possible that for these opponents (both prophets and political and religious leaders), the assurance of peace was mostly grounded in a false sense of security motivated by the traditions of Zion's inviolability and God's choice of the Davidic dynasty.¹³ Thus most of the uses of the concept *shalom* by Jeremiah in relation to the false prophets are negative, except in one case, Jeremiah 29:7, where he uses it positively to urge the exiles of Judah in Babylon to seek the peace of the city where they have been forced to live.

In the context of the exile, this is an interesting passage. In chapters 27 and 28, Jeremiah repeatedly warned his fellow citizens to submit to Babylon. Unfortunately, the people of Judah rejected his advice. As a consequence, the country was devastated, and many people were taken into exile.

In chapter 29, Jeremiah continues with the same message in a letter to the people of Judah who are already living in exile. Jeremiah asks them not to have a negative attitude towards Babylon or start another rebellion against it, but to live in peace and seek the peace¹⁴ of their new home. In this letter, Jeremiah was asking his compatriots in exile to become a constructive presence in Babylon.

In the context of Africa, this is an interesting passage. It is not uncommon to find African refugees and immigrants creating problems for the cities where

---

12. Of the 26 uses, the following 16 (22) references are of direct interest to the concept of peace as used in the Jerusalem cultic community: 4:10 (23:17); 6:14 (8:11) six references; 12:12; 14:13; 8:15 (14:19); 15:5; 28:9; 29:7 (three references); 29:11; 30:5; 33:6; 33:9; 38:4.

13. John Bright, *Covenant and Promise: The Future in the Preaching of the Pre-Exilic Prophets* (London: SCM, 1977), 140–41 expresses this idea of a false sense of security in Jerusalem during the time of Jeremiah well: "Men could tell themselves that, regardless of what the future might hold, no reason existed to worry about the nation's continued survival. Has not God promised to David a dynasty that will never end? Is not this temple-palace here in our midst on Mt Zion? Is it conceivable that he would ever abandon it, and the city in which it stands, to destruction? Perhaps the future will bring crisis after crisis – who knows? *But one thing is sure: this nation will always survive. God has so promised, and he does not alter the word that passed from his lips or lie to David.*" [Ps 89:33–37, emphasis added]

14. Most English versions and commentators translate the Hebrew word *shalom* as "welfare."

they live. For example, in July 2010, at least fifty people were killed and more than a hundred admitted to hospital as a result of three separate bomb blasts in Kampala, the capital of Uganda, as residents watched the 2010 World Cup final on giant screens. A Somali sheik Yusuf Sheik Issa responded to this carnage with the following statement: "Uganda is one of our enemies. Whatever makes them cry makes us happy. May Allah's anger be upon those who are against us."[15] He and other Somali extremists were not happy that Uganda had peace-keeping troops to Somalia and were promising similar attacks in all the countries that had sent soldiers to Somalia. The same justification was used by al-Shabaab for their attacks on the Westgate Shopping Mall in Nairobi, Kenya, on 21 September 2013, which killed at least 63 people, and on Garissa University in Kenya on 3 April 2015, which killed 148 innocent students.

It might be difficult to prove that these attacks were carried out by Somali refugees living in Uganda or Kenya. However, the attacks put the lives of refugees in both countries and the entire East Africa region in greater danger as Ugandan and Kenyan military and security agents carried out regular operations among Somali refugees to investigate whether any had connection with these attacks. In the same way, politicians in Kenya have been saying that the Dadaab refugee complex is providing sanctuary and support to members of the al-Shabaab.

Jeremiah's call for those in exile to live in peace and seek the peace of Babylon is a reminder of the need for foreigners to seek the good of the communities in which they find themselves.

Naming the Author of the Exile (v. 4)

In verse 1, it is stated that Jeremiah's letter was addressed to the surviving elders, the priests, the prophets, and all the other people from Jerusalem whom *Nebuchadrezzar* had taken into exile in Babylon. However, verse 4 states: "Thus says Yahweh, the Lord of Hosts, God of Israel, to all the exiles whom *I* have exiled from Jerusalem to Babylon."

There is an interesting combination of Nebuchadrezzar (v. 1) and Yahweh (v. 4) as the authors of the exile in these two verses which implies that there is a relationship between the Babylonian king and Yahweh. In fact, in the book of Jeremiah, Nebuchadrezzar is presented as Yahweh's partner in dealing with Judah and the surrounding nations (Jer 25:9–11). In 25:9, 27:6 and 43:10, Yahweh goes further by calling Nebuchadrezzar "my servant."

---

15. *BBC News Africa*, 12 July 2010.

In the Old Testament, the title "Yahweh's servant" is normally used for a few persons who had a special relationship with God and who were obedient to his will in the life of his people. These were people like Moses (Num 12:7; Josh 1:2, 7), David (1 Sam 22:8; 2 Sam 3:18; 1 Kgs 11:32, 34), and Isaiah the prophet (Isa 44:28).[16] So, this designation of Nebuchadrezzar is the only place where a foreign king is called Yahweh's servant in the Old Testament.

What this passage might mean is that Nebuchadrezzar is the instrument that Yahweh chose to bring divine judgement to his unrepentant people. In other words, after unsuccessfully using the prophets to warn Judah (25:4), now God sends his "servant," Nebuchadrezzar, to humiliate his people for their wickedness. A foreign king attacking Yahweh's people and destroying Yahweh's temple is indeed a terrible humiliation, and this picture reflects the prophet's understanding of God's work in history. Yahweh can use any human agent to help, warn, rescue, and punish. Though most people in our secularized world will deny it, it is important to remind our society that God is indeed in control of what looks like a godless world.

Later, verse 7 makes it clear that Yahweh had given Nebuchadrezzar the power and the authority to subjugate kingdoms and nations. As the instruments of God's judgement, the king of Babylon and Yahweh are indeed partners in the banishment of Judah. Nevertheless, it is important to note that this partnership is not without limit and restraint.[17]

Exhorting the Exiles to Settle down in Babylon (vv. 5–7)

Verse 5 is an admonition to the exiles to settle down in their new land. Yahweh, through his prophet, gives four clear directions about life in the new city.

Build houses and settle down

First, Jeremiah tells the exiles to build houses and live in them. This must have been a response to the question being asked by the newly arrived exiled people

---

16. John Hill, "'Your Exile Will Be Long': The Book of Jeremiah and the Unended Exile," in Martin Kessler (ed.), *Reading the Book of Jeremiah: A Search for Coherence* (Winona Lake, IN: Eisenbrauns, 2004), 154.

17. Walter Brueggemann, *Theology of the Old Testament: Testimony, Dispute, Advocacy* (Minneapolis, MN: Fortress, 1996), 510. He argues that the actual working out of "Babylonian policy reflects no such restraint, no mercy congruent with the intended mercy of Yahweh . . . This is why the book of Jeremiah, so long supportive of Babylonian policy as reflective of Yahweh's intention, culminates in a savage, extended oracle against Babylon (chapters 50–51)."

of Judah. This was a time of uncertainty, fear, terrible depression, and tension. Therefore, it was important to help them settle down and learn to cope with this new reality. They needed to develop a new metanarrative that provided a theological basis for their existence. In other words, they needed a change of mindset, to accept their situation and consider their stay in Babylon as positive.

Jeremiah's advice that they build homes in Babylon implies that they had not been there for a long time, and these first years must have been very difficult for them. There is a general agreement among scholars that life for the Judean captives was relatively pleasant. The argument to support this view being that when they were eventually allowed to go home, some did not want to return (Ezra 8:15). But this understanding of the exile can be misleading because we need to remember that the deportation was primarily Yahweh's punishment. Jeremiah 29 was uttered during the first years of the deportation. Adjustment takes time in a foreign land. The exiles left home under foreign military pressure, with beatings and terrible humiliation.

The Rwandan refugees who flooded the eastern part of DR Congo in June 1994 faced similar circumstances. On their arrival in eastern DR Congo, those who had cars and other precious items started selling them for derisory prices. I know some who sold luxury cars for $400 or less. Others "sold" their daughters to local Congolese people with the expectation that their new sons-in-law would help other members of the family to find food and shelter. Others did this for physical protection from the hostile local population that was overwhelmed by the number of refugees and from the undisciplined and corrupt Congolese army that was abusing helpless refugees. Whatever money they made from these sales did not sustain them for long. The situation of the Judeans deportees in Babylon might have been just as difficult at the beginning of the exile.

The exiles were also likely experiencing psychological suffering. Judeans thought of themselves as the people of the most powerful God who was protecting his nation from his immovable temple in Zion. Therefore, for the elites and the advocates of the long-trusted "official theology," the humiliation of being led captive to a foreign land, far from the temple (and therefore far from Yahweh) was agonizing. It was torture – both physical and spiritual.

Among the captives were the economically powerful, the rich people of Judah who owned properties and businesses in Jerusalem, who enjoyed a good life but who now found themselves far from these comforts. Thus I dispute the argument that Judeans enjoyed a good life in exile right from the beginning. This view needs to be reanalysed to discover what life was actually like during the first years of the exile, and how and what helped the deportees gradually adjust to living in Babylon.

Reflecting on the first experience of a refugee in a foreign land or in a refugee camp, Barry N. Stein writes,

> To the stresses and trauma inflicted on refugees before escape, during flight, and in refugee camp, one must add the difficulties and fears that face the refugees during resettlement. Acculturation, loss of status, identity confusion, language difficulties, poverty, concern for separated or lost family members, guilt, isolation, host hostility, and countless other factors add to the pressures on the refugee in a strange land.[18]

Psalm 137 offers a glimpse of the plight of refugees in their first years in exile. It was most likely composed by one who was in Babylon among the exiles. The opening stanza of the poem recalls how the Israelites refused to sing their sacred songs in Babylon for the amusement of their conquerors. These were enemies who had destroyed Jerusalem, who had looted and burned down Yahweh's temple, but who then had the effrontery and cruelty to ask the Israelite refugees to sing to them a temple song. The ultimate goal of this request was the humiliation of the exiles. It shows the attitude of the Babylonians towards Judeans, who had become objects of scorn. Given this poem and the reaction of the exiles, we cannot say that everything was fine for Judeans in Babylon, especially at the beginning of the exile. It is true that with Yahweh's help, they eventually adjusted to their new home and most of them were richly blessed. But I would think of Judah in exile (especially at the time this prophecy was uttered) as essentially a community that mourned because they were bereft of what they were accustomed to in life and longed for their homeland.

However, bereavement, longing, mourning, anger, and hope for a quick return could become an obstacle to the adjustment of the Judeans in Babylon. Prolonged longing for the homeland and strong hope for the quick return can delay the exiles' psychological arrival and hinder the process of adjustment. This is the reason for Jeremiah's letter in chapter 29. God has not forgotten them, and the promise of the return has not been denied; but for now, the exiles must accept the reality of their situation and prepare themselves for a long stay in the new land. The best way to show that they have accepted what has

---

18. Barry N. Stein, "The Experience of Being a Refugee: Insights from the Research Literature," in C. L. Williams & J. Westermeyer (eds.), *Refugee Mental Health in Resettlement Countries*, Series in Clinical and Community Psychology (Washington: Hemisphere, 1986), 5–23.

happened to them is by starting to establish themselves as a stable community in Babylon and the first step toward this is to build houses instead of living in temporary shelters, like most refugees do in Africa today long after arriving in new countries.

Plant gardens and eat their fruit

Second, Yahweh tells the exiles to plant gardens and eat their produce. Refugees and exiles who leave their homes because of wars and conflicts face nutritional challenges.[19] In Africa, most live in tents in refugee camps, separated from the local communities, and survive on food provided by the United Nations High Commissioner for Refugees (UNHCR) and other humanitarian agencies. They keep pressing the international community to quickly find solutions to their problems and those of their home countries. What this means is that refugees usually view themselves as temporary residents in these camps. Many of them are counting the days till they return home, marking the time meanwhile. Jeremiah's mission was to correct this way of thinking and tell the exiles from Judah that theirs would be a long stay in Babylon, which "must not simply be negative because their home for the indefinite future must be in Babylon, and it is there that they must build their lives."[20]

To rebuild life, one must engage in a meaningful activity like farming. But farming activities imply a certain attitude and effort, and often it is the citizens who own land, not refugees. A displaced person needs to accept the possibility of a long-term stay in a foreign land before they can start to negotiate for land to cultivate. Engaging in farming gives a them a sense of belonging to the new community. They can start regaining their lost identity in the new land. The sense of meaninglessness slowly disappears as the farmer starts producing food, linking with other local farmers, selling the surplus to local communities and markets, and at the same time buying from other farmers and local people. With this, the exiles/refugees start living a normal life and contributing to the local economy. In this way, the Judeans could become self-sufficient. Farming is an extremely integrative activity, maybe the most important in rural Africa, as expressed in the Bena (Tanzania) proverb: *Jembe na mundu ni baba na mama*

---

19. Neil Harris, Fiona Rowe Minnis and Shwan, "Refugees Connecting with a New Country through Community Food Gardening," *International Journal of Environment Research and Public Health* 11, no. 9 (September 2014): 9202–16, https://doi.org/10.3390/ijerph110909202.

20. Holladay, *Jeremiah 2*, 141.

(the hoe and sickle are your father and mother). By not farming, the exiles were neglecting this very important aspect of their life.

In Africa, refugees have been often considered as a drain on the host country, "imposing additional costs on an already hard-pressed public and social welfare budget, arresting economic growth, distorting markets, causing environmental degradation and putting political strains on already fragile and conflict-affected countries."[21] And the emergency relief plans of well-meaning humanitarian agencies like the UNHCR usually end up being long-term assistance efforts that easily lead to dependency among refugees. But Jeremiah conceives a different situation and encourages an entrepreneurial spirit among the exiles. He urges them not to fold their arms but to engage in farming and become a self-sustaining community.

The logic of Jeremiah's argument can be demonstrated in some parts of Africa where the arrival of refugees had actually contributed "to regional development as refugees could be settled on underutilized land and contribute to the local economy through increased agricultural production."[22] Karen Jacobsen quotes Oliver Bakewell on the complete integration of Angolan refugees that occurred in some parts of Zambia: "Land is abundant in Kanongesha and Zambian villagers commented that the arrival of refugees was welcome as [they] 'turned the bush into villages.' People can use as much as they can cultivate and the largest land users . . . were refugees."[23] Karen also describes how "in the Forest Region of Guinea . . . Liberian refugees gave a boost to rice production by increasing the cultivation of the lower swamp areas, which is common practice in Liberia but hardly known in Guinea."[24]

To be more contextual, Africa is now characterized by rapid urbanization. Many refugees find themselves in growing cities and not in villages. But Jeremiah would still urge them to develop an entrepreneurial spirit to help their integration in the new land. For example, in an important study on the

---

21. Roger Zetter, "Are Refugees an Economic Burden or Benefit?" *Forced Migration Review*, https://www.fmreview.org/preventing/zetter.

22. James H. S. Milner, *Refugees, the State and the Politics of Asylum in Africa* (Hampshire, UK: Palgrave Macmillan, 2009), 45.

23. Karen Jacobsen, "The Forgotten Solution: Local Integration for Refugees in Developing Countries," in *New Issue in Refugee Research* (Working paper no. 45, 2001), https://www.unhcr.org/research/working/3b7d24059/forgotten-solution-local-integration-refugees-developing-countries-karen.html.

24. Karen Jacobsen, "The Forgotten Solution," https://www.unhcr.org/research/working/3b7d24059/forgotten-solution-local-integration-refugees-developing-countries-karen.html.

life of refugees in Uganda, Alexander Bett showed that refugees can contribute meaningfully to the economy of a host nation even in an urban context:

> We found that actually many refugees don't just contribute from buying and selling goods or being even employees of Ugandan hosts. But actually, in some cases what was really surprising was that they create jobs in many cases in Kampala. The people who are entrepreneurial are employing Ugandan nationals.[25]

Unfortunately, Uganda, Zambia, and to some extent South Africa are the only countries in Africa where refugees have a certain degree of freedom of movement and the chance to work. All other countries have restrictive regulations on refugees and deprive them of the right to work. Yet, there are skilled and talented people among refugees who could contribute enormously to the development of local economies. Very often, refugees have nothing to offer because they have not been given the opportunity to do what they can. Africans need to change how they view refugees in their communities. Host communities need to see that refugees bring new opportunities and are not a threat. This might not be easy to do everywhere for political reasons, but Jeremiah challenges us to think differently and to adapt our regulations to help those who have come to us for refuge because of wars and conflicts in their home nations. Refugees have much to give to the host nations.

John Hill notices that in Jeremiah 29, Babylon is represented as a place in which the exiles can experience the very blessings that the Bible traditions associate with life in the land given by Yahweh to Israel.[26] But there is a huge difference between the new situation in Babylon and the settlement in Canaan as described in Joshua 24:13. In Canaan, cultivated land, cities, vineyards, and olive groves, all of which were technical and cultural achievements representing generations of work, were given to the Israelite settlers. In Babylon, however, they had to begin with the basics: building family homes for shelter and planting gardens for sustenance. In both situations, however, Yahweh's promise of blessings was assured.

---

25. Joe DeCapua, "Refugees Boost Local Economy," *VOA News*, 20 June 2014, https://www.voanews.com/africa/refugees-boost-local-economy.

26. Hill, *Foe or Friend?*, 127.

Get married and have children and grandchildren

Jeremiah did not only emphasize settling down in the land, he also called on the exiles to focus on the next generation, those who would be the bearers of a new future. Thus Yahweh, through his prophet, asks his people to "Take wives and have sons and daughters; take wives for your sons, and give your daughters in marriage, that they may bear sons and daughters" (Jer 29:6).

This passage reminds of the mandate to multiply that Yahweh gave to humankind in the book of Genesis. It also reminds of the great increase of the Israelites in Egypt before the exodus (Exod 1:7). Wherever they went and whatever the situation, God wanted his people to multiply. In this specific passage, the command to multiply is meant to guarantee a future generation of children who will survive the exile (v. 6).

Read carefully, the passage suggests that the exiles will be in Babylon for at least two generations. The text says that they have to marry and have children and give wives/husbands to these children so that they will also have children. Understood this way, Jeremiah 29 seems to say that the generation that went into exile has already lost the future. There is no hope for their returning home. It was therefore important that they focus on future generations, including those who will experience restoration in the land.

Such a message of the impossibility of return would have brought an extremely bitter realization to the exiles, especially those who believed there was still hope of an immediate return to Jerusalem. The message was as bitter for the exiles as it can be so for those of us who have difficulty investing in something whose gain we do not experience immediately. Many of us claim God's promises only for ourselves; we do not realize that some of them are meant for the benefit of those who come after us. This is the truth that Yahweh was trying to communicate to the exiles through Jeremiah. In other words, God was saying to them that the present was lost, and that their focus was to be on preparing the future generation that would return home from Babylon.

This passage speaks loudly to our own situation in Africa. Many countries have experienced years of wars and destruction with lasting consequences. Rebuilding Uganda after many years of bloody conflicts and wars (1971 to 1986) has taken years. It is the same with Liberia, Sierra Leone, DR Congo and other countries, where post-war reconstruction is painfully but slowly taking place. How many years will it take the Somali people to rebuild their country after they have destroyed it for decades? There will surely be at least one whole generation of Somalis who have no hope for a normal life in their land.

There is another interesting intertextual reading of these three verses (vv. 5–7) in the light of Deuteronomy and Isaiah. Deuteronomy 20 refers to the conduct of holy war in general, and in 20:5–7 it grants exemption to three categories of people: "anyone who has built a new house and has not dedicated it" (v. 5a), "anyone who has planted a vineyard and has not begun to use its fruit" (v. 6), "anyone who is engaged to a woman and has not married her" (v. 7). The reason for the exemption from war for people engaged in these activities is that these activities represent the blessings associated with the nation's life in the promised land, which was given to them by Yahweh. Nobody should, therefore, be deprived of their enjoyment. When the text of Jeremiah 29:5–7 is read in the light of Deuteronomy 20:5–7 and 28:30, it becomes clear that the activities associated with the blessings in the promised land are also being carried out in Babylon. Although there is a change in location, Yahweh's blessing on his people remains.

Another passage, Isaiah 65:21–23, is also clearly connected to Jeremiah 29:5–7. The passage offers a vision of the life of Israel in the land after the return from exile:

> They shall build houses and inhabit them;
>   they shall plant vineyards and eat their fruit.
> They shall not build and another inhabit;
>   they shall not plant and another eat . . .
>   and my chosen shall long enjoy the work of their hands.
> They shall not labour in vain,
>   or bear children for calamity;
> for they shall be offspring blessed by the LORD –
>   and their descendants as well.

Isaiah 65:21–23 is contained in what is called Deutero-Isaiah (Isa 40–66 including Trito-Isaiah), that speaks about abundant life in Israel after the restoration of Israel. What is surprising in Jeremiah 29 is that Yahweh does not need to wait for this future time to restore his people. The enjoyment of restoration can start even in the foreign land, in exile, considered as a place of banishment and suffering.

There is another lesson to be learned from Jeremiah 29:5–7. A growing Judean community would probably have an influence on the life of people living in Babylon. As the exiles multiplied, their influence would grow stronger. And one aspect of this influence would be spiritual since these were a unique people, defined by their conviction of being a chosen people of Yahweh. It is true that this spiritual conviction would have the potential of creating isolation from other people, but it would be considered a "witness presence" of Yahweh in a foreign land.

It is the same with African Christians today. Wherever they go, and under whatever conditions they get into Western countries, African Christian migrants/refugees carry their faith in Jesus Christ with them and can become a clear testimony of the vibrant African church. Though most Europeans are still hesitant to join these growing African-planted churches, this does not deny the real presence of the Holy Spirit working in Europe through African believers.

Seek the shalom of the city

It is possible to treat the exhortation in verse 7 with great scepticism. The capital city of the conqueror is the last place one would love to live in. Babylon was the last place in the world where the people of Judah would want to live because of the brutality of the invasions. For Judah, the Babylonians were the worst of all the enemies. Nobody would actually think about praying for the peace of Babylon. Instead, one would pray for its quick destruction! Like the Somali sheik Yusuf Sheik Issa (see p. 178), Judah was supposed to declare that "whatever makes them (the Babylonians) cry, makes us (the exiles) happy. May Yahweh's anger be upon those who are against us." From our own context, we can say that this is the attitude we would have towards the country whose army has brutally invaded our land.

Thus, the prophetic recommendation to pray for Babylon seems to be an impossibility in the context of war. According to Volz, this is the only place in the Old Testament where prayer for one's enemies and for unbelievers is commended (compare Matt 5:43–48; Rom 12:21; Titus 3:1–2; 1 Pet 2:18).[27] Bratcher calls it one of the most extraordinary and seemingly incongruous passages in Scripture.[28] Because Jeremiah had already been accused on several occasions of being in collaboration with the enemy, this passage could also be seen as another example to prove beyond any doubt that he continued to work for Babylon against his own nation.

Nevertheless, this was not the case. It should actually be understood as Yahweh's call to his people, to open their eyes. It is an invitation to see beyond political events, to see beyond the actions of Nebuchadrezzar's army. The commandment to pray for Babylon was the invitation to understand that Yahweh himself was dealing with his people because of their unfaithfulness. The central point in this call comes in verse 7a, when God commands his people to pray for the peace of the city "where 'I' have sent you into exile." In

---

27. Paul Volz, *Der Prophet Jeremia* (KAT 10; Leipzig: Diechert, 1928), 269.
28. Bratcher, "Jeremiah 1:1–10," n.p.

other words, Yahweh is asking the exiles to stop looking at Nebuchadrezzar with bitterness and to recognize him (Yahweh) as the one dealing with them. This change in perspective would help them to understand why they have been taken into exile. This new understanding of their presence in a foreign land would change them, and help them become a constructive presence there.

Thus, the important issue in verse 7 is how the deportation could possibly be seen in relation to Yahweh. In other words, the exiles were being invited to come to terms with the exile itself. If God was at work in the exile, then they needed to accept it in order to accept God's dealing with them. Such a change of attitude would bring several positive effects on the exiles. First, it would create internal healing. Second, the people of Judah would know that they are not in Babylon because of Nebuchadrezzar's powerful army but because of their unfaithfulness. They would also understand that Babylon is not the enemy but that they have been punished because of their breaking of the covenant. Moreover, they would know that Yahweh is still accessible to them through prayer. They would, finally, know that Nebuchadrezzar is not as powerful as they think but is simply an instrument in Yahweh's hand to help open the eyes of his people. With this positive attitude, prayer for Babylon would become a possibility. If God really was at work with the Babylonians and if in some sense Nebuchadrezzar was God's servant, then the welfare of the Babylonians was, indeed, inextricably linked with their own welfare. This is a powerful lesson for some of us in Africa. In times of war, we tend to condemn the enemy, but we forget that the destruction of our country starts with our own internal corruption that weakens us as a nation. Instead of looking at the real cause of our problems, we concentrate on condemning others.

For the exiles, the practical implication of this change of attitude will be an active and constructive presence in Babylon. Once Judeans are convinced that they are in the foreign land by Yahweh's will, they will stop complaining and being an inert presence. They will start to engage both with Yahweh and with other people in their new land. This engagement will be in prayer and in matters of daily life. The people who have not experienced peace for a long time in their own country will live in peace in a foreign land because Yahweh makes himself available to them outside their corrupted temple and their corrupted leadership. The exiles will now understand that Yahweh is not available only in the temple of Jerusalem. He can be worshipped everywhere. He is the Creator, the God of the entire universe who can be found wherever we seek him in truth, faithfulness, and justice.

However, this recommendation to settle in Babylon for a long time did not ignore the promise of restoration to the promised land. Verses 11 to 14 of

Jeremiah 29 clearly indicate that there is a future for the exiles in the promised land. In Jeremiah 32, Yahweh tells the prophet to symbolically buy a piece of land in the midst of Jerusalem's impending destruction, which came shortly after the transaction. This was an audacious prophetic action which clearly symbolized the future restoration of Judah. Jeremiah 32:15 concludes: "Houses and fields and vineyards shall again be bought in this land." What a message of hope!

There is much in today's world that creates despair over the future of our continent: poverty, wars, ethnic conflicts, climate change, Ebola, HIV/AIDS, and corruption, to name a few. However, the Bible is clear that there is a bright future for the people who have hope in God and in the Lord Jesus Christ. God has not given up on the world and Africa in particular. He is invested in the future destiny of humanity. Jeremiah is reminding us that in the deep crises in the continent, God's people need to act with courage, determination, and hope as a symbol of God's affirmation that the crises and devastation we know all too well will not have the final word. Terrifying times like ours call for a people of courage and faith, who like Jeremiah stand and put into action the hope for a brighter future that God has announced for humanity, whose manifestation is being observed everywhere in Africa, despite its deep turbulence.

Exhortation to Ignore False Prophets (vv. 8–9)

The question of falsehood in general and of false prophecy in particular is a recurring problem in the book of Jeremiah.[29] Throughout this chapter, I have argued that Jeremiah's concerns in this passage are practical and that he is calling for a change of attitude. I also argued that this was a time of deep national crisis and it was easy for false prophets to deceive the people, as they had been doing. There is no doubt that the exiles have been attracted to these false prophecies. Some have even claimed that Yahweh himself had raised up these prophets in exile (v. 15). God warns the exiles about the message of these prophets, given in the name of Yahweh, and the dreams they claimed to have had (see also 23:23–32). Jeremiah declares that they were deceivers and liars, for God did not send them. To listen to them would be to continue widening the gap between the people and Yahweh.

---

29. See Thomas W. Overholt, *The Threat of Falsehood: A Study in the Theology of Jeremiah* (Naperville, IL: Allison, 1970), and Thomas W. Overholt, "The Falsehood of Idolatry: An Interpretation of Jer. 10:1–16," *JTS* 16, no. 1 (1965): 1–2.

The warning of verses 8 and 9 is against an emotional and imaginative engagement in the illusion that false prophets were trying to propagate among the exiles. False prophets need to be silenced, and the actual voice of Yahweh needs to be heard. As W. Brueggemann nicely puts it, "no pretense based in religious fantasy can extricate God's people from their actual place in history. Prophetic faith is hard-nosed realism that is resistant to romantic, ideological escapism."[30] Those who try to let religion abrogate historical-political reality speak a lie. A correct reading of historical events can help us hear Yahweh's voice, if we are able to hear it correctly. This is true not only for Israel but also for most of us in Africa.

Conclusion

Let Babylon become the place of *shalom*! Let it temporarily become the new Judah! These two sentences can make a good summary of our argument in this chapter. In verses 1 to 4, Babylon is depicted as a place of exile, of suffering, of banishment and humiliation, for Judah. But in verses 5 to 9, Babylon changes its status and becomes the place of Yahweh's blessings. The people of Judah can experience the blessings of land and offspring, and they can live in peace. Babylon becomes the place in which all the blessings associated with life in the promised land can be experienced again. A new beginning is possible. Babylon becomes a new Judah where Yahweh can continue to bless his people.

Nevertheless, there is a condition for this blessing: the exiles have to forget about falsehood through false prophecy; they have to change their attitude, to accept their new reality, to accept that they have been taken to exile by Yahweh, not by Nebuchadrezzar, and that they must become a constructive presence in their new land. The time of exile must become a time of reflection on their own nation, with its corruption and injustice. With this changed attitude, they need to work and pray for the welfare of their new home as they have been doing for Jerusalem, the city of *shalom* (Ps 122:6). This prayer becomes a confirmation that Yahweh, the God of judgement, is also the God of deliverance; that the God of wrath is also the God of love who cares for his people wherever they find themselves.

As with Israel and Judah, our failures in Africa do not defeat God. He can forgive us and be with us in foreign nations or in any of the other places where we find ourselves as refugees or exiles.

---

30. Walter Brueggemann, *A Commentary on Jeremiah: Exile and Homecoming* (Grand Rapids, MI: Eerdmans, 1998), 258.

10

New Covenant and New Community

Jeremiah 31:31–34

³¹ "Behold, days are coming, says Yahweh,
   when I will make a new covenant
with the house of Israel
   and the house of Judah,
³² not like the covenant
   which I made with their fathers
when I took them
   out of the land of Egypt,
my covenant which they broke,
   though I was their husband,
      says Yahweh.
³³ But this is the covenant which I will make with the house of Israel after those days, says Yahweh:
"I will put my law in their midst
   and I will write it upon their heart;
and I will be their God,
   and they shall be my people.
³⁴ And no longer shall each man teach his neighbour
   and each his brother, saying, 'Know Yahweh,'
for they shall all know me,
   from the least of them to the greatest,
      says Yahweh;

for I will forgive their iniquity,
> and I will remember their sin no more."

Historical and Literary Context

Jeremiah 31 is part of the section of the book of Jeremiah referred to as The Little Book of Consolation (chs. 30–33), a term used to indicate that the subject of these four chapters has shifted from Jeremiah's ministry of proclaiming judgement through Babylonian invasions to concern with the future restoration of the people of God beyond the looming exile. In the words of Brueggemann, the oracle of promise in Jeremiah 31:31–34 "is the best known and most relied upon of all Jeremiah's promises."[1] However, he also mentions the following abuse of the interpretation of the same passage:

> It has frequently been preempted by Christians in a supersessionist fashion, as though Jews belong to the old covenant now nullified and Christians are the sole heirs of the new covenant. Such a distorted reading of the text has been abetted by the rendering of old and new "covenant" as old and new "*testamentun*," which was taken too easily and uncritically as the two "testaments" of Christian scripture . . . Such a supersessionist reading in fact asserts the rejection rather than the reconstruction of Israel, a point not on the horizon of these oracles.

This quotation is a warning that the passage must be interpreted carefully and not read too much through Christian glasses, as many Jeremiah students have wrongly done.

There is no indication of a precise date in the passage itself that can guide the interpreter to decide about the probable date, but in the whole context of The Little Book of Consolation there are some specific clues that can help to determine the time of this oracle. For example, 32:1–2 clearly indicates that this word came to Jeremiah from Yahweh in the tenth year of Zedekiah king of Judah, when the army of the king of Babylon was besieging Jerusalem, and when the prophet was in prison. In the same way, 33:1 indicates that the word of Yahweh came to Jeremiah for the second time (probably after the first one in 32:12) while he was still in prison. The content of the message is almost the same as that of 32:1–5, with an additional message that the Babylonians will indeed enter Jerusalem and destroy the city.

---

1. Brueggemann, *Commentary on Jeremiah*, 291.

It was during this time, when it was clear that the kingdom of Judah was coming to an end because of its rebellion, that Yahweh started giving prophecies of redemption. In other words, Jeremiah 31:31–34 indicates that the end of Judah had come, but that this was not the end of Judah's story because there was hope beyond the present darkness, and Yahweh himself was the agent of that hope. With these indications, I would argue that the period of the siege of Jerusalem by the Babylonian army,[2] before the fall and the destruction of Jerusalem in 587 BC is the most probable date of this oracle.

Most commentators recognize 31:31–34 as coming from Jeremiah.[3] In fact, Rudolph and Weiser go further than any other scholars by arguing that the passage is one of *ipsissima verba jeremiae*.[4] Carroll and Nicholson[5] are among the few who deny the authenticity of this passage. For them the idea of Yahweh rescuing his people without repentance, as I argued in relation to Jeremiah 31:31–34, contradicts the theology of Jeremiah and of all Israelite prophets:

> So to encounter a passage in a prophetic book which promises a golden future and a new covenant without repentance, and which envisages a period when there will be no need for such moral change by the people because Yahweh will change them automatically, is to enter a world where the prophets have conceded defeat and have withdrawn from the moral struggle... If people will not change, then to hope for God to change them is to move from the moral sphere to piety and transcendentalism. It is in this sense that the motif of the new covenant is a counsel

---

2. According to John Bright (*Covenant and Promise: The Future in the Preaching of the Pre-Exilic Prophets* [London: SCM, 1977], 184), the Babylonian army arrived in Palestine late in 589 BC, and the siege of Jerusalem probably began in January 588 (compare Jer 52:4) and continued until July 587 when the city fell (Jer 52:6). During that time, the prophet Jeremiah was desperately trying to convince the leadership of Judah to take the right decision. See also Oded Lipschits, *The Fall and Rise of Jerusalem: Judah under Babylonian Rule* (Winona Lake, IN: Eisenbrauns, 2005), 72–84.

3. A. C. Welch, *Jeremiah: His Time and his Work* (Oxford: Blackwell, 1928), 228–29. Welch recognizes the authenticity of this passage and argues that it is related to both Judah and Israel (the Northern Kingdom). J. P. Hyatt, *Jeremiah* (Nashville: Abingdon, 1956) argues that though the idea of the covenant in that passage is Jeremianic, the prophecy in its current formulation must have been thoroughly reworked after the book had received a Deuteronomic redaction. See also R. Martin-Achard, "Quelques Remarques sur la Nouvelle Alliance chez Jérémie," in C. Brekelmans (ed.), *Questions Disputées de l'Ancien Testament* (Duculot: Gembloux, 1974), 141–64 and Holladay, *Jeremiah 2*, 197.

4. See Wisser, *Jérémie, Critique de la Vie Sociale*, 221–24 for detailed discussion concerning Jeremianic authenticity of the passage.

5. E. W. Nicholson, *Preaching to the Exiles* (New York: Schocken, 1970).

of despair if it is to be attributed to Jeremiah (contrast the role of repentance in restoration in Jer. 31:18–20).[6]

However, despite their strong opposition, my view is that this passage goes back to Jeremiah himself, and that the idea of the new covenant was not alien to the man from Anathoth who dearly loved his nation. Moreover, we do not do justice to God's word when we reject the idea of redemption through a new covenant in Jeremiah (characterized by the giving of a new heart by Yahweh) simply because it appears as alien to the prophet's message and ministry. What Carroll and others who follow his idea forget is that Yahweh sometimes acts in ways that are incommensurable with those of human beings, and does unexpectedly intervene in the existence of his people to renew life where it has been threatened and disrupted. For example, according to the Scriptures, Yahweh did this with Moses in Exodus in order to help the suffering Israelites in Egypt. It seems to me that in Jeremiah 31:31–34 (as in Jeremiah 24:4–7), human ability has reached its end, and something has to be done to reverse the situation. With the deportations and the destruction of the temple, Judah's national theology ceased to function, its intelligentsia no longer worked; its alliances and counter-alliances were proven useless. It is in a situation such as this that we expect Yahweh's intervention in a way that nobody can fully explain. If we are able to explain everything that Yahweh does, he will cease to be God, the creator. This is why the idea of the new covenant is indeed new in a manner that our logic and that of the Judeans can hardly explicate. Yahweh takes his people to the limit (5:3), but he does not leave them there. He initiates a new action that reorients them towards a new and better relationship with him.

Promise of a New Covenant (31:31–32)

The passage is introduced by the phrase "behold days are coming." This passage invites the hearers to turn toward the future, toward what Yahweh plans to do for his people after the disastrous events during the proclamation of the oracle.

Carroll recognizes that the whole passage is full of elements alien to the Jeremianic core, and unfortunately this led him to dismiss the whole passage as non-Jeremianic.[7] Probably what Carroll does not perceive is the use of the adjective "new" (*hădāšâ*), qualifying the word covenant (*běrît*) in the sentence.

---

6. R. P. Carroll, *From Chaos to Covenant: Uses of Prophecy in the Book of Jeremiah* (London: SCM, 1981), 220.

7. Carroll, *From Chaos to Covenant*, 217.

This is truly a new element that posits a deep discontinuity between the first part of Jeremiah's ministry (before the fall of Jerusalem) and the second part (after the fall and during the exile).

Another new element concerning this covenant is that it includes both Israel and Judah ("I will make a new covenant with the house of Israel and the house of Judah"). Wisser, like Bright, thinks that the phrase "and the house of Judah" is a late addition to avoid a misunderstanding that in this passage, the prophet is referring only to the northern kingdom, by analogy to the poetic passages in Jeremiah's prophecy that deal only with Judah.[8] For Hans W. Wolff, the whole saying about the new covenant was initially promised to Israel and not to Judah, and it was only after 587 BC that the promise given to Israel was applied also to the house of Judah by a new prophetic voice.[9]

It is actually interesting to realize that God is still speaking about the two kingdoms even in the passage concerning the new covenant. It might even be true that the passage is a late editorial addition. But my argument will take another route and posit that the prophet might have talked about the two kingdoms here and then about only one kingdom in verse 33 ("But this is the covenant which I will make with the house of Israel") to signify that the past division between them (as the characteristic of the people during the time of the old covenant) is over and that the new thing God is going to do for them also includes the unification of their divided communities. In other words, a literary reading and a stylistic focus on verses 31–34 can help us to see how God is moving from two kingdoms (v. 32) to only one (v. 33).

Yahweh's plan for his people is that they might live in unity. The division of Israel into two kingdoms was not what God wanted, though he allowed it as a consequence of their sins and bad leadership. Sin and bad leadership bring disruption and division in the community, but when God intervenes to bring change in the heart of his people, this change also affects relationships at both the individual and public/national levels and recreates unity. The importance of unity in every dimension of human society can never be overestimated. Both for Israel and for us today, lack of unity is liable to lead to devastation. At the national level, the structure of a nation cannot stand unless unity is strengthened at all levels of the society. Unity contributes to the organic harmony of the nation and protects the country from troubles from inside and outside. Nations cannot succeed without unity. But unity is only possible with good leadership, following the model of what Yahweh is doing in this passage.

---

8. Wisser, *Jérémie, Critique de la Vie Sociale*, 221.
9. Hans W. Wolff, *Confrontations with Prophets* (Philadelphia: Fortress, 1983), 51.

For Israel, when God brings in the promised change, it will renew relationships in the society and recreate a united and perfect kingdom. The new covenant will create a transformed society. By way of implication, and with reference to the New Testament and the African context, the transformation that should have been brought by Jesus Christ to the millions of Africans who call themselves Christians should also have positively affected their relationships with one another (toward unity) and with God. Said differently, we cannot claim to be Christians and be unable to live together in a harmonious society. Also, Africa cannot continue to claim to have become a Christian continent without being able to build better, harmonious and united communities. If this is not happening, then we need to seriously question our understanding of the word and will of God and our faith as Christians. Unity is especially important for Africans because we are living in deeply divided nations. The future of Christianity on the continent depends on how we solve this dichotomy between Africa being a deeply religious continent that claims to be Christian while at the same time African societies are terribly fragmented and full of hatred, division and wars (genocide).

Africa is made up of thousands of ethnic groups. There is a need of a theology that helps to celebrate this diversity instead of making it a curse for the continent. Our diversity and differences make us need one another, they point to the fact that there is no one ethnic group, one community, or one country that can be self-sufficient. Moreover, the differences in African society are not only related to cultural and ethnic diversity. There are also differences between rich and poor, old and young, men and women, educated and uneducated, physically normal people and those living with disability, etc. These differences are part of our humanity and turn us toward one another, whether in need, compassion, or love. How can African theologians and church leaders articulate this beauty of our diversity and point out its strengths instead of making it one of our greatest weaknesses?

Verse 32 says that the new covenant is "not like the covenant which I made with their fathers when I took them out of the land of Egypt, my covenant which they broke, though I was their husband, says Yahweh." The covenant that was inaugurated between Yahweh and his people at Sinai (Exod 19:1–24) is the background to the announcement of the new one.

There are two relative clauses in this verse, both introduced by *ashĕr* (which/that): "the covenant *which* I made with their fathers . . . my covenant *which* they broke." Each clause is used to qualify the word (old/first) "covenant." They draw a strong contrast between the two parties that signed the first covenant: on the one side, there was Yahweh, the faithful "master/husband,"

and on the other side, there was Israel (their fathers), the unfaithful vassal. This contrast is also underlined by the use of the pronouns "I" and "they/their" in the same sentence.

In short, the passage highlights the fact that the first covenant has been broken. The defaulting party had experienced the necessary consequences of that breach. The mention of Egypt in this passage points out that unfaithfulness has been a characteristic of Israel's history since its earliest days (since the deliverance from Egypt: Deut 9:6–21; Judg 2:1–3, 20), and that the whole history of Israel is one of breaking the covenant and even going after other gods. Carroll is right when, commenting on this passage, he states: "If ever an institution was created which was a complete failure from the beginning it must be the deuteronomistic covenant!"[10] A brief glance at some of the prophets will further demonstrate Israel's breach of the covenant: "For you are not my people, and I am not your God" (Hos 1:9 NIV); or "I reared children and brought them up, but they have rebelled against me" (Isa 1:8 NIV); "They have turned back to the iniquities of their forefathers, who refused to hear my words; they have gone after other gods to serve them" (Jer 11:10). There was a need for a new covenant. But the sentence "not like the covenant which I made with their fathers . . . my covenant which they broke" implies that the new covenant will be different from the first one and unbreakable.

Substance of the New Covenant (vv. 33–34)
A new heart

In Hebrew, verse 33 starts with the disjunctive *kî* (but) in the sentence "but this is the covenant which I will make with the house of Israel" to introduce the contrast between the old and new covenants. The key contrast is the mode in which the covenant is received. The second part of the verse is introduced by the sentence "I will set my law in their midst and I will write it upon their heart." This describes the method by which the law in the new covenant will be transmitted from Yahweh to Israel. Thompson rightly argues that heart here equals the will and mind.[11] The old covenant was written on external objects such as stones (Exod 31:18; 34:28–29; Deut 4:13; 5:22) or in books (Exod 24:7), but the new one will need to be written internally, that is, in the wills and minds of people. The ancient covenant was transmitted through an intermediary (Moses) and subsequently mediated through the prophets

---

10. Carroll, *From Chaos to Covenant*, 217.
11. Thompson, *Jeremiah*, 581.

and the priests. But the new one will be transmitted directly into the heart of the people. Brueggemann understands the transforming power of the new covenant in this way:

> The commandments will not be an external rule which invites hostility, but now will be an embraced, internal identity-giving mark, so that obeying will be as normal and as readily accepted as breathing and eating. Israel will practice obedience because it belongs to Israel's character to live in this way. All inclination to resist, refuse, or disobey will have evaporated, because the members of the new community of covenant are transformed people who have rightly inclined hearts. There will be easy and ready community between God and reconstituted Israel.[12]

Unterman thinks of the transmission of the law in the new covenant as "an internal act, which takes place within the recipient and transforms the Torah into an organic part of the individual."[13] Andrew G. Shead describes it as God's palimpsest, his overwriting of an original sinful text with his words.[14] McKane calls the writing of the new covenant "a deep symbiosis of Divine Law and human understanding of it."[15] Wolff describes it as a heart transplant: "the heart of stone which is impervious to impressions will be surgically removed, and a new heart of flesh, living and functioning, will be implanted instead."[16]

Each of the above descriptions and explanations tries to say something about the nature of this new covenant, though I must confess that we are still speculating on what it will really look like. Nevertheless, there are two important points to be underlined in this passage:

First, in Jeremiah 17:1, we read: "the sin of Judah is written with iron stylus, engraved with a stylus point of hard stone." This statement describes the nature of Judean society: deeply corrupted and impossible to change. Now, Yahweh will have to "surgically" (to repeat Wolff's expression) remove this unbelieving heart and replace it with a new one that will enable new human relationships in the community and a new life with Yahweh himself (Jer 31:31–34).

---

12. Brueggemann, *A Commentary on Jeremiah*, 293.
13. Unterman, *From Repentance to Redemption*, 98.
14. Andrew G. Shead, "The New Covenant and Pauline Hermeneutics," in Peter Bolt and Mark Thompson (eds.), *The Gospel to the Nations: Perspectives on Paul's Mission* (London: Inter-Varsity Press 2000), 38.
15. McKane, *Jeremiah 2*, 820.
16. Wolff, *Confrontations with Prophets*, 55.

Two kinds of societies are described. The one described in Jeremiah 17:1 is characterized by deep corruption and total decay, with no hope of change. That was what Judean society was like when the prophet uttered this prophecy: an exhausted country was heading towards total dissolution, with all signs of true life disappearing one after another, until nothing was left but death. With the exile in 587 BC, Judah reached this dissolution. The voice we hear speaks of relinquishment of the old society that pretends autonomy. But in Jeremiah 31:31–34, we hear a new voice and read of a new society created by God and characterized by its obedience to Yahweh. The old society is incarnated in the political claims of the Davidic dynasty, the ritual pretensions of the Jerusalem priesthood and temple, the public arrangements of power, that were practised and trusted in the royal temple system of Jerusalem with its official theology.[17]

After the relinquishment of this old society, Jeremiah announces the coming of a new mode of social existence, a new society that is trustfully obedient to the norm of the covenant. Brueggemann summarizes the two worlds with these words:

> The world is perceived under the twin aspects of relinquishment and receiving. That perception of reality is based in an unshakeable theological conviction: God's powerful governance is displacing the present idolatrous order of public life and is generating a new order that befits God's will for the world. This theological conviction is not rooted in political observation, economic analysis, or cultural yearning. It is rooted decisively in the notion of who God is and what God wills.[18]

A new community

As in Jeremiah 24:4–7, here the writing of the law will not be done on the hearts of scattered individuals. In fact, in Hebrew, the word "heart" in verse 33 is in the singular with a plural pronoun (i.e. their heart)[19] to signify that it will be a community matter, a corporate will and mind. Shead sees in this

---

17. See a good discussion in Brueggemann, *Hopeful Imagination*, 5.

18. Brueggemann, *Hopeful Imagination*, 4. However, we need to add to this quotation that the new order will necessarily have an impact on political, economic, cultural and religious aspects once Israelites return to their land. In other words, what happens in the heart must have sociopolitical (cultural) and religious effects.

19. Only Holladay (*Jeremiah 2*, 198) and Shead ("New Covenant and Pauline Hermeneutics") have noticed that the word "heart" designating the people of Israel is in the singular. All other commentators translated the word as plural.

corporate will and mind the universality of the new covenant.[20] His argument can easily be judged as an attempt to take this text out of context and let it hastily speak for the New Testament community. Yet, different elements in the passage emphasize the fact that the writing of the law in the heart will enable relationships that will create a harmonious community.

Yahweh states that after writing the law within the heart of Israel, he will become their God and they will become his people. This statement is reminiscent of the end of verse 32, which speaks of Israel breaking the covenant. In covenantal language and in the context of Ancient Near Eastern society, breaking of a covenant by either party put an end to the relationship. So according to Near Eastern legal regulations, the people had ceased to be Yahweh's people (though Yahweh himself remained faithful and did not stop being their master).[21] Thus what was needed was the restoration of the relationship to its original status. Accordingly, the new covenant is about the restoration of a broken covenant, it is about the restoration of the relationship between Yahweh and his people.

The writing of the law in the heart will create solidarity in the community. Verse 34 states: "And no longer shall each man teach his neighbour and each his brother." In the book of Jeremiah, all references to neighbours and brothers are negative and are associated with telling lies, deceit, enslavement and perversion of Yahweh's word:

> Let each man be on guard against his fellow, and put no trust in any brother; for every brother is a deceiver and every friend a slanderer. Each man deceives his neighbour. (Jer 9:4–5)

> But you turned about and profaned my name, and have taken back every one of you his male and female slaves, whom he had set free, to where they wished, and have compelled them once more to be your bondmen and bondwomen. (Jer 34:16)

---

20. Shead, "New Covenant and Pauline Hermeneutics," 38.

21. This goes beyond the ordinary understanding of the covenantal relationship in Ancient Near Eastern society. In that society, when one party broke the covenant, the relationship ceased to exist. But Yahweh who called his people into existence would not stop being their God though they were no longer his people (since they put an end to the right relationship). This is why we see him initiating a new relationship. In fact, it is difficult to think of Yahweh as an equal partner in the treaty. The fact is that he is God and consequently cannot be bound by human convention as Canaanites gods were. He is therefore free to act as he wants and to change the course of history whenever he wants to.

But 31:34 talks about a learning community, a transformed community, a community that is willing to know Yahweh's way together and to grow together, though there will be no need for teaching one another about Yahweh's instruction. This actually denotes the ideal community that Yahweh wanted to create in Israel right from the start.

This passage speaks strongly to our situation in Africa, which is terribly affected by divisions of various kinds, including divisions in the churches that were supposed to unite Africans. There is also the appalling reality of ethnic divisions in some countries. Ethnicity refers to a group identity, more specifically to a group of people who define themselves by the consciousness of descending from a common ancestor and who share some common past memories and links. This consciousness is unfortunately sometimes fuelled by opposition to other ethnic groups, resulting in the deterioration of human relationships and the fragmentation of the society.

Ethnic divisions and the conflicts they create have been one of the major problems in the continent. Such conflicts result in death and lasting deep divisions between groups of people. Where such conflict is recurrent, solidarity becomes mostly determined by ethnic origin, even among Christians. It is not uncommon to see Christians travelling a long distance on Sundays in search of churches led by pastors belonging to their ethnic group. Some churches in Africa have become tribal churches, and many of them are breaking apart because of the divisions caused by tribalism. In such churches, Christian ministry becomes a rivalry between ethnic groups rather than a collaboration between believers. Sometimes, this rivalry even breaks out in real clashes between members. Even appointment to church leadership positions can be politicized, which is why leadership standards are often so low in our churches and denominations. Jeremiah 31:31–34 challenges us to live together and grow together as God's community of faith. Here again, the restored relationship with Yahweh has an ethical effect; it is meant to bring about harmonious relationships in the community. The ethnicity or tribalism that is practised in our churches is a clear sign that something is just as wrong with our Christianity as it was with Israel and Judah.

According to Jeremiah, the writing of the Torah in the heart of the covenanted people will result in the true knowledge of Yahweh: "they shall all know me" (v. 34). Here the expression "to know Yahweh" is to be understood in its technical sense as denoting a mutual legal recognition of Yahweh as suzerain (Lord) and the Israelite community as his servant after all conditions for the treaty have been met. In the Near Eastern context, this is an ideal relationship between the suzerain and his obedient vassal whereby the vassal fulfils all the requirements given by his master and the latter provides care and protection for his subject. In the context of the Old Testament, it also means that Israel as a community will perfectly know Yahweh's will and will obey his law that is now written on its heart.

There has been a debate as to what the word "Torah" refers to in this passage. G. A. Ostborn[22] and W. D. Davies[23] reject the idea that the Torah of the new covenant will be the same as the one given at Sinai. Duhm accepts that in this passage, the word "Torah" does designate the same law that was first given to Israelites at Sinai.[24] However, for him this also means that verse 34 is to be considered as the work of a late editor (and rejected) because the legalism contained in the law cannot fit with the concept of the new covenant as described in verses 31–34. My understanding is that the word "Torah" is indeed used in the same sense as the law in the old covenant, but this use does not necessarily compel us to consider verse 34 as non-Jeremianic. It seems to me that our problem today is in thinking of the Torah simply and solely in terms of legalism instead of considering it as Yahweh's commandment in general. In my estimation, Dennis R. Bratcher is among the few who have found a good definition of the Torah that might fit this context:

> The OT concept of Torah is a lifestyle of nurtured and nurturing relationship with God and others, subsuming every facet of life to a dynamic (growing) and joyful acknowledgment of God as supreme Sovereign and Lord of the earth. Torah is not primarily a book to obey or rules to follow; it is a path of walk, a way of life to lead. And yet that walk must authentically reflect the character of the God who has called people to walk it.[25]

Therefore, according to Bratcher, Torah is "primarily a relational concept, providing the community of faith an anchor point in God's grace from which it can live out its identity as the people of God."[26] Thus, my argument is that what will be different in the new covenant is not the Torah but the way the restored community will be enabled to internalize it and then externalize it in social

---

22. G. A. Ostborn, *Torah in the Old Testament: A Semantic Study* (Lund, 1945), 155.
23. W. D. Davies, *Torah in the Messianic Age and/or the Age to Come* (JBL Monograph Series, 1952), 26–28.
24. Quoted by Unterman, *From Repentance to Redemption*, 99.
25. Dennis R. Bratcher, "Torah as Holiness: Old Testament 'Law' as Response to Divine Grace" (Paper Presented to the Thirtieth Annual Meeting of the Wesleyan Theological Society, Dayton, Ohio, 5 November 1994), http://www.crivoice.org/torahholiness.html.
26. Bratcher, "*Torah as Holiness,*" http://www.crivoice.org/torahholiness.html.

forms that reflects Yahweh's identity and grace. I understand the internalization of the Torah in the community of the new covenant as the value principles that will structure the people's thought and imagination, guide their action, and form their world view. In other words, Torah will become an Israelite culture, their way of daily life in all its aspects.

Reading this text from our context, its message is that if we want real change in our nations, we must find a way to let Christian principles and values guide our thinking, our mentality, and our action. Christian prayers should not remain simple recitations, and the songs and sermons in our churches should shape us so that our inner selves can guide our daily activity and thinking. In brief, our vision must be in conformity with biblical values. Whatever we do as Christians must reflect our Christian values. This is how the Torah or law is to be understood in the context of the new covenant, and this is what knowing Yahweh would mean for all people.

Shared knowledge in the community

The new community will also be characterized by a common, shared access to the "knowledge" of the law "for they shall all know me, from the least of them to the greatest, says Yahweh." This shared knowledge evidences a fundamental egalitarian commitment in the community. In the new covenant community, knowledge will not simply be the privilege of the few, the powerful, and the rich, as it was in the Israel of the old covenant, and as it is in most of our societies today. We all know that in our societies access to information and knowledge is exceedingly unequal and that control over knowledge is a real source of power. The transmission of this knowledge occurs within limited socially and politically constituted networks of elite people, institutions, and organizations that tend to control the common people. Understood this way, knowledge becomes a tool to be used to gain power. It can also be manipulated to dominate or oppress others. This kind of power relies a great deal on the possession of knowledge. But in regard to this passage from Jeremiah, Brueggemann comments:

> On the crucial matter of connection to God, the least and the greatest stand on equal footing. No one has superior, elitist access, and no one lacks what is required. All share fully in the new

relation. All know the story, all accept the sovereignty, and all embrace the commands.[27]

Brueggemann's view makes a lot of sense to me, especially as an African. People who have power know that knowledge is indeed power. Their children attend the best universities abroad, whereas poor citizens have no option but to send their children to local universities with very poor infrastructure, where they are taught by poorly paid professors. The powerful know that by giving the best education to their children, those children will come back to replace them and so they will maintain power in the corrupted system of the nation. In such settings, knowledge is the privilege of only a few in the land. Sadly, the situation is often similar in the church, with children or relatives of bishops and superintendents receiving scholarship for higher theological education. They too are expected to eventually replace their parents and perpetuate their control of church leadership and administration. This nepotism is often a source of tension and division in the church. But in the community of the new covenant, knowledge will be democratized. The African church should follow this model in empowering all church members, where possible, for the ministry. But we all know that democratizing knowledge in the community is a threat to the establishment both in the church and in the government.

A forgiven and forgiving community

The last statement in verse 34 concerning Yahweh's forgiveness is introduced by the conjunction *kî* (for), in the sentence "for I will forgive their iniquity, and I will remember their sin no more." The difficulty with this statement is that it comes at the end of the section, after the prophet had already described the character of the new community under the covenant. The logic would suggest that the issue of forgiveness be dealt with before the people enter the new covenant (i.e. a new relationship) with Yahweh. The question then becomes: Should the phrase "for I will forgive their iniquity, and I will remember their sin no more" be restricted to the actions described in verse 33 and a section of verse 34 as a once-for-all forgiveness, or should it mean that forgiveness is an ongoing feature of the new covenant? In other words, will Yahweh forgive the iniquity of his people before he writes his law on their heart and before they come to know him, or will forgiveness of iniquity be a long process during the period of the new covenant? It seems to me that forgiveness has to come prior

---

27. Brueggemann, *Commentary on Jeremiah*, 294.

to the events described in verses 31–34 concerning the new covenant. It is in fact this forgiveness that will allow newness in the relationship. Put differently, the forgiveness spoken about in this passage will probably take place after judgement and before the initiation of the new relationship between Yahweh and his people. In this way, the new community will always remember that they belong to Yahweh by grace because of forgiveness. In other words, the new covenant community is a forgiven community. Wolff rightly claims that the forgiveness of sin is the bedrock and the cornerstone of the new covenant.[28]

Forgiveness and the African church

The concept of a forgiven community is important for the church today, especially for our people in Africa. Jeremiah 31:31–34 reminds us that we are in the church because we are a forgiven people, forgiven by Yahweh through the blood of his son Jesus Christ. The practice of forgiveness should thus characterize us in the church. We should not indulge in the resentful, careful management of old hurts in a region infested by perpetual tension but should seek an authentic yielding of the past for hope. By forgiving one another and making peace with one another, we will demonstrate that we truly belong to the new community of redeemed people, having received redemption through the blood of Jesus, which sealed the beginning of the new covenant (Luke 22:20; 1 Cor 11:25). All Christians should be aware that they are both members of a forgiven and a forgiving community.

For most of us, however, including genuine Christians, being a forgiving community sounds impossible to achieve. Countries in Africa have experienced genocide, wars, ethnic/tribal conflicts, apartheid and other mass crimes in which hundreds of thousands, if not millions, of people have lost their lives. These killings have sometimes been perpetrated by neighbours and friends. Violence perpetrated by individuals who know their victims well makes forgiveness and the rebuilding of communities incredibly challenging. In such contexts,

> forgiveness and reconciliation never come easily. They express no hint of romance, only the courage and risk-taking of people willing to confront their anger and find constructive ways to deal with the past. For those who decide to forgive or reconcile, a constant

---

28. Wolff, *Confrontations with Prophets*, 59–60.

motivation echoes through each of their stories: a desire to live at peace with themselves and those around them.[29]

I experienced the difficulty and pain of forgiveness on one of my pastoral visits in 2011. My wife and I were visiting a group of churches in the area still controlled by rebels of the Front for Patriotic Resistance in Ituri (FRPI) who had killed more than 1,200 people in my community nine years earlier. As usual, the rebel leader had to be informed of my visit in the region, and he agreed to send a bodyguard who was posted at the entrance of the house where my wife and I were staying. When I saw the armed man who was "protecting" me, I felt intense pain and fear, for he was one of the brutal militiamen who had exterminated my people. I personally had lost thirty-four close relatives (cousins, nephew, aunts, sisters, etc.). His name was prominent among the killers. But there he was, sent to "guard" me and my wife, without any apology.

Did I know what he was thinking about or why his commander, hiding in the bush, chose him as my temporary bodyguard? What should have been my reaction? My wife and I took time to pray for peace and we decided that we would take lunch together and have an opportunity to talk to him about his life and about Jesus. After four days spent in that situation, something changed in my life. God gave me grace to feel free to look at those killers as human beings who also struggle with life. Our bodyguard told us that often he does not know why he does the things that he does. He confessed that he did not know why he was still living in the bush.

How deeply are Christians, especially in some parts of Africa, affected by the estrangement that can result from these kinds of situations? Will the church be able to take up the challenge and help Christians to forgive one another and remember that we are a forgiven community and must remain a forgiving community? What kind of nurturing should be adopted to help Christians live together as a forgiven community? This is an important area of need in the African church because the absence of forgiveness and reconciliation is hindering its witness in many parts of the continent. The church needs to urgently model true reconciliation that is based on God's forgiveness because many post-war national reconciliation and reunification efforts have failed to bring about the unity that results from true reconciliation.

In many cases, there have been initiatives asking people to forget the past and to integrate militia group members in the national army without judging

---

29. Phil Clark, "The Complexity of Forgiveness and Reconciliation in Central Africa," Fetzer Institute, https://fetzer.org/blog/complexity-forgiveness-and-reconciliation-central-africa.

them for the wrong they have done. As a result, some of the masterminds of these conflicts move quickly into the capital cities and become political leaders or very influential in government. Once in power, these individuals push for a false kind of reconciliation that is based on trying to deal with the history of violence by suppressing its memory. But there can be no reconciliation without justice. Robert J. Schreiter argues:

> The first form of false reconciliation tries to deal with a history of violence by suppressing its memory. By not adverting to the fact that violence has taken place, this approach is supposed to put the violent history behind us and allow us to begin afresh. Not surprisingly, this kind of reconciliation is often called for by the very perpetrators of violence who, either having seen what they have done or having realized the potential consequences of their actions, want to get on to a new and different situation. They want the victims of violence to let bygones be bygones and exercise a Christian forgiveness. While reconciliation as a hasty peace bears a superficial resemblance to Christian reconciliation, it is actually quite far from it.[30]

Forgiveness and reconciliation involve a deep repair to human lives, especially to "the lives of those who have suffered. That repair takes time, time that can make the participants feel insecure, but necessary time nonetheless for beginning a new life."[31] The objective of reconciliation should be a new life and a new community whose reconciliation is based on the gospel. This is the message of Jeremiah 31:31–34. God took time to warn his people, and after they rejected his warning, he sent them into exile, before he could start any meaningful work of forgiveness.

It is here that the church in Africa can play a great role of reconciliation. But which church? Has not the church been negatively affected by conflict too? Has the church in Africa also become part of the problem? In 2003, the Vatican had to depose the Catholic bishop of Bunia Diocese in DR Congo for his involvement in the bloody ethnic conflict in the area that claimed the life of over 50,000 people. It is reported that a huge quantity of ammunitions and guns serving a tribal militia belonging to his ethnic group was found in his house. The bishop's case is just one of the many such cases in our region.

---

30. Robert J. Schreiter, *Reconciliation: Mission & Ministry in a Changing Social Order* (Maryknoll, NY: Orbis, 1992), 19. See also Robert J. Schreiter, *The Ministry of Reconciliation: Spirituality & Strategies* (Maryknoll, NY: Orbis, 1998).

31. Schreiter, *Reconciliation: Mission & Ministry*, 21.

Some church leaders in Africa might not be useful instruments of change in the society. However, the church in Africa has other resources (theological, social, intellectual, etc.) for enabling reconciliation, but it needs to recognize and acknowledge that it too can be part of the problem.

Conclusion

In the new covenant community, true knowledge of God will be a corporate knowledge, given to the whole community, to affect the relationship between the people and their God and the relationships between people. In relationship with God, knowledge will create the faithfulness that was missing in the old covenant. As a result, the whole community will know Yahweh, from the least to the greatest. The community that knows Yahweh is also one that has internal harmony. This is the kind of society that Yahweh wants to establish on earth. The church is called to reflect the image of such a community until the return of the Lord to establish his kingdom, which will be the perfect covenant human community.

In the present, the church's primary responsibility is to strive to build a community of *shalom* here and now as an image of the true *shalom* that will come when the kingdom of God is fully established. The church in Africa must courageously and decisively engage in serious theologizing that yields practical steps for building coherent and integrative Christian communities in a conflict-torn continent. Otherwise, the church will fail to be salt and light and become an empty shell, a place of entertainment.

In the covenant community, the knowledge of Yahweh will also be democratized (i.e. every member will know the Lord). Access to knowledge will no longer be for the few powerful or the rich who use knowledge to take advantage of the weak and foreigners. Instead, the community of the new covenant will be a learning community, a community that strives to grow together in the perfect knowledge of Yahweh (i.e. in being right with God and with one another). But creating this kind of community in Africa will remain a pipe dream unless we learn together to go beyond sacralizing our tribes and our selfish interests and strive to create a harmonious community.

For the church, Jeremiah's message in 31:31–34 means that we lie and our faith is false if we continue to claim that we know Yahweh while we still kill and hate others. The presence of these evils among us is a sure sign that we have not yet known the Lord or been transformed by him. This point is also an invitation to all, even those who have been victims of violence, to demonstrate that we are able to forgive those who have wronged us. This is the power of the Christian life, "the power of forgiveness over retaliation, of suffering over violence, of love over hostility, of humble service over domination."[32]

Forgiveness creates newness in the lives of people and a transformation of their heart to know Yahweh and serve him with genuine devotion. Members of a forgiven community know Yahweh (obey his commandments) and make every effort to forgive one another as he has forgiven them. Paul reminds us in 1 Corinthians 12:12–31 that, as Christians, we belong to the new covenant community; a community that is called forth by Yahweh himself and which should be characterized by love for one another and forgiveness for one another as Yahweh himself has forgiven us through Christ.

To conclude this chapter on the new covenant and new community, it is important to remind the African church that our covenantal hope is not meant to be kept only in the believing community but must be articulated in the entire society that we are serving. Since we know that this world will one day be liberated to become a community that covenants with God, that lives in total peace, that distributes its produce (including knowledge) equally, that values all its members, that rejects all kind of acts that destroy unity, and whose members forgive each another, there is an urgent need for the church to articulate, anticipate, and practice the transformation that is sure to come. Then the prayer "your kingdom come, your will be done, on earth as it is in heaven" will become a true expectation for all believers. This expectation will grow and spread across all societies in Africa, bringing renewal to its people as they await the fulfilment of the new covenant.

---

32. Kwame Bediako, "De-sacralization and Democratization: Some Theological Reflections on the Role of Christianity in Nation-Building in Modern Africa," *Transformation: An International Journal of Holistic Mission Studies* 12, no. 1 (January 1995): 5–11, 10.1177/026537889501200102.

Bibliography

Adewale, Samuel A. "Crime and African Traditional Religion." *ORITA* 26, no. 1–2 (1994): 54–66.

Ake, Claude. "What Is the Problem of Ethnicity in Africa?" *Transformation: Critical Perspectives on Southern Africa* 22 (1993): 1–14.

Anderson, Bernhard W. *The Living World of the Old Testament*. London: Longmans, 1967.

Asamoah, Kwame, Emmanuel Yeboah-Asiamah, and Alex Osei-Kojo. "Demons of Transitional Democracies: Politics of Insults and Acrimony in Ghana." *Journal of Social Science Studies* 1, no. 1 (2014): 49–61. http://dx.doi.org/10.5296/jsss.v1i1.4725.

Atuobi, Samuel M. "Corruption and State Instability in West Africa: An Examination of Policy Option." http://www.kaiptcorg/Publications/Occasional-Papers/Documents/no_21.aspx.

BBC News Africa. "Somali Militants 'behind' Kampala World Cup Blasts." 12 July 2010. https://www.bbc.com/news/10593771.

———. "South Africa's Jacob Zuma 'Sorry' over Nkandla Scandal." 1 April 2016. http://www.bbc.com/news/world-africa-35943941.

Bediako, K. "De-sacralization and Democratization: Some Theological Reflections on the Role of Christianity in Nation-Building in Modern Africa." *Transformation: An International Journal of Holistic Mission Studies* 12, no. 1 (1995): 5–11.

Bratcher, Dennis R. "Jeremiah 29:4–7." *The Voice: Biblical and Theological Resources for Growing Christians*, 2009; n.p. http://www.textweek.com/prophets/jer1.htm.

———. "Torah as Holiness: Old Testament 'Law' as Response to Divine Grace." Paper Presented to the Thirtieth Annual Meeting of the Wesleyan Theological Society, Dayton, Ohio, 5 November 1994. http://www.crivoice.org/torahholiness.html.

Bright, John. *Covenant and Promise: The Future in the Preaching of the Pre-Exilic Prophets*. London: SCM, 1977.

Brueggemann, W. *The Prophetic Imagination*. Philadelphia: Fortress, 1978.

———. *Theology of the Old Testament: Testimony, Dispute, Advocacy*. Minneapolis, MN: Fortress, 1996.

Center for African Studies. "Swahili Proverbs: *Methali za Kiswahili*." http://swahiliproverbs.afrst.illinois.edu/lying.html.

Chenu, Bruno. *Prophétisme et Église*. Abbaye de Saint Maurice: Edition numérique, 1981.

Chuter, David, and Florence Gaub. "Understanding African Armies." *EU Institute of Security Studies*, April 2016. https://www.iss.europa.eu/sites/default/files/EUISSFiles/Report_27.pdf.

Clark, Phil. "The Complexity of Forgiveness and Reconciliation in Central Africa." *Fetzer Institute*. https://fetzer.org/blog/complexity-forgiveness-and-reconciliation-central-africa.

Clive, Gabay, and Sophie Harman. "Rwanda: The Politics of Success, Silence and Genocide Leverage." *News Stories*. Queen Mary University of London. 17 April 2014. http://www.qmul.ac.uk/media/news/items/ hss/128742.html.

Craigie, Peter C., Page H. Kelley, and Joel F. Drinkard Jr. *Jeremiah 1–25*. Word Biblical Commentary. Dallas, TX: Word Books, 1991.

Davies, W. D. *Torah in the Messianic Age and/or the Age to Come*. Journal of Biblical Literature Monograph Series 7. Philadelphia: Society of Biblical Literature, 1952.

DeCapua, J. "Refugees Boost Local Economy." *VOA News*, 20 June 2014. https://www.voanews.com/africa/refugees-boost-local-economy.

de Lubac, Henri. *The Splendor of the Church*. New York: Sheed & Ward, 1956.

Diamond, A. R. Pete. *The Confessions of Jeremiah in Context. Scenes of Prophetic Drama*. Sheffield: Sheffield Academic Press, 1987.

Diamond, A. R. Pete, and Louis Stulman, eds. *Jeremiah (Dis)placed: New Directions in Writing/Reading Jeremiah*. New York: T&T Clark, 2011.

Diamond, A. R. Pete, Kathleen M. O'Connor, and Louis Stulman, eds. *Troubling Jeremiah*. Sheffield: Sheffield Academic Press, 1999.

Éla, Jean-Marc. *My Faith as an African*. Trans. John Pairman Brown and Susan Perry. Eugene, OR: Wipf & Stock, 2009.

Elmer, Martens A. *Jeremiah*. Believers Church Bible Commentary. Scottsdale, PA: Herald, 1986.

Erinosho, Laye. "Sociology, Hypocrisy, and Social Order." *African Sociological Review* 12, no. 2 (2008): 85–97. http://www.jstor.org/stable/24487607.

Esler, Phillip F. *Community and Gospel in Luke-Acts: The Social and Political Motivations of Lucan Theology*. Cambridge: Cambridge University Press, 1987.

Eslinger, Lyle M. *Kingship of God in Crisis: A Close Reading of 1 Samuel 1–12*. Sheffield: Sheffield Academic Press, 1985.

Gathogo, Julius. "The Challenge of Money and Wealth in Some East Africa Pentecostal Churches." *Studia Historiae Ecclesiasticae* 37, no. 2 (2011): 133–151.

Geschiere, Peter. *Modernity of Witchcraft*. Charlottesville, VA: University Press of Virginia, 1997.

Gould, David J. "Patron and Clients: The Role of the Military in Zairian Politics." In *The Performance of Soldiers as Governors*, edited by Isaac James Mowoe, 57–144. Washington: University Press of America, 1980.

Hadey, J. "Jérémie 29: Demain n'est pas Hier . . ." *Lire et Dire: Etudes Exégétiques en vue de la Prédication* 64 (2005): 3–8.

Hans-Joachim, K. *Theology of the Psalms*. Trans. Keith Crim. Minneapolis, MN: Fortress, 1992.

Harris, Neil, Fiona R. Minniss, and Shawn Somerset. "Refugees Connecting with a New Country through Community Food Gardening." *International Journal*

of Environment Research and Public Health 11, no. 9 (2014): 9202–9216. doi.org/10.3390/ijerph110909202.
Hart, Bentley D. *Atheist Delusions: The Christian Revolution and Its Fashionable Enemies.* New Haven, CT: Yale University Press, 2009.
Hill, John. "'Your Exile Will Be Long': The Book of Jeremiah and the Unended Exile." In *Reading the Book of Jeremiah: A Search for Coherence*, edited by Martin Kessler, 149–61. Winona Lake, IN: Eisenbrauns, 2004.
———. *Foe or Friend? The Figure of Babylon in the Book of Jeremiah MT.* Leiden: Brill, 1999.
Hirsch, Susan F. "Putting Hate Speech in Context: Observation on Speech, Power, and Violence in Kenya." Unpublished paper, prepared for George Mason University. https://www.ushmm.org/m/pdfs/20100423-speech-power-violence-hirsch.pdf.
Hizkias, Assefa, and George Wachira. *Peace-Making and Democratization in Africa: Theoretical Perspectives and Church Initiatives.* Nairobi: East African Educational Publishers, 1996.
Hobbs, T. R. *2 Kings.* Word Biblical Commentary, vol. 13. Nashville, TN: Thomas Nelson, 1986.
Holladay, W. L. *Jeremiah 1.* Hermeneia. Philadelphia: Fortress, 1986.
———. *Jeremiah 2.* Hermeneia. Minneapolis: Fortress, 1989.
Hyatt, J. P. *Jeremiah.* Nashville: Abingdon, 1956.
Jacobsen, K. "The Forgotten Solution: Local Integration for Refugees in Development Countries." In *New Issue in Refugee Research.* Working paper no 45, 2001. https://www.unhcr.org/research/working/3b7d24059/forgotten-solution-local-integration-refugees-developing-countries-karen.html.
Kä Mana. *Christ d'Afrique, Enjeux Ethiques de la Foi Chrétienne en Jésus Christ.* Paris: Karthala, 1994.
Kabongo-Mbaya, Philip B. "Churches and the Struggle for Democracy in Zaire." In *Peace-Making and Democratisation in Africa*, edited by Hizkias Assefa and George Wachira, 130–152. Nairobi: East African Educational Publishers, 1996.
Karimi, F., and M. L. Gumuchian. "Nelson Mandela Buried, Ending Journey That Transformed South Africa." *CNN*, 15 December 2013. http://www.cnn.com/2013/12/15/world/africa/nelson-mandela-qunu-funeral/.
Katho, Bungishabaku R. *Jérémie et Lamentations.* Carlisle: LivresHippo, 2017.
Katongole, Emmanuel. *The Sacrifice of Africa: A Political Theology for Africa.* Grand Rapids, MI: Eerdmans, 2010.
Kempe, Ronald H. *From Crisis to Renewal: Development Policy and Management in Africa.* Leiden: Brill, 2012.
Keown, Gerald L., Pamela J. Scalise, and Thomas G. Smothers. *Jeremiah 26–52.* Word Biblical Commentary 27. Dallas, TX: Word, 1995.
Kirk, Andrew J. *Liberation Theology: An Evangelical View from the Third World.* Atlanta, GA: John Knox Press, 1979.

Laarman, E. "Power, Might." In *International Standard Bible Encyclopedia*, vol. 3, edited by Geoffrey W. Bromiley, 926–29. Minneapolis: Fortress, 1986.

LaSor, W. S. "Nebuchadnezzar." In *International Standard Bible Encyclopedia*, vol. 3, edited by Geoffrey W. Bromiley, 506–508. Minneapolis: Fortress, 1986.

Leistner, E. "Witchcraft and African Development." *African Security Review* 23 (2014): 53–77.

Lichfield, John. "The Parisian Treasures of African Tyrants: French Government May Seize Mansions and Luxury Cars of Corrupt Regimes." *Independent*, 13 July 2013. http://www.independent.co.uk/news/world/europe/the-parisian-treasures-of-african-tyrants-french-government-may-seize-mansions-and-luxury-cars-of-8706535.html.

Lundbom, J. R. *Jeremiah 1–20: Anchor Bible 21A*. New York: Doubleday, 1999.

———. *Jeremiah 21–36: Anchor Bible 21B*. New York: Doubleday, 2004.

———. *Jeremiah 37–52: Anchor Bible 21C*. New York: Doubleday, 2004.

Martin-Achard, R. "Quelques Remarques sur la Nouvelle Alliance chez Jérémie." In *Questions Disputées de l'Ancien Testament*, edited by C. Brekelmans, 141–64. Duculot: Gembloux, 1974.

Maxwell, John C., and Jim Dornan. *Becoming a Person of Influence: How to Positively Impact the Lives of Others*. Nashville: Thomas Nelson, 1997.

Mbembe, Achille. "Jean-Marc Éla: le veilleur s'en est allé: L'hommage de Achille Mbembe." *Africultures*. 27 January 2009. http://africultures.com/jean-marc-ela-le-veilleur-sen-est-alle-8355/.

McComiskey, Thomas E. "Hosea." In *An Exegetical & Expository Commentary: The Minor Prophets*, edited by Thomas E. McComiskey. Grand Rapids, MI: Baker, 1992.

McConville, J. G. *Judgment and Promise: An Interpretation of the Book of Jeremiah*. Leicester, UK: Apollos, 1993.

Mekonnen, A. *The West and China in Africa: Civilization without Justice*. Eugene, OR: Wipf & Stock, 2015.

Mendelsohn, I. "On Corvée Labor in Ancient Canaan and Israel." *Bulletin of the American Schools of Oriental Research* 167 (1962): 31–35.

Mendenhall, George E. "The Monarchy." *Interpretation* 29, no. 2 (1975): 155–70.

Mfonobong, N. "An African Dictator's Son and His Very Lavish Toys." *Forbes*, 7 July 2011. http://www.forbes.com/sites/mfonobongnsehe/2011/07/07/an-african-dictators-son-and-his-very-lavish-toys/#1e879f044913.

Mills, D. H. "African Leaders Lack Wisdom." *Ghana Web*, 29 December 2016. https://www.ghanaweb.com/GhanaHomePage/NewsArchive/African-leaders-lack-wisdom-Bishop-Heward-Mills-463110.

Milner, James. *Refugees, the State and the Politics of Asylum in Africa*. Hampshire, UK: Palgrave Macmillan, 2009.

Morgan, G. Campbell. *Studies in the Prophecy of Jeremiah*. London: Fleming A. Revell, 1931.

Mottu, Henry. *Les Confessions de Jérémie : Une Protestation Contre la Souffrance*. Genève: Labor et Fides, 1985.
Mugambi, Jesse N. K. "Problems and Promises of the Churches in Africa." In *The Church and the Future in Africa: Problems and Promises*, edited by Jesse N. K. Mugambi, 193–204. Nairobi: All Africa Conference of Churches, 1977.
New Humanitarian, The. "A Refugee's Story." 18 August 2011. http://www.irinnews.org/report/93527/kenya-somalia-refugees-story.
Niringiye, D. Z. *The Church: God's Pilgrim People*. Downers Grove, IL: IVP Academic, 2015.
Nzongola-Ntalaja, G. "The Role of Intellectuals in the Struggle for Democracy, Peace and Reconstruction in Africa." *African Journal of Political Science* 2, no. 2 (1997): 1–14.
O'Donovan, O., and Joan L. O'Donovan. *From Irenaeus to Grotius: A Sourcebook in Christian Political Thought*. Cambridge: Cambridge University Press, 1999.
Oded, Lipschits. *The Fall and Rise of Jerusalem: Judah under Babylonian Rule*. Winona Lake, IN: Eisenbrauns, 2005.
Okeja, U. B. "Magic in an African Context." In *Magic and the Supernatural*, edited by Scott E. Hendrix and Timothy J. Shannon, 101–106. Oxford, UK: Inter-disciplinary Press, 2012.
Ostborn, Gunnar A. *Torah in the Old Testament: A Semantic Study*. Lund: H. Ohlssons Boktryck, 1945.
Overholt, T. W. "The Falsehood of Idolatry: An Interpretation of Jer. 10:1–16." *Journal of Theological Studies* 16, no. 1 (1965): 1–12.
———. *The Threat of Falsehood: A Study in the Theology of Jeremiah*. Naperville, IL: Allison, 1970.
Perdue, Leo G. *Wisdom and Cult: A Critical Analysis of the Views of Cult in the Wisdom Literatures of Israel and the Ancient Near East*. Missoula, MT: Scholars Press, 1977.
Piwang-Jalobo, George. "The Legacy of St Janani Luwum: 1922–1977." Unpublished paper, 2006.
Polk, T. *The Prophetic Persona: Jeremiah and the Language of the Self*. JSOT Supplement 32. Sheffield: Sheffield Academic Press, 1984.
Raitt, Thomas M. *Theology of Exile: Judgment/Deliverance in Jeremiah and Ezekiel*. Philadelphia: Fortress, 1977.
Reventlow, H. G. *Liturgie und Prophetisches Ich bei Jeremiah*. Guterlsoh: Mohn, 1963.
Roberts, J. J. M. "In Defense of the Monarchy: The Contribution of Israelite Kingship to Biblical Theology." In *Ancient Israelite Religion*, edited by Patrick D. Miller, Paul D. Hanson, and S. Dean McBride, 377–96. Philadelphia: Fortress, 1987.
Rodway, J. A. *The Vitality of the Individual in the Thought of Ancient Israel*. Cardiff: University of Wales Press, 1949.
Sanneh, Lamin. *Whose Religion Is Christianity. The Gospel beyond the West*. Grand Rapids, MI: Eerdmans, 2003.

Sarbah, Bartholomew A. "Awake Mother Africa." 5 October 2011. http://www.poemhunter.com/poem/awake-mother-africa/.

Schreiter, Robert J. *Reconciliation: Mission & Ministry in a Changing Social Order*. Maryknoll, NY: Orbis, 1992.

———. *The Ministry of Reconciliation: Spirituality & Strategies*. Maryknoll, NY: Orbis, 1998.

Shead, A. G. "The New Covenant and Pauline Hermeneutics." In *The Gospel to the Nations: Perspectives on Paul's Mission*, edited by Peter Bolt and Mark Thompson, 33–50. London: Inter-Varsity Press, 2000.

Slavin, Susan L., and Carolis Salvador. *What's So Blessed about Being Poor? Seeking the Gospel in the Slums of Kenya*. Maryknoll, NY: Orbis, 2013.

Smith, Daniel J. *A Culture of Corruption: Everyday Deception and Popular Discontent in Nigeria*. Princeton: Princeton University Press, 2016.

Smith, Mark S. "Jeremiah 9:9: A Divine Lament." *Vetus Testamentum* 37 (1987): 97–99.

Soédé, Nathanaël Y. *Cri de l'Homme Africain et Christianisme. Jean-Marc Ela, Une Passion pour l'Opprimé*. Abidjan: Seprim Ivoire, 2009.

Stein, B. N. "The Experience of Being a Refugee: Insights from the Research Literature." In *The Series in Clinical and Community Psychology: Refugee Mental Health in Resettlement Countries*, edited by C. L. Williams and J. Westermeyer, 5–23. Washington: Hemisphere Publishing, 1986.

Stuart, F. *The State in the Light of the Scripture*. Potchefstroom: Potchefstroom University, 1988.

Tarimo, A. "Politicization of Ethnic Identities." *Journal of Asian and African Studies* 45, no. 3 (2010): 297–308.

Thompson, J. A. *Book of Jeremiah: New International Commentary on the Old Testament*. Grand Rapids, MI: Eerdmans, 1980.

Unterman, J. *From Repentance to Redemption: Jeremiah's Thought in Transition*. Sheffield: Sheffield Academic Press, 1987.

Volz, P. *Der Prophet Jeremia*. KAT 10. Leipzig: Diechert, 1928.

Von Rad, Gerhard. *Wisdom in Israel*. London: SCM, 1972.

Walvoord, J. F., and R. B. Zuck. *The Bible Knowledge Commentary: Old Testament*. Colorado Springs, CO: Chariot Victor, 1985.

Weinfeld, M. "Judge and Officer in Ancient Israel and in the Ancient Near East." *Israel Oriental Studies* 7 (1977): 65–88.

———. *Deuteronomy and the Deuteronomic School*. Oxford: Oxford University Press, 1972.

Welch, A. C. *Jeremiah: His Time and His Work*. Oxford: Blackwell, 1928.

William, A. D. *The Earth Is God's: A Theology of American Culture*. Maryknoll, NY: Orbis, 1997.

Wisser, L. *Jérémie, Critique de la Vie Sociale: La Connaissance de Dieu et la Justice Sociale dans le Livre de Jérémie*. Geneva: Labor et Fides, 1984.

Wood, C. E. "With Justice for All. The Task of the People of God: A Biblical Theology." Unpublished class notes, Nairobi Evangelical Graduate School of Theology, 1998.
Wood, L. *A Survey of Israel's History.* London: Pickering & Inglis, 1970.
Wrong, M. *In the Footsteps of Mr. Kurtz: Living on the Brink of Disaster in Mobutu's Congo.* New York: HarperCollins, 2001.
Zetter, R. "Are Refugees an Economic Burden or Benefit?" *Forced Migration Review*, 2012. https://www.fmreview.org/preventing/zetter.

www.ingramcontent.com/pod-product-compliance
Lightning Source LLC
Chambersburg PA
CBHW071740150426
43191CB00010B/1645